Anthropology

FOR

DUMMIES®

Anthropology
FOR
DUMMIES®

by Cameron M. Smith, PhD
with Evan T. Davies, PhD

WILEY

Wiley Publishing, Inc.

Anthropology For Dummies®

Published by
Wiley Publishing, Inc.
111 River St.
Hoboken, NJ 07030-5774
www.wiley.com

For general information on our other products and services, please contact our Customer Care
Department within the U.S. at 800-762-2974, outside the U.S. at 317-572-3993, or fax 317-572-4002.

For technical support, please visit www.wiley.com/techsupport.

Wiley also publishes its books in a variety of electronic formats. Some content that appears in print may
not be available in electronic books.

Library of Congress Control Number: 2008931633

ISBN: 978-0-470-27966-3

Manufactured in the United States of America

10 9 8 7 6 5 4 3 2 1

WILEY

About the Authors

Cameron M. Smith's fascination with humanity was sparked on a 1984 trip to Mexico's Maya ruins; by 1987, he was a student of both Harvard University's early human archaeology field school at Kenya's Leakey research station and the University of London's Institute of Archaeology. He then went to Durham University in northern England for a Joint Honours BA in Anthropology & Archaeology, followed by an MA in Anthropology at Portland State University (in Portland, Oregon) and a PhD from Canada's Simon Fraser University.

Since 2002, Dr. Smith has taught a wide variety of courses as an Adjunct Associate Professor at Portland State University's Department of Anthropology; he has also taught at Washington State University and Linfield College.

Dr. Smith's scientific works have been published in journals such as the *American Journal of Physical Anthropology* and the *Journal of Field Archaeology* and books published by International Monographs in Prehistory and Oxford's British Archaeology Reports. His research has been supported by the National Endowment for the Humanities and the National Science Foundation-funded Barrow Arctic Science Consortium.

Reaching out from the academic world, Dr. Smith has written popular-science articles for *Scientific American MIND*, *Archaeology*, *Playboy*, *Spaceflight*, *Skeptical Inquirer*, *South American Explorer*, *The Next Step*, *Cultural Survival Quarterly*, *The Bulletin of Primitive Technology*, and other magazines. *Anthropology For Dummies* is Dr. Smith's second book. His first, written with Charles Sullivan, was *The Top Ten Myths About Evolution* (Prometheus, 2006).

Outside his academic pursuits, Dr. Smith enjoys mountaineering, art, and arctic exploration. He is a Life Fellow of the Royal Geographical Society, a Fellow of The Explorers Club and a member of the Society for Human Performance in Extreme Environments. His Web site, www.cameronmsmith.com, covers his recent writing, academic, and expedition activities.

Evan T. Davies received his BA from Cornell University where he began his studies in anthropology. He earned a PhD in cultural anthropology from Rice University, and has conducted fieldwork throughout Europe, the South Pacific, and in many locations throughout sub-Saharan Africa. His doctoral dissertation reported on the land use patterns of the BaAka foragers of the central African rainforests whose subsistence and hunting strategies he studied while living with them through the seasons. He has recently become involved with the protection of archaeological sites in Iraq.

Dedications

From Cameron: I dedicate this book to all the anthropologists who have spent careers investigating fundamental questions about humanity, and to their hosts, the indigenous folk of everywhere from Africa to Australia.

From Evan: To my parents, and every good teacher I ever had.

Authors' Acknowledgments

From Cameron: I'd like to thank my parents, professors Donald E. and Margit J. Posluschny Smith, for stimulating my interest in the human species in the first place and then supporting my education, worldwide, for many years.

I also thank all of my professors, from Britain to Canada and the United States, from physical anthropologists to cultural anthropologists to linguists and many, many archaeologists. There are too many to name, though I can highlight Professors Brian Hayden, Kenneth M. Ames, Anthony Harding, Anthony Bilsborough, and the late Jack Nance.

Although I wrote the bulk of this book, I turned to my friend Dr. Evan T. Davies to draft Chapter 12 on how cultural anthropologists do their field-work. Dr. Davies' experience runs from field experiences in the Congo to New Guinea and the Near East, and I thank him for his work on this chapter.

I've been privileged to have the friendship of many fascinating people who have led to many fascinating discussions, all of which simmer for months and eventually find their way into my overall writing style and content. These folks include my occasional coauthor Chuck Sullivan, my brothers Mark and Julian, and my friends John Haslett, W. McRee Anderson, and Todd Olson. I especially thank Ms. Christine Calfas for her companionship and compassion.

I also thank all the members of the Leora writing group in Portland for their great advice and good humor on various writing projects.

I also want to thank my agent, Matt Wagner, of Fresh Books literary agency, for suggesting this project in the first place, as well as Senior Project Editor Alissa Schwipps, Acquisitions Editor Lindsay Lefevere, Technical Editor Robert J. Meier, PhD, and the artists at Wiley Publishing for their great work, support, and patience.

None of these folks are dummies, and neither are my readers; the title of the book is tongue-in-cheek. So, finally, I thank all of you readers for taking the time to think about humanity in a new way.

From Evan: I'd like to thank Steven Tyler, professor of anthropology and linguistics at Rice University, for some very helpful guidance during the writing; the members of the Explorers Club for their continued inspiration to a new generation of field researchers; and Dr. Cameron M. Smith, colleague and friend. May we have at least 20 good years of expeditioning left in us.

Publisher's Acknowledgments

We're proud of this book; please send us your comments through our Dummies online registration form located at www.dummies.com/register/.

Some of the people who helped bring this book to market include the following:

Acquisitions, Editorial, and Media Development

Senior Project Editor: Alissa Schwipps

Acquisitions Editor: Lindsay Lefevere

Copy Editor: Megan Knoll

Editorial Program Coordinator: Erin Calligan Mooney

Technical Editor: Robert J. Meier, PhD

Senior Editorial Manager: Jennifer Ehrlich

Editorial Assistants: Joe Niesen, Jennette ElNaggar, David Lutton

Cover Photo: © Workbook Stock

Cartoons: Rich Tennant (www.the5thwave.com)

Composition Services

Project Coordinator: Erin Smith

Layout and Graphics: Reuben Davis, Melissa K. Jester, Christine Williams

Proofreader: Context Editorial Services

Indexer: Valerie Haynes Perry

Special Help

Alicia South, Tracy Brown Collins, Jennifer Connolly, Joan Friedman, Natalie Harris

Publishing and Editorial for Consumer Dummies

Diane Graves Steele, Vice President and Publisher, Consumer Dummies

Joyce Pepple, Acquisitions Director, Consumer Dummies

Kristin A. Cocks, Product Development Director, Consumer Dummies

Michael Spring, Vice President and Publisher, Travel

Kelly Regan, Editorial Director, Travel

Publishing for Technology Dummies

Andy Cummings, Vice President and Publisher, Dummies Technology/General User

Composition Services

Gerry Fahey, Vice President of Production Services

Debbie Stailey, Director of Composition Services

Contents at a Glance

Table of Contents

Introduction

· ·

Right now, someone somewhere is digging up an ancient relic — perhaps a stone tool a million years old or the remains of an ancient Greek wine jug. That one artifact may not be much, but it's a piece in the vast jigsaw puzzle of humanity's ancient past.

Right now, someone somewhere is interviewing a hunter–gatherer — maybe in the Arctic or in Africa. That one interview — maybe about why the hunter-gatherer is going to split away from the main group with his family — may not be much, but it's a page in the encyclopedia of human cultural behavior.

Right now, someone somewhere is decoding ancient Neanderthal DNA, trying to identify how living humans are related to this fascinating proto-human species. The fragment of DNA is microscopic, but it can tell humanity a tremendous amount about our biology and evolution.

And right now, someone somewhere is studying a rapidly vanishing language — maybe in Polynesia or Southeast Asia — by learning it from a tribal group's elders. The words and phrases she's learning are short, but each language provides a new way to understand the world in a uniquely human way.

All of those someones are anthropologists, like me — people who professionally study the human species in all its aspects, from biology to culture. Of course, it's not just anthropologists who love to learn about humanity; people from every culture and walk of life have an interest in what humanity is today and what it's been in the past.

And that's why I've written *Anthropology For Dummies* — to share what remarkable things anthropologists have discovered and continue to discover with folks like you who are fascinated with the human species (or at least fascinated with passing your Intro to Anthropology class). Join me for a grand tour of the human species, across the world and through millions of years. If that doesn't get your blood going, I can't help you!

About This Book

The study of humanity today (and for the past few million years) has created a vast storehouse of anthropological knowledge printed in millions of pages of research reports and thousands of books. Even professional anthropologists simply can't keep up with the speed and volume of published research. I can't possibly recount what all this research has revealed, but I can — and in this book I do — boil down 150 years of anthropological discoveries into a nuts-and-bolts reference describing the essentials of human evolution, both cultural and biological. I also describe just how anthropologists work so you can understand the pros and cons of different methods.

If you're taking an introductory course in Anthropology, this book can help clarify some ideas that can be pretty confusing and aren't often clearly explained, even in textbooks. If you're reading this book out of sheer curiosity, let me assure you that I've trimmed away a lot of technical material that may otherwise get in the way of your understanding the essential lessons of anthropology. Lots of popular-science books cover some aspects of anthropology, but few if any really cover anthropology as a whole in a clear, no-nonsense way. I've worked hard to provide just such a handbook in *Anthropology For Dummies*.

Each chapter is divided into concise sections, and each section breaks down the essentials of anthropology, including

- ✔ Terms and definitions
- ✔ The lowdown about competing theories
- ✔ How anthropology understood certain topics in the past and how it understands them today

I've written this book so that you can start anywhere; if you're most interested in human language, you can jump to that chapter and understand it without knowing about human evolution. But because every aspect of humanity is tied to some other aspect, I'd be surprised if you don't eventually end up reading it all!

Conventions Used in This Book

I use the following conventions throughout the text to make things consistent and easy to understand:

- ✔ All Web addresses appear in `monofont`.
- ✔ New terms appear in *italic* and are closely followed by an easy-to-understand definition.
- ✔ **Bold** text highlights key words or concepts in some bulleted lists and the action parts of numbered steps.

It's tough to write a book about humanity without using the collective term "we," so when I use it, keep in mind that I'm talking about humanity at large and not anthropologists (unless otherwise noted).

I often refer to the past because humanity is an old species, and we can learn a lot from our past. When I do this, I often use the convention *BP* for "before present" (which basically means years ago). When talking about the history of Western civilization, I use the conventional terms *BC* for "Before Christ" and *AD* for "Anno Domini" (which marks the year of Christ's birth); some instead use *BCE* ("Before the Common Era") and *CE* ("Common Era") to avoid valuing the timescale of Western civilization, but these terms still just point exactly to BC and AD. Because so much information about the past uses BC and AD, I stick with this convention. Don't worry, I'm not pushing a religion or valuing one timescale over another; I'm just using a common way to indicate the passage of time.

Some physical anthropologists now use the term *hominin* to refer to any human or human ancestor; however, this change hasn't been complete, and many news reports still use the term *hominid*. Until all anthropology makes this switch, I'm sticking with hominid to mean any large, bipedal (walking on two legs) primate, which basically means modern humans, some ancient human ancestors, and some of their closest biological relatives.

Anthropologists often use the terms *society* and *culture* interchangeably. I do this as well. It's an old convention that's not technically accurate, but unless you're studying for your PhD, the difference isn't that important. (Don't worry; I define both society and culture in the book so you're aware of the difference.)

Finally, when I refer to the scientific names of various life forms, I capitalize the genus but don't capitalize the species, or subspecies. For example, modern humans are all *Homo sapiens sapiens*. I don't always use subspecies names (like the second *sapiens*), and sometimes, for convenience, I just indicate the genus with a capital letter while writing out the species name, as in *H. sapiens*. Don't worry, this kind of terminology isn't a large or important point of this book, and these designations will all be very clear when you find them in the chapters.

What You're Not to Read

I've written this book so that you can both find information easily and easily understand what you find. And though it'd be great if you read every word, I've set off some text off from the main information, text you can live without if you're just after the reference material. Don't get me wrong — this stuff is interesting material. But if you're just after the nuts and bolts, you can come back to these items later:

- **Text in sidebars:** Sidebars are shaded boxes that usually give detailed examples or flesh out historical perspectives on the topic at hand.

- **Anything with a Technical Stuff icon:** This icon indicates information that's interesting but that you can live without. Read these tidbits later if you're pressed for time.

- **The stuff on the copyright page:** No kidding. You'll find nothing here of interest unless you're inexplicably enamored by legal language and Library of Congress numbers.

Foolish Assumptions

I don't think I'm going too far out on a flimsy limb to make these assumptions about you as a reader:

- You're someone — just about anyone who can read, really — interested in the human species. Bring that interest to the reading and you'll be rewarded.

- You're taking an Introduction to Anthropology course and your textbook just isn't making things clear; all you want is a friendly, digestible resource that gives you the info you need in plain English.

- You either believe that evolution happens or that it's a sound biological theory. Evolution is the basis of modern biology, and nothing in the world of living things makes sense without it. Even if you have some doubts about evolution, I'm assuming that you can keep your mind open to the fact that humanity is very ancient; evolution is a foundation of the scientific study of our species.

- You're anyone who wants a handy reference to settle a friendly argument about some aspect of humanity. When did the first civilizations arise? How many human languages exist? What did our earliest ancestors eat? You'll find these answers and plenty more.

How This Book Is Organized

I've divided this book into five tidy parts. The following sections describe what each part covers.

Part 1: What 1s Anthropology?

Anthropology is the study of the human species, from DNA to language. It's such a massive field that the first thing to do is sketch out just what anthropology does and doesn't study. You also discover some important facts about how anthropology developed as a scientific discipline.

Part 11: Physical Anthropology and Archaeology

Physical (or biological) anthropology focuses on humanity as a biological phenomenon — just another member of the 200+ primate species on Earth today. This part explores humanity's oldest natural relatives — the primates — and the human species itself. Also in this part, I discuss evolution (the foundation of all modern biology), showing how it's essential to understanding humanity biologically. I also introduce you to *archaeology* (the study of ancient cultures) and show you how it works and what it has learned about the prehistory of our species, from cave art to the great civilizations of the ancient world. Finally, I take you through some of humanity's earliest action, from migration to farming to full-on civilization.

Part 111: Cultural Anthropology and Linguistics

Cultural anthropology studies all facets of modern living cultures, from their religions to their ways of adapting to change, resolving conflict, and more. *Linguistic anthropology* is the study of *language,* humanity's distinctive way of communication. This part covers what culture really is, why it differs worldwide, and how different human language is from other animal communication (and why that's a key characteristic of our species). It also discusses how hotbed issues like race, gender, religion, and politics relate anthropologically.

Part IV: So What? Anthropology, the Modern World, and You

In this part, I cover the main ways that the study of anthropology can cross over into daily, real-world life. I show you how cultural anthropology can help humans resolve political friction and conflict, how physical anthropology and archaeology are important to better understanding history, and how anthropology can create more efficient responses to climate change and some other big issues facing our species today.

Part V: The Part of Tens

This part is all about you: It gives you some ideas about careers in anthropology, recommends some anthropologically themed books and movies for your enjoyment, and boils down the ten most important lessons of this entire book.

Icons Used in This Book

To make this book easier to read and simpler to use, I include some icons that can help you find and fathom key ideas and information.

Any time you see this icon, you know the information that follows is so important that it's worth reading more than once.

This icon presents historical, case-specific, or otherwise interesting information that you can read for further understanding; however, the info isn't necessary for grasping the concept.

This icon warns about potential traps that can derail you in your quest to understand anthropology.

Where to Go from Here

I've organized this book so that you can go wherever you want to find complete information. Want to know about the evolution of civilization, for example? Check out Chapter 10. If you're interested in Neanderthals and why they went extinct, you want Chapter 7. If the complexities of language or religion flip your switch, head for Chapter 13 or 16. You get the idea. You can use the table of contents to find broad categories of information or the index to look up more specific topics.

If you're not sure where you want to go, you may want to start with Part I. It gets you started with what anthropology studies, and how, and you can follow your interests from there.

Part I

What Is Anthropology?

In this part . . .

What's anthropology, and why should people study it? This part answers these questions and sketches out the history of *anthropology,* the study of humanity at large. It also introduces you to the four subfields of anthropology.

Chapter 1

Human Beings and Being Human: An Overview of Anthropology

- -

In This Chapter

▶ Discovering what anthropology is and how it studies the human species

▶ Exploring the Indiana Jones stuff: Physical anthropology and archaeology

▶ Checking out how cultures and languages fit into anthropology

▶ Finding out how modern anthropology analyzes human issues today

- -

*W*hy isn't everyone the same? Why do people worldwide have differences in skin and hair color and ways of greeting one another? Why doesn't everyone speak the same language?

Questions like these have fascinated humanity for as long as we have written records — and I'm sure people thousands and even tens of thousands of years before writing was invented asked the same things (in whatever language they used.) *Why don't those people do things the way I do? What's wrong with them, anyway?* Of course, people from that other group just on the next hilltop were scratching their heads and asking exactly the same questions.

Enter *anthropology*, the study of humanity. In this book I tell you what you need to know about anthropology, what anthropologists have discovered about humanity, and what anthropologists mean when they say that there are many ways of being human. I also tell you how anthropology works, and what anthropologists have learned about humanity, both modern and ancient.

And knowing all this is important if, as a species, we want to understand ourselves. Biologically, humanity needs to know itself if it's going to make good decisions about everything from medicine to genetically engineering food crops; that knowledge comes from anthropology. And culturally, knowledge of our past can help us understand what we are today, for better and worse; that knowledge, today, also comes from the field of anthropology. In Part I of this book — specifically in Chapters 2 and 3 — you find out how anthropology studies humanity from these biological and cultural perspectives. Finally, Part IV of this book also shows how anthropology can help humanity deal with some real, real-world problems.

Digging Into Anthropology's History

For a long time the answers to profound questions about humanity came largely from religious texts. For example, when European explorers realized that the New World wasn't India, the Native Americans — millions of people nobody was expecting to find — were explained from a biblical perspective as remnants of the lost tribes of Israel.

But since the late 19th century AD another perspective has emerged, the scientific study of humanity called *anthropology*. At first anthropology was a quaint and pretty simple affair, studied as a sort of hobby by all kinds of Naturalists and pseudoscientists. But when people started to realize how much anthropology could teach humanity about itself, they began to take it more seriously. Anthropology became a science, the science of humanity at large.

In Chapter 2, you can get a grip on anthropology's history and how it changed over time from being a pseudoscience to today's highly technical study of human DNA and ancient fossils. In Chapter 3, you can find more detail about how anthropology has developed over time, affecting how it goes about learning about humanity in the first place.

The questions that anthropologists have asked (and ask today) are in part a reflection of the times; for example, today a lot of people are investigating the effects of climate change on ancient human populations. Knowing the potential for bias, anthropologists are careful about making assumptions.

Getting Acquainted with Anthropology's Subfields

Anthropology has a complex, colorful, and sometimes checkered history. As you find out in Chapter 2, the field has gone through several transformations, and today there are more ways of doing anthropology than you can shake a stick at.

Now, the study of humanity is a vast undertaking, so anthropologists have divvied up the task into four main subfields:

- ✓ Physical anthropology
- ✓ Archaeology
- ✓ Cultural anthropology
- ✓ Linguistics

As you study anthropology, keep in mind that to really understand humanity, anthropologists need to know about each of the subfields. For example, an archaeologist studying an ancient civilization needs to know what a physical anthropologist has to say about that people's bones, what the people ate, or how they practiced medicine. And today, cultural anthropologists can't know much about a culture unless they have a good knowledge of that culture's language system.

Physical anthropology

Physical differences between groups of humans are easily visible; mainland Europeans tend to be lighter-skinned with straight hair, and folks from Africa are typically darker-skinned with curlier hair. These are biological differences, and the goal of *physical anthropology* — the study of humanity as a biological species — is to understand how and why these variations on the human theme came about. Physical differences among living humans aren't all that physical anthropology is concerned with, but understanding human variation (especially genetic differences) worldwide and through time is an important part of the field.

In Part II of this book, I boil down the main discoveries of physical anthropology to date so that what's left is the skeleton, the essentials. This material is what physical anthropologists know today and a little about what they're studying and hoping to learn in the future. Chapter 4 introduces you to the primate order, your home in the animal kingdom. Chapters 6 and 7 take you to Africa, the cradle of humanity, to cover the fossil evidence of human evolution.

Like all anthropology, physical anthropology has its fingers in a lot of different pies, from the study of fossils, to DNA analysis, documenting and explaining differences in cold- or heat-tolerance among people worldwide, the study of disease, population genetics, and a dozen other topics. Chapter 19 introduces you to the cutting edge study of physical anthropology, focusing on the magnificent molecule called DNA.

Archaeology

It's hard to get to know someone without knowing a little about their past, and the same goes for humanity; a lot of what we do today — good and bad — is based on the acts and decisions of our ancestors. To understand humanity any further than skin deep requires looking into the past. This is the business of archaeologists.

But the past can be foggy (on a good day) because history — the written record — can only take us so far (and if you believe everything written in the ancient historical texts, well, I've got some oceanfront property in Utah you may be interested in). However well-meaning they may have been, historians have had their biases like everyone else. And, of course, the ancient historians didn't write down everything, especially if they were unaware of, say, the entire New World (North and South America).

Archaeologists are the people who try to fill in the gaps of history by studying the material remains of ancient cultures. It's archaeologists who get excited over discovering an ancient piece of pottery, not necessarily for that piece of pottery alone (though it may be beautiful) but because of what it can tell humanity about its past.

Archaeologists don't just focus on correcting or fleshing out the historical record; they also study the roughly 2.5 million years of humanity *before* writing was invented.

Chapter 5 tells you how archaeologists learn about the past, from carbon dating to meticulous excavation. Chapter 7 tells you about the spread of modern humans out of Africa and across the globe, and Chapter 8 gives some exciting examples of how humanity adapted to every environment imaginable, including the Arctic and the Pacific.

Cultural Anthropology

Humanity has more facets than just where we came from, our relations to the other primates, or how our ancient civilizations rose or fell. You also have to consider the whole original question of why people today differ worldwide. How come traditional Polynesian clothing is different from traditional clothing in the Sahara? Why do many Asian folks eat with chopsticks but others use a fork and knife? Why is it okay for a man to have several wives in one culture but not in another culture?

Unfortunately, the common sense answers are rarely right — chopsticks aren't some archaic precursor to fork and knife, they're just a different way of getting food into the mouth. Similarly, the ways in which people find marriage partners in traditional Indian society (perhaps by arranged marriages) and traditional German society are just different. Cultural anthropologists study why these variations exist in the first place, and how they're maintained as parts of cultural traditions, as elements of a given society's collective identity.

Part III of this book covers cultural anthropology, the study of living human cultures. Overall, these chapters give you the nuts and bolts of what cultural anthropologists have learned about living human cultures. Chapter 11 tells you just what culture for anthropologists really means (no, it's not the opera or stuffy wine-and-cheese parties) and how critical it is for human survival.

In Chapter 12 you see that all human cultures are basically *ethnocentric*, meaning that they typically believe that their own way of doing things — from how they eat to how they dress — is proper, right, and superior to any other way of doing things. This feeling of superiority can lead (and has led) to everything from poor intercultural relations to ethnic cleansing. Cultural anthropologists, and the knowledge and understanding they generate while studying the many different ways of being human, can help smooth out intercultural communications; how they do this is also covered in Chapter 12. It can help humans understand other perspectives.

Part III also explains why race and ethnicity can be such volatile issues (Chapter 14), how humanity organizes identity (from family groupings to gender categories) and keeps track of who's related to whom (Chapter 15), and the basic characteristics of humanity's various religious traditions and political systems (Chapter 16).

Linguistics

Depending on whom you ask, humanity as a whole speaks something like 6,000 human languages. Chapter 13 explains what language is as well as how linguistic anthropologists investigate how language evolved in the first place — one of the most fascinating questions in all of anthropology. In laying out a clear definition of language, linguistic anthropologists have had to compare human communication with the communication systems of other living things. All of what they've learned — from the fascinating study of how humans acquire language to the layers of meaning that seem to only be present in human communication — give humanity a better understanding of just how unique and precious language is.

That uniqueness is in jeopardy, though, because languages become extinct every year as more people take up just speaking just one of the handful of main languages spoken worldwide today.

Making Sense of Anthropology's Methods

Anthropology's methods also range from lab analysis of DNA to taking notes on Sicilian (or any culture's) body language. Each of these methods helps better understand the many ways of being human. The following list gives you an overview of some of these methods:

- ✔ Evolution is the foundation of modern biology, and physical anthropologists — who study humanity from a biological perspective — rely on it. Check out Chapter 3 for the lowdown on exactly what evolution is and isn't and how it helps anthropologists study humanity.

- ✔ Archaeology isn't just Indiana Jones dodging bad guys and saving priceless treasures. Chapter 5 covers the methods of archaeologists, from keeping track of where objects are found to dating them by the carbon-14 method.

- ✔ Do cultural anthropologists really get grants to go to other countries and observe human behavior? Yes, but there's a lot more to it than that! Chapter 12 covers the methods of cultural anthropology, from observation to immersion in a subject culture.

- ✔ The complexity of human language is one of the main characteristics distinguishing us from non-human animals. Chapter 13 shows you how anthropologists think about and study language.

Applied Anthropology: Using the Science in Everyday Life

Part IV of this book introduces the many ways that the lessons of anthropology are relevant in daily life. Anthropology isn't just studied by scruffy professors clothed in tweeds (although I have to admit that yes, I do have a tweed jacket, and yes, I've worn it to an anthropological conference . . . once). Anthropologists are employed by many companies and government agencies, bringing what they know of humanity to the tables of commerce, international diplomacy, and other fields as *applied anthropologists*.

Applied anthropologists help humanity get along in a very literal sense. Chapter 17 shows how the lessons of anthropology are important to understanding and preventing cultural conflict.

Anthropology also helps humanity survive. Humanity faces enormous challenges, from overpopulation to language extinction and climate change (covered in Chapter 18) and common-sense solutions to these problems just aren't working. But with a subtler understanding of why humanity is the way it is, applied anthropologists are better suited to implementing changes, particularly on the community level, than many government officials who may know a lot about high-level politics but little about cultural traditions and values in the smaller communities they govern.

Chapter 19 takes you into the lab, where anthropologists are analyzing DNA with methods that can help you find out where your genetic roots lie. This chapter shows you that they ultimately lie in the great continent of Africa.

Finally, Chapter 20 has some exciting examples of how archaeological discoveries help us flesh out the history books. The common people of the ancient world — and unless you're royalty, that means your ancestors — didn't write much, but archaeology has given them a voice. Here you can find out about the lives of common laborers of ancient Egypt, American slaves, and the vanished Greenlandic Norse.

Chapter 2

Looking Into Humanity's Mirror: Anthropology's History

In This Chapter
▶ Figuring out exactly what anthropology studies
▶ Discovering how anthropology defines humanity and culture
▶ Reviewing the historical roots that led to modern anthropology

*I*n 1949, anthropologist Clyde Kluckhohn published "Mirror for Man," an introduction to the study of anthropology, the study of humanity (anthro meaning "of humanity" and logy meaning "the study of"). Since then, attitudes have changed a little (most people now speak of "humanity" rather than "mankind"), but Kluckhohn's words still ring true: "Anthropology holds up a great mirror to man and lets him look at himself in his infinite variety."

Anthropology is the mirror of our species; a place for humanity to reflect on itself. But you have to do that looking, and the discovering that comes from it, with care. If you want to understand anything, you need to see everything, warts and all. As a species we've found time and again that our cultural biases — our *ethnocentric* way of thinking that our culture is superior to all others — are simply wrong; humanity has found many ways to be human. Anthropology studies those many paths.

What does humanity see in the great mirror of anthropology? Before answering this question, you need to understand where anthropology came from. It didn't just pop up out of nowhere, and it wasn't invented overnight: it was cobbled together, refined, reinvented, crafted, and then reimagined and reinterpreted such that today anthropology is a very diverse field holding up many mirrors for humanity.

Rather than give you a comprehensive history of the discipline of anthropology — which would take a separate book — in this chapter I introduce the main *ideas* that paved the way to modern anthropology. As with any idea, you see that some were products of their times and have since fallen by the wayside, and others were eternal from the start and continue to fascinate anthropologists.

Getting to the Heart of Anthropology

An exciting passage of Homer's *Odyssey* finds Odysseus and crew spying distant figures on an island they're about to land on and wondering about the people they'll encounter. Do those strange folk plant crops in an orderly fashion or do they forage for their food? Do they revere the gods and have laws and lawful assemblies? Or are these some other kind of people — savages, maybe? Savages, of course, would be people who didn't do things the Greek way . . .

Homer wrote nearly 3,000 years ago, but the questions Odysseus asked were already ancient. *Look, over there: People different from us! What are they like?*

Anthropology is rooted in the question of what Other (with a capital *O*) people are like. But up from the roots has grown a whole plant, an anthropology that not only looks at Others but also looks at itself and all of humanity. Anthropologists today continue to learn about the human species by studying people outside Western civilization, but they also scrutinize humanity as a biological species, investigate how the modern world came to be by examining the past, and obsess over details of uniquely human characteristics such as language. Anthropologists have even taken up the study of anthropology *itself*, some saying, in effect, that the mirror is cracked and that to understand humanity better, they must understand the history of anthropology itself.

By examining the history of their own discipline, anthropologists have gone from *silvering* the mirror — applying the reflective coating to the glass — to gluing it back together and, today, trying to keep it clean. Because culture changes so quickly, the questions that each generation of anthropologists asks tend to change, so maintaining this mirror for humanity isn't easy. In fact, some would say that each generation has its own mirror, and that questions *should* change as culture changes.

On the surface, I'd agree: As times change and we learn new things, we need to ask new questions. But at the same time, I'm confident that the following topics will always be central to humanity's investigation of itself — to the field of anthropology:

- ✓ **What are the commonalities among humans worldwide?** That is, what does every human culture do?

- ✓ **What are the variations among humans worldwide?** That is, what things do only some cultures do?

- ✓ **Why do these commonalities and variations exist in the first place?** In other words, why aren't all human cultures the same?

> ✔ **How does humanity change through time?** Is it still evolving, and if so, how?
>
> ✔ **Where has humanity been, and what can that show us about where humanity is going?** That is, what can we learn about ourselves today, from our past?

To answer these and other questions, one foundation of anthropology is the *comparative approach,* in which cultures aren't compared to one another in terms of which is better than the other but rather in an attempt to understand how and why they differ as well as share commonalities. This method is also known as *cultural relativism*, an approach that rejects making moral judgments about different kinds of humanity and simply examines each relative to its own unique origins and history.

Because humanity qualifies as one of many biological species in the animal kingdom, another foundation of anthropology is *evolution*, the change of species through time. As I discuss throughout this book, both human biology and culture have evolved over millions of years, and they continue to evolve. What's more, human biology can affect human culture, and vice versa. For example, over time, human brains became larger (biological change) leading to increased intelligence, language, and eventually writing (a cultural change in the way humans communicate). Anthropologists call human evolution *biocultural* evolution to illustrate this dual nature of human change.

Dazed and Confused: What It Is to Be Human

The problem with being human is that it leads to questions. Eighteenth-century German philosopher Immanuel Kant wrote that three fundamental questions were "What can I know? What ought I to do? What may I hope?" Just like Rene Descartes' momentous phrase "I think, therefore I am," each of Kant's little nuggets can lead to a lifetime of introspection. If anthropology is a mirror for humankind, the individual human mind is itself a hall of mirrors. It's a wonder we can make any sense of anything!

To start, you need some definitions. These terms come up again throughout this book, but it's important to get a handle on them sooner rather than later.

Humanity refers to the human species, a group of life forms with the following characteristics:

✔ *Bipedalism* (walking on two legs)

✔ Relatively small teeth for primates of our size

✔ Relatively large brains for primates of our size

> ✔ Using modern language to communicate ideas
>
> ✔ Using complex sets of ideas — called culture (discussed later) — to survive

Standing on two legs and having particularly small teeth and large brains are all anatomical characteristics, and they're studied by anthropologists focusing on human biological evolution. Surviving by using a wide array of cultural information (including instructions for making a fur cloak in the Arctic or a pottery canteen in the desert Southwest) is the use of culture (defined in the next section). It's studied by other anthropologists, and even more study the evolution of language.

Humanity is a general term that doesn't specify whether you're talking about males, females, adults, or children; it simply means our species — *Homo sapiens sapiens* — at large. The term *humanity* can be applied to modern humans *(Homo sapiens sapiens)* as well as some of our most recent ancestors, placed more generally in *Homo sapiens,* without the subspecies (the second *sapiens*) suffix. Exactly when *Homo sapiens* evolved into *Homo sapiens sapiens* is a complex question based on when humans became *anatomically* modern and when they became *behaviorally* modern. I introduce these questions a little later in this chapter and investigate them in detail in Chapter 7.

Two types of culture

The next most important definition is that of *culture,* which is the whole set of information a human mind uses to describe what the world is like and what's appropriate behavior for living in that world. *Cultural differences* are basically different conceptions of what is appropriate in a given situation. For example, women in traditional Tibetan culture often have more than one husband, whereas men in traditional Tajikistan (a country in central Asia) often have multiple wives. Each culture, then, has specific ideas about what's appropriate marriage-wise, but the difference between what each considers appropriate is pretty major.

When anthropologists speak of *different cultures,* on the other hand, they mean different groups of people each possessing a unique set of ideas for what's appropriate — in this case, the Tibetans and the Tajiks.

Anthropologists often use the words *society* and *culture* interchangeably, as I do in this book. Strictly speaking, a society can contain several cultures, so it's a larger unit than a single culture (for example, American society today encompasses Irish, Hispanic, and Japanese American cultures, to name only three). Culture, then, includes ideas about identity (for example, what the word *brother* means), nature (what *wild* means as opposed to *tame*), social relationships (how to greet the queen of England as opposed to how to greet your darts partner) and so on, as well as artifacts.

Some anthropologists extend culture to the objects (called *artifacts*) that humanity makes or uses to aid in survival. In this case, culture is both the information stored in the brain (shared among a group) and the objects that group uses to survive. For example, artifacts (also called *material culture*) include the distinctive Inuit harpoon carved from bone and used to hunt seals. Not all artifacts have such obvious survival value, though. The specially made drum a shaman uses in a healing ritual isn't directly related to staying alive—gathering calories—but as far as the shaman is concerned, that specific drum is very important. It has to be made the right way and carry the right tone; otherwise, the healing would be jeopardized. In this way, the drum is just as important to survival as the harpoon.

The idea of extending culture to encompass artifacts sees all of culture as the *extrasomatic means of adaptation*. That is, whereas other life forms survive via bodily (*somatic*) adaptations, humanity relies not so much on its anatomy as its culture, its *extrasomatic* means of adaptation and survival.

Two types of modernity

The term *humanity* can be a little tricky because anthropologists use it to refer to our species, *Homo sapiens sapiens*, as well as some of our most recent ancestors in the more general species *Homo sapiens* (lacking the very specific subspecies *sapiens*.) When the human species should be referred to as *Homo sapiens* versus *Homo sapiens sapiens* depends on whether you're talking about being *anatomically* or *behaviorally* modern.

Anatomical modernity is being anatomically indistinguishable from modern, living populations. This term really comes into play only when anthropologists are looking at the bones of ancient human-like creatures and asking whether these creatures are human; strictly speaking, if anthropologists can't distinguish the bones they're looking at from those of modern populations, the bones are anatomically modern.

Behavioral modernity is behaving in a way that's indistinguishable from modern, living populations. This label also really comes into play only when anthropologists are looking at the complexity of behavior in the past — for example, at the objects made by ancient proto-humans. Asking whether the creatures that made these objects were behaviorally human is a tough question that I re-examine in Chapter 7, but for the moment it's enough to know behaviorally modern people employ *symbolism*, the use of one object to stand for another. Blood, for example, is a common substance, but humanity can also use it — or its properties, such as the color red — symbolically to activate emotions, memories, and actions in other people. This uniquely human capacity for the complex use of symbols is a big part of behavioral modernity.

-Isms and the Making of Anthropology

Like most scholarly disciplines, anthropology wasn't just tidily invented overnight; I think of it as a Frankenstein's monster of ideas and questions culled from other disciplines, cobbled and stitched together into a more-or-less functional whole. (You can read more about the various subdisciplines of anthropology in Chapter 3.)

But even before anthropology existed as a discrete academic field, its foundations were being laid by people doing other things that would later be called anthropology (or act as guidelines for building anthropology). Herodotus, a 6th-century Greek scholar, described the peoples and antiquities of Egypt, and Julius Caesar described the people he encountered in France (the Gauls) and southern England (the Britons) in the 50s BC; people have been interested in other people for a long time. But these reports were often curios or written as political statements, and they were largely descriptive; they showed what *was* (more or less) but didn't go into too much detail about *why*. They offered few systematic explanations.

It wasn't until the 19th and 20th centuries AD that people systematically went out from the centers of Western civilization (in Europe and North America) with the specific goal of studying Other people. Even then, figuring out how to apply what they learned about others to what they already knew about humanity at large took some time. When this did begin to happen, though, the seed of anthropology was watered, and a new discipline began to grow.

Harsh words for early anthropology

Although Europeans began to substantially colonize the New World and other "discoveries" in the 17th century, the colonialist endeavor wasn't fully realized and backed up by industrialization until the 19th century. Early *ethnographies* — documents describing non-European cultures authored by people who lived for some time on those cultures — were often little more than intelligence reports for use in exploitation.

In 1966, Claude Levi-Strauss, a leading anthropologist of his time, wrote that cultural anthropology and ethnography were rooted in a historical context in which "... the larger part of mankind [was made] subservient to the other, and during which millions of innocent human beings have had their resources plundered and their institutions and beliefs destroyed, whilst they themselves were ruthlessly killed, thrown into bondage, and contaminated by diseases they were unable to resist."

Colonialism

Early anthropology is rooted in the efforts of Western civilization to better understand the lands it was colonizing. This isn't revisionist history or Western-civilization bashing — it's just plain fact.

For example, in 1902 the *Report of the Philippine Commission* stated that "Since the first arrival of the Portuguese in Eastern waters, the mind of the Malay has appeared to the European as a closed book. Both races have ever misunderstood and mistrusted each other. Out of mutual ignorance and fear have followed hatred, oppression, and retaliation . . . this government is attempting to rear a new standard of relationship between the white man and the Malay. The success . . . will depend . . . on our correct understanding and scientific grasp of the peoples whose problems we are facing."

The problems the report refers to were Western problems revolving around how to make better workers of the Malaysians, and the solution was a scientific understanding of these folk to be achieved through the new science of anthropology. Specifically, this new science would use one of its principal tools, ethnography, to help the colonial effort. *Ethnography* is the direct observation of a group of people by living near or among them, and making records of what one observes.

This kind of study is hardly surprising today, but keep in mind that for a long time knowledge of what went on in non-Western cultures wasn't based on direct experience but on superficial reports from outsiders, reports that often judged — with Western civilization's basic biblical morality — what had been observed. Actually putting observers into the cultures they were to be investigating was a new move.

Colonialist ethnographies had some distinctive characteristics:

- **Racism:** Particularly, the idea that non-Western people were inferior to Westerners and therefore had to be educated to the best of the colonial powers' ability (but would always remain inferior to Westerners).

- **Social Darwinism:** Particularly, the idea that non-Western people either were destined to be Westernized (in which case they should be helped to achieve Westernization — for example, by having their customs banned and replaced with Western customs) or were doomed to extinction (in which case not much could be done for them but to document them like living museum exhibits before they became extinct).

- **Ethnocentrism:** The idea that Western civilization was at the pinnacle of human evolution, and that all other ways of life were inferior; note that this view isn't exclusive to Western civilization — many cultures worldwide believe it as well.

Although early anthropology was colored by its involvement with colonialism, by the 1950s many anthropologists recognized that ethnographies being produced under the colonialist paradigm weren't as objective as they could be; in 1969, the American Anthropological Association formed a Committee on Ethics. By the mid-1970s, guidelines for ethical ethnography were being published, and today graduate students undergo rigorous ethical and human-relations training before doing fieldwork.

Federally funded anthropological research by U.S. researchers normally requires a review and approval by the government's Institutional Review Board to ensure that "human subjects research" doesn't harm the very people it's researching.

Although anthropologists still must consider plenty of ethical issues when doing research among other human beings, I'm confident that most ethnographic anthropologists today don't work for colonialist efforts or efforts counter to the interest of the people they study; in fact, my impression is that most ethnographers today do the opposite: work in the interest of the folks they study. At the same time, most of them — in one way or another — are working to answer some of the basic questions I outline in the section "Getting to the Heart of Anthropology" earlier in the chapter.

Antiquarianism

You can find the roots of *archaeology* (a branch of anthropology that studies the ancient past) in a distinctly nonscientific interest in the past. Many motivations initially drove this *antiquarian* (prescientific) interest: Ancient Sumerian royalty commissioned excavations that could show their connections to mythical culture heroes, 16th-century French traders could sell *curios* (unusual articles) to royal families across Europe, and 19th-century eligible English bachelors could clutter their parlors with artifacts meant to demonstrate their owners' high education and interest in the esoteric. Only in the 1850s did appreciable numbers of investigators — who began to call themselves archaeologists — start to carefully document what they excavated.

Like colonialist ethnography, antiquarian archaeology had some distinctive characteristics:

✔ **A focus on large, visible archaeology:** In particular, large ruins — such as the walled city of Troy, the pyramids of Egypt, or the Parthenon — that were relatively easy to find and analyze. (This propensity for size also led to a focus on the royal families of the ancient world because they were associated with these large monuments, whereas common people were buried elsewhere and essentially ignored by archaeologists until the 1960s.)

> ✔ **A focus on the Western world:** Early archaeologists largely believed that the West was at the pinnacle of evolution, and all other societies were either going to become Western or become extinct.
>
> ✔ **A focus on monetary value:** Many sought antiquities not for their value as knowledge but as items that could be sold.
>
> ✔ **A concept of shallow time:** Until the 1860s, many believed that the Earth was only a few thousand years old and that most explanations of the ancient world were in the Christian Bible.

Although archaeology began without distinctively scientific goals, by the early 1900s people knew that the Earth was very ancient and that evolution had shaped humanity as early as millions of years ago, and archaeologists had begun to make very careful records of what they found. You can check out more about modern archaeological methods in Chapter 3. For the moment, you just need to know that although the study began in antiquarianism, it developed into a modern science that has revealed a great deal about the human past.

Scientism

By the 1930s, anthropology was underway as a distinctive academic field worldwide, with anthropologists trying — in different ways — to examine some of the basic questions outlined in the section "Getting to the Heart of Anthropology" earlier in this chapter. Bodies of theory even developed, each a different lens through which to interpret the cultures worldwide (which were being documented by ethnographers). Essentially, people applied a scientific approach to the study of humanity.

This development could go too far, as when people improperly applied biological concepts to cultural change (resulting in the idea of *social Darwinism*, a mistaken idea I examine in Part III of this book), but essentially it was a step in the direction of objectivity, of trying to filter out ones' own cultural preconceptions when thinking about or documenting other cultures. It was an attempt, then, to combat ethnocentrism.

Although some today subscribe to the *postmodern* philosophy, which essentially states that all knowledge is socially constructed and that you can never get out of the box (you're hopelessly imprisoned in an ethnocentric shell) — I don't buy it. I believe human beings *can* be somewhat objective and make accurate statements about what they observe. Although each person wears his own culture's lenses, everyone can learn that some things apply to all cultures regardless of which lenses they're most accustomed to.

Ole Wurm and the circus strongman

The roots of modern scientific archaeology are in Europe, where, from the 1650s to the 1850s, all manner of men sought to find and bring home antiquities and curios of the ancient world. This checkered crew included genuine naturalists, such as Danish prehistorian Ole Wurm, legions of vaguely interested wealthy British bachelors, and Giovanni Belzoni, the Italian-born charlatan, circus strongman, and explorer of the Egyptian pyramids.

Wurm (1588–1654) was a Danish professor of medicine with an interest in, well, everything. Paying students to collect objects and curios any time they traveled abroad, Wurm assembled an impressive collection of artifacts, skeletons, fossils, rocks, ancient statuary, artifacts, and other bric-a-brac. Working under the impression that the world was just a few thousand years old, Wurm organized the objects in his museum — not according to age, but by how much they resembled one another. This was a start at systematically organizing the

many new objects being discovered by explorers, but it was different from today's archaeology because it lacked an understanding of the actual age of the Earth and humanity.

By the time he was 25, Belzoni (1778–1823) had fled from a monastic school in Rome and started a 12-year career as a strongman in an English circus. Traveling to Egypt in 1815, he quickly began an extraordinary new career as an "Antiquarian." Within a few years he had sent many ancient Egyptian relics back to London's British Museum, including multi-ton stone statues. In 1818 he used what some called his engineering genius to locate a passage into the Great Pyramid at Gizeh; although he found that it had already been looted, his exploits were enough to excite the public with tales of treasure-hunting and relics from past ages. Though he wasn't a professional scholar, Belzoni is credited with encouraging the public to take an interest in the ancient world.

Don't get bogged down by the hierarchy of scientific terminology regarding observations. An *observation* is something that you've seen or otherwise carefully documented; a *hypothesis* is a statement that suggests the relationship between two variables (for example, the *liquid* state of the variable *water* will change to the *solid* state when the variable *temperature* is sufficiently decreased). A *theory* is a more fully developed, complex form of hypothesis, and a *fact* is a statement — normally based on multiple confirmed hypotheses — that can account for many well-documented observations.

The attempt to add some scientific objectivity to anthropology led to the recognition and adoption of two very important perspectives:

✔ The *emic* perspective is that of a person within a culture — it's the insider's view. For example, it's a New Guinea highlander's concept of what constitutes murder, even though a Western scientist may have a different perception of that word.

> ✔ The *etic* perspective is that of a person from outside a culture — it's the outsider's view. For example, it's a scientist's definition of murder that he or she wants to use in comparing many different societies' punishments for having killed another person.

Although remaining emic or etic in your fieldwork or observations isn't always easy, know that anthropologists strive for both emic and etic knowledge (as opposed to early anthropologists, who focused on etic knowledge). You can read more about emic and etic perspectives in Chapter 12.

Holism

Another idea that came into anthropology with science was the concept of *holism*, which is the recognition that all parts of a human culture are more or less interdependent. Turns out studying one single aspect of a culture wasn't working for anthropologists. For example, kinship — how people reckon their relations with other members of society — intersects with economics, and economics intersect with religion and politics.

Anthropologists had to recognize that the many facets of the human experience were interrelated. This discovery didn't make humans easier to study, but it was better than laboring under the impression that human societies would be easy to figure out. Anthropologists are still trying to figure out how to understand the interrelations of the many facets of human culture, but at least they're no longer deluded by the idea that every cultural institution, for example, meshes perfectly with some other institution so that both would function easily. This idea (one of many *functionalist* conceptions) simply didn't recognize that people are messy, and cultures are hard to draw lines around. Because of this nonuniformity, cultural anthropology can be hard to study.

Holism doesn't mean that all parts of a society work in perfect harmony; all cultures appear to have some disunity or friction.

Anthropology Today

By the 1960s, anthropologists weren't content to simply study humanity — they wanted to apply what they'd learned about humanity to pressing real-world problems such as poverty. This approach, called *applied anthropology,* is an important facet of anthropology today, shaping some anthropologists' research plans (and entire careers) as well as determining where the lessons the anthropologist has learned will be applied.

Today, anthropology is a multidisciplinary study, one that draws on evidence from many studies in many different academic disciplines. Throughout this book I describe the discoveries of generations of anthropologists worldwide. Keep in mind that such discoveries draw on all sorts of lines of evidence to flesh out the human story. You can read about these other kinds of evidence, and the subfields of anthropology, in Chapter 3.

Chapter 3

Actually, Four Mirrors: How Anthropology Is Studied

*A*nthropology, the study of humanity by humans, isn't easy. Like any life form, the human species has many fascinating facets — from its biology to its language and deep history — and Western civilization has only been studying these facets in a truly systematic way for about 150 years. And much has changed even in those 150 years, both worldwide and within anthropology, such that anthropologists have to study the history of their own discipline to understand how much of what's already been done is still important and what's essentially out of date.

Still, anthropologists press on, believing that with care, diligence, sensitivity, a few research dollars, and plenty of graduate students willing to work for next to nothing, humanity can indeed learn important lessons about itself.

In this chapter, I describe the main ways that anthropologists examine humanity. Each of the subfields — physical anthropology, archaeology, linguistics, and cultural anthropology — are normally the career of a single anthropologist, but a full understanding of our species demands that you combine information from all these fields (see Figure 3-1). Therefore, anthropologists often proudly tell you that they're four-field anthropologists, focusing on one facet of humanity but tying their findings in with all others. In the same way, I'm going to break anthropology out into its four subfields, but remember, discoveries in these individual fields have effects on the others.

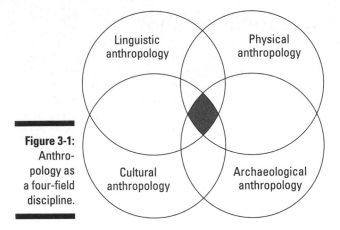

Figure 3-1:
Anthro-
pology as
a four-field
discipline.

Physical Anthropology and the Evolutionary Basis of Biology

One of Charles Darwin's great contributions to civilization was to demonstrate that humanity was part of the world of living things, not separate from it. For thousands of years, Western civilization, backed up by the biblical story of creation, held humanity as a special creation fundamentally different from all other living things. By Darwin's time, many were beginning to question this assessment, but the cultural pressure to conform to the dominant religion prevented most from saying so out loud. But Darwin's ideas and the many it fertilized set the foundation for a new study: the study of humans as living, evolving creatures in many ways no different from the rest of animal life. Today, anthropologists have countless reams of data, much of it based on studies of DNA — the molecule that shapes all Earth life — to back the claims Darwin made in 1859.

And so today they also have *physical anthropology,* the study of humanity as a biological phenomenon. What species are we most and least like? Where and when did we fist appear? What were our ancestors like? Can we learn about human behavior from the behavior of our nearest relatives, the chimpanzees and gorillas? Is our species still evolving? How do modern human genetics, population growth, and other current issues play out from a biological perspective? These are all questions physical anthropologists ask.

You say you want an evolution

You can find the answers to these and many other questions about our species in the study of *evolution,* the change through time of the properties of a living species. That's because evolution is the foundation of the life sciences. Many kinds of life forms have become extinct (like the dinosaurs), but each of today's living species (including humanity) has an evolutionary ancestry that reaches far back in time. Today, people understand that these principles can reveal a lot about the world of living things.

Evolution is often called a theory by people outside the scientific community, but many biologists would prefer to see it advanced to fact status. In a technical sense, gravitation is also a theory, but physicists have such good evidence for it that they universally accept it as fact.

Evolution, like anthropology, is studied by scientists. The scientific method both subjects share is a relatively simple process of generating knowledge based on three main stages of investigation. First, the scientist makes observations about the relationships among variables (such as air temperature and its effect on water). She then forms a *hypothesis,* or a statement about what effects she believes those variables will have on one another. (For example, she may hypothesize that exposure to cold air will cause water to freeze.) To test her hypothesis, she performs experiments to see whether her predictions are correct. If her hypothesis holds up under this extensive testing, she accepts the hypothesis as fact; if the experiments fail to produce the predicted results, she rejects the hypothesis. The key here is experimentation. What matters isn't whether the scientist is a professor or an undergraduate but whether the data support the hypothesis. Every scientific claim is entirely open to questioning and scrutiny. Science recognizes no authorities; every statement is open to further investigation. In this way, science is the most democratic way of generating knowledge.

Replication, variation, and selection

Until the mid-1800s, many questions about the human species, the age of the Earth, and other basic inquiries were answered by looking to one document: the Christian Bible. People argued that it contained all the answers humans would ever need, so no further investigation was necessary. The age of the Earth? An Irish archbishop calculated it as about 6,000 years based on biblical statements. The origins of humanity? Clearly laid out in the first pages of Genesis: God created humanity. Whatever one thinks of the morality prescribed by the Bible — and it offers plenty of good messages — it's clear today that these so-called facts are simply incorrect, dating from an age in which little was empirically known about the age of the earth, the origins of humanity, or even that our own planet wasn't at the center of the universe but only one of many.

Evolution is a process, not a thing. In fact, it's a single word used to describe the *cumulative effects* of three independent facts. Importantly, these attributes of evolution can be (and are) observed in nature every day. They are

- ✔ **Replication:** The fact that life forms have offspring
- ✔ **Variation:** The fact that each offspring is slightly different from its parents, and its siblings
- ✔ **Selection:** The fact that not all offspring survive, and those that do tend to be the ones best suited to their environment

Figure 3-2 shows these characteristics in more detail.

Regardless of your personal views on the topic of evolution, the three processes of evolution aren't arguable. Whether it's in the form of zebra calves, salmon fry, or human infants, life forms replicate. Also, all offspring aren't clones; variation occurs in small ways and significant ways, but it occurs. And if it weren't for selection, the world would be swarming with every mosquito, beetle, and tadpole ever born; the fact that it isn't verifies that not all of these creatures born survive into adulthood. Finally, it's not arguable that the offspring best suited to their environment tend to pass their genes on to the next generation.

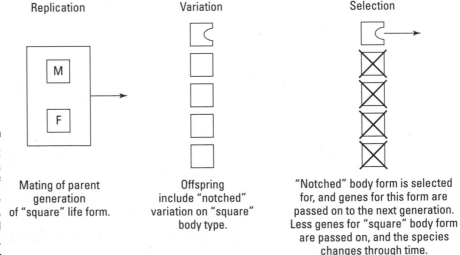

Figure 3-2: Evolution as the result of replication, variation, and selection.

Replication — Mating of parent generation of "square" life form.

Variation — Offspring include "notched" variation on "square" body type.

Selection — "Notched" body form is selected for, and genes for this form are passed on to the next generation. Less genes for "square" body form are passed on, and the species changes through time.

When replication happens, the variable offspring are born into an environment that basically either selects *for* or *against* them; if two dragonflies are pursued by predators (like birds), the one with a better build for its environment is most likely to survive. It's been selected for rather than against, and it's therefore more likely than its less-fit sibling to pass on the genes that made it. Now the genes that made a fit dragonfly go on to make the next generation of dragonflies, which are slightly fitter than the parent generation. Essentially, that's evolution: selection acting on the variable offspring, leading to the change through time of the characteristics of the organism.

Groups of living things that can interbreed and have healthy offspring are called *species*. Groups of similar species diverge into further groups, forming a biological classification hierarchy that I discuss in Chapter 4. In this chapter, just remember that a *genus* is the level above species. Humanity is in the genus *Homo* and the species *sapiens*, yielding the scientific name *Homo sapiens*.

Speciation

Sometimes groups of living things move from one environment to another, as when air currents carry insects from one island to another or some subpopulation of a species of squirrel somehow crosses a river and is cut off from its original population. When this happens, new selective environments may reshape the population so much that if it were to rejoin its ancestral population, the two couldn't interbreed. This event is called *speciation*, and it's what most people think of when they think about evolution: one life form gradually changing into another.

Because speciation can take a long time (anywhere from thousands to millions of years), it's hard to observe. Still, you can see it in the fossil record, where billions of years of Earth life have left traces of their change through time. And that record speaks clearly, even though it has gaps here and there (because geological forces have wiped out some fossils, for example, or animal and plant remains simply didn't fossilize due to geochemical factors), telling anthropologists that yes, all living species have long evolutionary histories, including *Homo sapiens* and all its living and past relatives in the primate order. This is where physical anthropology comes in, to investigate that evolutionary past.

More facets of physical anthropology

The evolutionary principles underlying physical anthropology touch everything that physical anthropologists study. In this section, I outline a few of the main fields of physical anthropology; you can read about yet more subfields and discoveries in the other chapters in this part of the book.

Why being human can make evolution hard to understand

Although the world of biology widely accepts evolution, the topic can be hard to understand for several reasons. Leaving aside deliberate mischaracterization of evolution by those with a religious agenda, I'm talking about how being human itself obscures our view of evolution.

By this I mean that although humans evolve, we do so in some ways profoundly different from other species. For the last 100,000 years our outward, physical bodies haven't evolved too terribly much; modern human skeletons are essentially indistinguishable from those of 100,000 years ago. And yet humanity has changed a great deal; most of us now live in massive cities, instead of as highly mobile foragers, and most of us eat foods grown on farms rather than collected from across vast landscapes. So what has changed, and how does it make evolution hard to understand?

What have changed are our minds and the cultures we carry in them. *Culture,* really, is the mind's set of instructions for what the universe is like and what you're supposed to do about it. (You can read about culture in more detail in Chapter 11.) *Doing* is the crux: We humans evolve proactively, inventing artifacts and cultural practices to survive in new environments, not reactively like every other species; other species don't even know they're evolving through time. Consider the Arctic, which was widely colonized after about 1,500 years ago by folks who invented dog sleds, whale-hunting equipment, watercraft, and igloos.

This purposive invention leads us, I think, to see living things the way we see our artifacts: as finished products of some kind of intent. It's hard to imagine that some mind didn't make the elm tree for some purpose, because we ourselves invent and build things for specific purposes. But evolution provides a competing idea about how those things came to be, one that can be hard to reconcile with humanity's purposeful tendencies.

Primatology

One specialty of physical anthropologists is the study of living primates, a field called *primatology.* (Some biologists also study primates, but without expressly looking for what they can teach humanity about itself.) Primatological physical anthropology studies primate behavior, biology, evolution, and anatomy. Each of these fields ties into the other, such that what anthropologists learn about behavior informs — and is informed by — what they learn about biology and so on. For example, you can't fully understand the anatomy of a species without knowing about its evolution because anatomical characteristics — like a prehensile tail, or new kinds of teeth — don't just pop up out of nowhere; they accumulate (or vanish) as selective pressures change and shape the organism.

Anthropologists study primate behavior by using the principles of *ethology*, the study of animal behavior. Although approaches vary, they often emphasize

- ✔ Observation of the animal in its natural environment for long periods — for example, across seasons and years rather than just a few weeks at a time

- ✔ Careful consideration of the interplay between behavior, environment, and anatomy, accounting for all that's known about the species

- ✔ A search for and explanation of patterns of behavior

- ✔ A search for and explanation of variations from patterns of behavior

When I say "animal behavior," I really should say "nonhuman animal behavior" because humans are, of course, animals. But the dividing line between humans and all other life forms has been so ingrained in Western civilization for so long that the phrase "animal behavior" is tough to shake.

Unfortunately, study of many primates in their natural habitats is becoming impossible as primate species go extinct or their habitats are reduced. (You can read more about the peril in which many primate species exist in Chapter 4.) Unfortunately, primatologists must resort to studying many primate species in enclosure settings such as zoos. Considering that humanity has only been doing extensive and broad, comparative primatology for a few decades and is only just sketching out an understanding of the living primates, this situation is a real shame.

Palaeoanthropology

Palaeoanthropology (*palaeo* meaning "old") specifically studies the human species and its relatives in the ancient past, particularly focusing on the early proto-human species, known as the *hominids*. (You can check out more on hominids in Chapter 6; for more on the difference between hominids and hominins, head to the Introduction.) Palaeoanthropology is extremely diverse and involves finding ancient human fossils, excavating them (and any artifacts found with them), interpreting the skeletal remains to understand the anatomy, and reconstructing hominid behavior as well as evolutionary relationships. To accomplish all this, most palaeoanthropologists have a strong background in the following fields:

- ✔ **Evolution:** Because the foundation of biology must be comprehensively understood to make sense of the fossil record

- ✔ **Skeletal anatomy:** Because *fossilized bone* (bone turned to stone by a geochemical process) is the bread and butter of palaeoanthropology, understanding how the body's skeletal tissues reflect daily life, disease, stress, and other factors is critical to reconstructing ancient ways of life

✔ **Geology:** Because fossils are often found in complex geological circumstances

✔ **Archaeology:** Because archaeologists must exercise great care to excavate fossils, the principles of keeping track of where they find items and carefully bringing them back to the lab are important

Some people even specialize within these divisions; some palaeoanthropologists focus on certain parts of the skeleton (like the teeth, the hand bones, or the pelvis), some focus on specific geological layers (to best understand them to the exclusion of all others), and some focus on *palaeoecology*, reconstructing entire ancient ecosystems in which early hominids evolved.

One of the main contributions of palaeoanthropology to the human understanding of humanity is to fill in the missing links of the evolutionary chain connecting modern people to our most ancient ancestors. Unfortunately the term *missing link* is something of a misnomer because species aren't so easy to define or draw lines around when you know them from fossil material only. But fossils can tell a lot about ancient life, and they do indeed show us, as a species, where we've been both figuratively and literally. (You can read more about fossils in Chapter 6.) Today, hundreds of fossil specimens bear some resemblance to modern people, and more ancient human-like forms. Because new species don't pop up out of nowhere today, anthropologists can reasonably assume that these hundreds of fossils don't represent early proto-humans that simply popped up and then vanished but rather members of our own lineage that slowly changed over time. They're better thought of as shades from an evolutionary spectrum than links in a chain, but the latter metaphor has stuck, and it's a tough one to fight.

Because the fossils of the earliest human ancestors are in Africa, fieldwork is complex and can be difficult; most of it occurs in the countries with the best infrastructure, like South Africa, Kenya, Tanzania, and Ethiopia. Modern projects are normally large-scale, incorporating diverse international research teams. They commonly train African students as well, so that even in the past 20 years, the authors of scientific reports are increasingly Africans themselves.

The biocultural animal

One thing that makes physical anthropology particularly complex is that humanity evolves not only as a result of biological factors but also because of cultural factors. For this reason, anthropologists call it *biocultural evolution*. *Culture* — which I discuss more thoroughly in Chapters 2 and 11 — is basically the set of ideas that dictate how you see and act in the world. Although humans survive by using both their biology and cultural information, all other animals survive mainly through their biology and by relying on instinct rather than such cultural information.

The Koobi Fora research project

Just two years into my undergraduate study of archaeology, I was lucky enough to participate in a field school project in the Koobi Fora research project in northern Kenya. Run from the National Museum of Kenya and based on a landform called Koobi Fora on the eastern shore of Lake Turkana (once Lake Rudolf), the project was begun by Richard Leakey in the 1960s. Today it's run by his daughter, Dr. Louise Leakey, who orchestrates a team of 16 principal scientists from institutions as diverse as the Free University of Amsterdam, the Smithsonian Institution, and Australia National University.

Research at Koobi Fora has revealed more than 200 early hominid fossils dating between about 4 million and 700,000 years ago. As a student, I vividly remember crawling across the baking desert and finding chips of stone eroding from an ancient lake-shore; picking one up, I realized it had been buried for more than a million years, and my career was locked in that moment.

Currently, Rutgers University runs a field school at Koobi Fora; you can check it out at `www.rci.rutgers.edu/~kffs/`. You can also keep up with the research on the project's Web site at `www.kfrp.com`, which has a blog during field seasons and many photographs of fieldwork.

For example, cultural, not instinctual, information tells you certain kinds of wood are good for making a digging stick. You don't know about different kinds of wood instinctually but because detailed information about the properties of different kinds of wood was passed on to your mind culturally — through some form of language — by your parent generation or your peers.

This difference may seem trivial, but it's actually very important. For example, consider the following cultural behaviors and their possible involvement with biological evolution of our species:

- The earliest use of stone tools corresponds with increased consumption of animal protein. More animal protein in turn changes the hominid diet and potentially its anatomy.

- The use of clothing (itself a cultural artifact) allows human bodies to survive in environments they wouldn't normally survive in. For example, the human body is naturally best-suited for equatorial environments, not the Arctic, but the invention of heavy coats and other such clothing enables that body to survive Arctic temperatures.

Palaeoanthropologists are deeply concerned with understanding how cultural, noncultural, and biocultural evolutionary factors shaped humanity through time.

Is the human species still evolving?

One of the most common questions asked of anthropologists is whether the human species is still evolving. Have we reached a pinnacle? Will we become giant-brained, fragile-bodied space-dwellers, using only a single finger to press buttons in the far future?

The simple answer is that yes, we're still evolving; if we have offspring (replicate), if those offspring aren't clones (variation), and if not all of our offspring survive to sexual maturity (selection), then by definition, the human species is evolving. But it's natural to ask whether we're still evolving because — in developed countries at least — humanity has used medicine and other means to eliminate a lot of the pressures that once took so many of our children. With so many selective pressures defeated (at least in

the short term), you may easily conclude that significant genetic evolution has stalled in developed countries in the last century or so.

But what's still evolving, and very quickly, is human culture, and this process is just as important as human genetic evolution. Human culture changes very rapidly, and the changes affect millions. Imagine the differences between the U.S. (say, in clothing and musical styles, concepts of race and religion, and the ethnic diversity of the population) in 1950 and in 2000 — some pretty major changes occurred in the late 1960s (for example, the success of the civil rights movement). Whether the changes are good or bad is another matter; for the moment, the important idea is that yes, humanity is still evolving and in a very significant way.

Considering that analyzing and understanding a single fossil skull can take years (in addition to what may have been an extensive search and excavation), it's no surprise that palaeoanthropology requires patience. But perhaps you should also give palaeoanthropologists some slack when they go a little crazy over new fossil discoveries. After all, it's a slow business . . .

Archaeology: The Study of Ancient Societies

Archaeology studies ancient societies through their material remains, which you may know as artifacts. These artifacts number in the billions and pepper the globe, each a piece to the puzzle of our ancestors' lives. Every arrowhead, every stone net-weight, every clay pipe-stem and shard of glass, every mud brick and gnawed bone and corroding sword have something to tell about the lives of past human societies, and the archaeologists' job is to fit the puzzle back together.

Fitting the puzzle back together isn't easy. Archaeology isn't that technically difficult or even expensive (compared, to, say, nuclear physics or chemistry), but it takes a long time to do well. Because artifacts are so numerous, and archaeologists are eager to extract as much information from each object as possible, excavations of archaeological sites can take years, even generations.

Archaeological research has many goals but normally adheres to some common principles:

- Establishing *chronologies,* or sequences of events in the ancient world, such as dating *when* the first occurrence of writing, farming, or the use of fire

- Establishing *spatial understanding* of the chronicled events, such as *where* the first writing, farming, or use of the wheel occurred, and what that can reveal about their invention

- Understanding the evolution of ancient cultures through time so as to better understand why certain societies survived and others went extinct, or answer other large questions, such as what prompted the change from small-scale chiefdoms to large-scale civilizations

Archaeologists establish chronologies by carefully noting the age of artifacts recovered in excavations. They must carry excavations out carefully so they can record the exact position of artifacts; this care is critical to understanding the artifacts' ages for many reasons (which you can read more about in Chapter 5).

Carefully recording where artifacts are found is another way to achieve spatial understanding. If a stone bowl came from a cave in southern Mexico, you don't want to confuse it with one found in northern Peru. This obvious logic extends all the way down to the centimeter, such that archaeologists work long hours carefully recovering artifacts with whisk brooms and other delicate instruments.

Archaeology and evolution

Evolution is characterized by change; to understand ancient cultural evolution, archaeologists often focus on what changed through time in the ancient society they're investigating.

For example, around 10,000 years ago people in the Danube River valley of southeastern Europe were highly mobile foragers who left only short-lived campsites for archaeologists to discover, but by about 7,000 years ago, they were a rather sedentary people, living in riverside villages that you would normally associate with farming people. However, the folk of these villages, including the fascinating site of Lepenski Vir, weren't farmers; they continued to hunt and gather. Something, then, changed in their culture, and archaeologists want to know what it was.

Explaining how cultures changed through time is one of the most contentious issues in the field of anthropology. Many models have been proposed to account for cultural change, including

- ✔ **Cultural ecology:** These approaches consider the most important changes in human culture to be traced back to ecological issues, such as food and water supply. These factors are certainly important, but some argue that cultural ecology misses the importance of factors such as religion and even the individual human, turning people into automatons that simply react to environmental changes.

- ✔ **Postmodernism:** Postmodern approaches place a high value on the ability of such factors as gender, ideology, religion, myth, and the individual to change culture over time.

- ✔ **Marxism:** These approaches focus on the organization of labor and the negotiation of social inequalities (haves and have-nots) in society. They have been interesting and useful for some archaeological investigations, but don't work so well when ancient labor wasn't organized as it is in the industrial world, and labor divisions and social inequalities weren't very prominent (as in the many millions of years of foraging societies).

Archaeologists have proposed dozens of other lenses through which to envision and understand cultural change through time, and they're fascinating. But none, in my view, has entirely explained everything, and I know that most archaeologists agree with me. Culture is complex, people are complex, and all kinds of events have happened in the past to shape cultural change. I say this in a few other places in this book: Single-factor models never seem to pan out.

Archaeology deals with change through time as reflected by the artifacts used by ancient humans, so its limit goes back to around 2.5 million years ago, the age of the earliest (known) artifacts. Archaeologists commonly mutter "We don't do dinosaurs!" when people ask whether they're excavating a dinosaur because the dinosaurs — studied by palaeontologists — became extinct around 65 million years ago.

More facets of archaeology

Like all the fields of anthropology, archaeology even has its own subfields; I describe two of the most important ones — dealing with the prehistoric and historic periods of human evolution — in the following sections.

Cultural evolution

Combining the terms *cultural* and *evolution* is enough to make some anthropologists see red. That's because for a long time (from the late 1800s through the 1950s), anthropology labored under a mistaken concept of how culture changed through time, crudely grafting Darwinian evolution to the concept of culture. When this mistaken view was overturned in the mid-20th century, many anthropologists also threw out an evolutionary approach to culture, a move that has many archaeologists — me included — a little steamed.

The mistaken idea was that all human societies were on a Darwinian track toward Civilization and that those that didn't make it were — however unfortunately — simply being selected against or weeded out by the pitiless forces of nature. This idea roughly categorized foraging peoples (like Australian Aborigines, most Native Americans, and polar hunting folk) into the category of Savagery, followed by small-scale farmers (like the chiefdoms of Hawaii or New Guinea) in the category of Barbarism, which could only evolve into — and rightly *should* evolve into, according to the idea — Civilization. That Civilization was typified by the Victorian white male of London was a nuance few noticed. This misconception of how culture changed (that all cultures were on the same track) was clearly and carefully used to justify colonial efforts worldwide that were considered beneficial; after all, Civilization was being brought to the Savages.

For many reasons, this theory revealed itself to be a flawed understanding: Human societies, it turns out, don't have an automatic drive towards being white Victorian males. But this flaw isn't enough to entirely ditch the concept that culture changes through time by an evolutionary process.

Archaeologists, deeply concerned with the change in cultures through time, have most carefully examined cultural change, and they are most convinced that it does change by an evolutionary process. Culture doesn't ride on the genes — it's taught by language. Every society has its own way of surviving, but the principles of evolution apply to culture in some important ways. I don't dwell on them in this book, but if you're interested, you may want to start with some more advanced readings in archaeology, such as textbooks that cover archaeological theory.

Prehistoric archaeology

The earliest writing systems go back to about 6,000 years ago, and the entire period between that time and the time of the first stone tools (the first artifacts), around 2.5 million years ago, is called *prehistory*.

Prehistoric archaeology studies this period with many of the same concerns as historic-period archaeologists. However, some aspects of prehistoric archaeology are unique:

  ✔ **A concern with ecology and adaptation:** Whereas most peoples written about in the historic period were agriculturalists, people of the prehistoric period were mostly foragers who moved across landscapes to hunt and gather their food; figuring out what they ate and how they got their hands on it (adapted) is a central focus of prehistory.

✔ **A focus on stone, bone, and antler artifacts:** Before the historic farming societies, artifacts made from these materials were the most likely to have survived decay over the millennia. Wood was also important, but not much has survived.

✔ **A concern with egalitarian social organization:** Unlike the farming societies, which ranked members according to how much they did or didn't have, prehistoric societies were essentially socially equal.

Keep in mind that just because some societies took up writing around 6,000 years ago, not all did; many remained foragers or other folks outside the growing civilizations. These people included the Native Americans, people who lived in the Americas for well over 10,000 years before the arrival of European explorers. Those explorers wrote down what they observed of the Native Americans, so documents do exist that describe people on the margins of history. But of course the Native Americans had their own histories, told as oral traditions, so they weren't people without history.

Historic archaeology

Historic archaeology takes advantage of the fact that about 6,000 years ago, some human groups invented language and began to write down things that can tell about the past. In a way, because I'm primarily a prehistoric archaeologist, I envy historic archaeologists; they have a lot more information to go on when they start their research. On the other hand, when I start looking into the billions of pages of historic records about the ancient world, I realize that the historic record presents as many problems as it does solutions.

Historic archaeology proceeds with many of the same concerns and methods as prehistoric archaeology, but it often addresses two issues of particular importance.

History, as the saying goes, is written by the winners, which is another way of saying that each story has (at least) two sides. The use of propaganda, the convenient omission of inconvenient facts from state records, and the wholesale creation of "facts" are nothing new; these occurred in every ancient civilization, from Sumer to the Incan empire. Unless you're happy to simply believe what ancient governmental records tell you about their illustrious (and they're always illustrious) leaders, historic archaeology is a good way to test that written record against artifacts in the ground.

Written records of the ancient world often dealt with the royalty and their activities, military conquests, or religious ceremonies and ideas, but they rarely discussed the common people — the peasants — who formed the bulk of the population of every ancient civilization. And unless you're directly descended from royalty — and I mean without a drop of commoner's blood in your veins, which is pretty unlikely — the history of the common person is partly your history. Historical archaeology sometimes focuses on these forgotten ancestors, fleshing out the history books with a fuller picture of the ancient world.

Linguistic Anthropology

Linguistic anthropology studies human language, the animal kingdom's most uniquely powerful — and at the same time subtle — system of communication between individuals.

Language is basically a system of information transmission and reception; humans communicate these messages by sound (speech), by gesture (body language), and in other visual ways such as writing. Because language is one of humanity's most distinctive characteristics, I devote all of Chapter 13 to a detailed examination of what language is and how it may have evolved.

Linguistic anthropology traditionally focuses on several key issues, each resulting from a new research paradigm developed over the last 60 or so years. Interestingly, these interests haven't steamrolled the previous ones but rather incorporated and complemented earlier types of investigations. The following list details some of those key issues:

✔ Classification of languages, to identify which languages evolved when and where

✔ Understanding of language structure, units, and grammar

✔ Identification of the ways language constructs identity, ideology, and narratives

Another topic of considerable interest has been when, where, and among what species modern human language first appeared and how it evolved. This is one of the great questions of anthropology, but it's such a massively complex topic that all you really need to know at this level is that, at present, no single model or theory has convinced all anthropologists just how language first evolved. People have presented some compelling theories, but anthropologists are still evaluating them. You can read more about these theories in Chapters 7 and 13.

Nonhuman animal communication

Nonhuman animals also communicate; this reminds humanity that we're not as different from other animals as people often like to think.

Although chimpanzees and gorillas have been taught several varieties of basic sign-language and can use these signs to assemble basic sentences — on the order, generally speaking, of a three-year-old human's sentences — it's important to remember that chimps and gorillas haven't invented or evolved language on their own in the wild. This fact suggests that the capacity to do something (learn language) doesn't necessarily indicate that it will occur in the wild.

Nonhuman animal communication is different from human communication and language, though, in certain ways:

- **Nonhuman language is symbolically simple.** A monkey's screech for "hawk" (an aerial predator) is surely distinct from a squawk for "python" (a ground predator), but "hawk" or "python" are ALL these sounds can mean. On the other hand, humans can use language to say "That guy is a real python," attaching the ideas of the person to the idea of snake-like qualities.

- **Nonhuman words are phonemically simple.** That is, although human words can be constructed from many sounds (like the word *constitutional*) nonhuman "words" are usually formed of two or fewer sounds.

- **Nonhuman language is grammatically simple.** Although human sentences can be constructed from many words (like "I broke the glass that was sitting on the edge of the table"), nonhuman "sentences" are very rare, and grammatical rules for their assembly are lacking.

Spoken language

Human spoken language, in contrast to nonhuman communication, has the following characteristics:

- **Human language is extraordinarily fast,** communicating information at a high speed.

- **Human language is extraordinarily dense,** communicating a lot of information per unit of time.

- **Human language is extraordinarily subtle,** with the use of metaphor being common and radically multiplying the potential meaning of any word, sentence, or even idea.

Gesture and body language

In addition to spoken human language, we also use *gesture,* or what Adam Kendon, editor of the scholarly journal *Gesture,* has called "visible action as utterance." Gesture isn't exactly the same as a word; it's more of a reinforcement of what you're saying aloud. And it's very important. You can imagine how using the wrong gestures in the wrong circumstances could cost you heavily!

Gestures vary widely worldwide, but some common patterns occur.

- ✔ You can use gesture to point.
- ✔ You can use gesture to indicate a state of mind.
- ✔ You can use gesture to reinforce what you're saying.
- ✔ You can use gesture to negate what you're saying (for instance, to indicate sarcasm).
- ✔ You can use gesture to mark beginning or ending points in a conversation.

The boy who cried Whorf

One of the most fascinating and controversial concepts in linguistic anthropology is the Sapir-Whorf hypothesis, forwarded in the 1930s by linguists Edward Sapir and Benjamin Whorf. The two argued that language does as much to create human reality as it does to reflect the real world.

In 1940, Whorf wrote, "We dissect nature along lines laid down by our native languages. The categories and types that we isolate from the world of phenomena we do not find there because they stare every observer in the face; on the contrary, the world is presented in a kaleidoscopic flux of impressions which has to be organized by our minds — and this means largely by the linguistic systems by our minds. We cut nature up, organize it into concepts, and ascribe significances as we do, largely because we are parties to an agreement to organize it in this way — an agreement that holds throughout our speech community and is codified in the patterns of our language. The agreement is, of course, an implicit and unstated one, but its terms are absolutely obligatory; we cannot talk at all except by subscribing to the organization and classification of data which the agreement decrees."

In other words, although an objective reality exists — jump off a cliff and you will die, whether you call it "flying" or "dying" — your impressions of that world are strongly shaped by the vocabulary you have to describe that world. For me, the lesson is to increase your vocabulary, to learn other languages or at least words from other languages — you don't know what new things you may find in the world.

These are fascinating issues considering that the first languages most likely had a strong gestural component, and you could potentially discover much about them by studying modern gesture. Figure 3-3 shows some polite gestures of 17th-century Europe; the upper left gesture is "adoration," the upper right "reconciliation," the lower left "impatience," the lower right "demonstration," and the middle "benediction." You can easily imagine using these gestures in your own communication; think about how different communication is without them . . . for example, over e-mail.

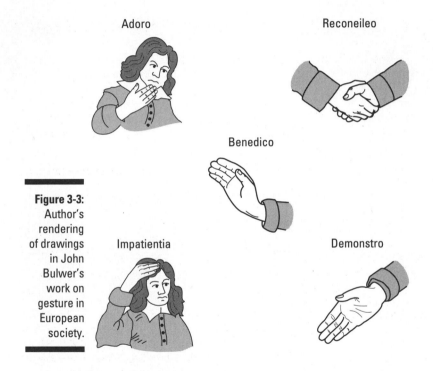

Adoro

Reconeileo

Benedico

Impatientia

Demonstro

Figure 3-3: Author's rendering of drawings in John Bulwer's work on gesture in European society.

Cultural Anthropology: The Study of Living Societies

Whereas archaeology studies ancient cultures, *cultural anthropology* focuses on living societies. Some reasons include

  ✔ **An attempt to identify cultural similarities worldwide:** Such similarities may offer very important insights into what it is to be human.

- ✔ **An attempt to identify cultural differences worldwide:** Such differences can illustrate the diverse ways humans have found to survive across the globe and, in some cases, through time.

- ✔ **An attempt to correct supposedly common-sense ideas about humanity:** This process is important because most cultures worldwide believe their own way of living is the most appropriate and right for all of humanity.

Putting the culture in cultural anthropology

Whatever end you hope to achieve through cultural anthropology, the means are going to be a study of culture. Culture has been defined in many ways; I give you a definition in the section "The biocultural animal" earlier in this chapter, and you can take graduate-level courses just to grapple with culture theory. Generally speaking, culture encompasses everything from attitudes toward material objects to philosophical, political, and religious concepts.

Cultural anthropology: An equal-opportunity whistle-blower

Attempting to rectify common-sense evaluations of the rest of the world is a sort of corrective for human perception of itself. The idea that one's own culture is the best and most appropriate way to live is called *ethnocentrism*, and it's been used to justify discrimination against people outside ones' own culture for centuries and worldwide. Keep in mind that just because a cultural practice exists doesn't necessarily mean that it's good for the culture at large; like slavery, it may benefit a relative few at the expense of many. Robert G. Edgerton's book *Sick Societies* demonstrates that many human cultural adaptations are actually *maladaptations*, adaptations that are actually bad for the society rather than beneficial. For example, some agricultural practices provide high yields in the short run but may burn out the soil in the long run.

Western civilization isn't shy about pointing out obvious problems of its own — such as racial discrimination or the fact that women make significantly less money than men — and should remain open to the possibility that such problems are possible in other cultures. In this way, cultural anthropology isn't just a discipline focused on bashing Western civilization; it's an objective science that doesn't idealize *any* society over another.

Important features of culture include the following:

- ✔ **Culture isn't genetic; it's learned.** Each new generation doesn't receive it in genes but from parents, siblings, and anyone else in the culture (largely through language).

- ✔ **Culture is shared among a population, but it allows variation within it.** Individuals of a culture may have their own interpretations of the culture's set of descriptions of the universe and instructions for how to live properly in it. This discrepancy is important because it recognizes a major characteristic of humanity: *individuality,* the fact that humans aren't typically of one mind but rather are individuals with a great deal of individual personality.

- ✔ **Cultural information is often symbolic.** *Symbols* — which are linguistic, visual, and gestural metaphors that stand for something else — are heavily influential in the communication of culture from one generation to the next.

Although cultural information rides in the brain, humans can also express it physically. Material objects — for example, seagoing canoes, totem poles, or sports cars — are also expressions of certain cultural ideas. Even the most apparently utilitarian artifacts, like writing pens, can and often do carry cultural information. A glitter-spangled, bubblegum-pink pen is more likely to belong to an adolescent girl than to a public official; the official probably requires a fancier pen to project a certain image in public ceremonies. Material objects, then, constitute culture; some call the study of such items the study of *material culture.* Because archaeologists study ancient cultures through their artifacts — which are material culture — they've made the most thorough studies of material culture.

Attempting to explain why humans do what they do

Cultural anthropologists have devised many fascinating and complex bodies of theory to explain humanity and the diversity and commonalities of human cultures. Among them:

- ✔ **Evolutionary approaches** (including materialist approaches) that seek explanations by looking for the adaptive advantages of various cultural practices — such as cannibalism or social ranking — worldwide. These theories seem to explain some things, but critics argue that they ignore the significance of individual action, which is sometimes known as *agency*.

- ✔ **Functionalist approaches** that understand elements of culture as each working in an integrated way to promote the culture's welfare. Critics claim that these approaches ignore the importance of conflict, which is always present in culture (particularly those with social rank or class differences).

✔ **Postmodern approaches** that focus on conflicts, individual agency, and other nonstandard aspects of culture. Critics argue that such approaches, though they admirably give voice to common people, often ignore physical, material, and evolutionary realities of the fact that humans are evolving animals.

As with single-factor attempts to describe all of cultural change, I can confidently say no one explanation of the complexity of culture has convinced all anthropologists of its validity; single-factor models never seem to pan out.

One of the most important tools for the cultural anthropologist is the *ethnography*, a document describing some aspect of some culture, written by a trained observer — a cultural anthropologist who often participates, to some degree, in the culture he's observing. See Chapter 12 for more on ethnographies.

Participant observation

Cultural anthropologists gather their raw data — information about life in traditional societies — in a number of ways, but a major technique is *participant observation*. This method includes living with or among the people they observe and even taking part in those peoples' activities, such as foraging or religious ceremonies.

Cultural anthropology versus sociology

People often confuse cultural anthropology with the related discipline of sociology, but you can note at least two clear distinctions between the two fields:

✔ **Cultural anthropology focuses on nonindustrial societies.** These groups are often called *traditional* societies because they have many things in common with societies that existed before the recent, massive global changes associated with post–World War II globalism. On the other hand, sociology tends to focus on industrial or Western civilization (particularly urban civilization).

✔ **Cultural anthropology tends to rely on direct interviews with the members of traditional societies.** Many of these people don't read or write, and sociologists tend to gather data with questionnaires.

Academic departments of sociology and anthropology often have close connections and sometimes merge, but their theoretical backgrounds are very different. Sociology's roots are in economics and anthropology's in the humanities. Although they share some similarities, it's probably best to keep these fields separate.

Early anthropologists didn't spend too much time thinking about how to do this work effectively and were often so scientifically detached from the people they were studying that they came away with inaccurate reports. As the pendulum has swung the other way in the last few decades, some anthropologists became so personally involved with the societies they were investigating that their own reports were too personal and still missed real understanding. Cultural anthropologists have to tread a fine line between these extremes.

Today, most cultural anthropology graduate students spend a long time studying how to do participant observation before simply heading out to do it. They often study

- Effective and respectful ways to introduce themselves to a community they want to study. (How would you react if someone from, say, New Guinea arrived at your doorstep and asked whether she could live with you for a few months, just out of her own curiosity?)
- Culturally sensitive ways to negotiate difficulties.
- The language(s) of the region they will study.
- Everything ever written, filmed, recorded, or speculated about the society they will study.

Once doing actual field research, cultural anthropologists stay on track by maintaining both emic and etic perspectives.

The emic perspective

An *emic* perspective focuses on how the people being observed think rather than how the cultural anthropologist may think. For example, for an emic understanding of a landscape, an anthropologist may ask a native hunter to draw out his own idea of what the land looks like. This image may be very different from what it looks like on a printed map, but in some ways that map is irrelevant to the hunter's life.

The etic perspective

An *etic* perspective focuses on the observer being an objective scientist capable of seeing patterns that even a native of the culture at hand may be unaware of. Anyone who has had the experience of someone telling her how she's behaving — even if she can't see it herself — recognizes the benefit of this perspective. Here, an analysis of the hunter's movement across the landscape would focus on the map derived from a satellite image.

Notes from the field

My colleague, Dr. Evan Davies, spent months with the BaAka of central Africa. His doctoral dissertation, describing his experiences, is a combination of emic and etic descriptions. Following is an etic description of the phenomenon of *social fission* as an example of what anthropologists can learn from fieldwork:

"There are two major seasonal changes throughout Central Africa that affect the subsistence strategies of the BaAka, the rainy season which lasts roughly from to April to October and the dry season, which runs the rest of the year with the exception a few brief periods of rain during the winter months. During the dry season, the game animals in the forest must congregate around the major water sources (rivers and their tributaries) in the forest, and are hunted with relative ease by the BaAka. During this time, the BaAka live in semi permanent villages close to towns and embark into the forest on day hunts. They are usually able to catch enough game during a day spent hunting to last them several days. A village sized band of approximately 75 people may therefore spend

the months of the dry season hunting every fifth day or so, and the rest of the time will be spent in their village cooking, eating and resting, repairing their dwellings and their tools."

"With the advent of the rains in the spring, the game animals hunted by the BaAka have more water sources available to them, and so are no longer forced to frequent the perennial sources of water that as they did during the dry season. Because the animals are more dispersed in the forest, the BaAka must travel further into the forest and remain for longer periods of time to catch enough to feed themselves.

For this reason, it is no longer advantageous for these hunter gatherers to travel in a large single group as they did during the dry season, when game was plentiful. It is more helpful for members of the group to fragment into smaller, nuclear family sized groups and spread out into the forest much as the game they are hunting, and so, during the rainy season we witness social fission among the BaAka."

Applied anthropology and global culture

Applied anthropology is a kind of cultural anthropology that applies what's known abut human culture to various pressing, real-world issues such as discrimination against women, the implementation of Third-World aid programs, or child-labor issues. For at least the last decade, about half of cultural anthropology PhDs haven't gone into academics but rather into agencies such as the UN to assist in improving culturally sensitive communications worldwide.

The Society for Applied Anthropology (www.sfaa.net/) lists its mission as promoting " . . . interdisciplinary scientific investigation of the principles controlling the relations of human beings to one another, and the encouragement of the wide application of these principles to practical problems." Essentially, this means applying what anthropologists have learned about human culture at large — and the culture in question specifically — to policy statements and implementation. In effect, applied anthropology remedies the solution of distant bureaucrats making momentous decisions about a culture's way of life from on high. Rather, this bottom-up approach recognizes that simply imposing change is less effective and respectful than working with people to stimulate change that works for them.

Anthropologists have played important roles in all kinds of applications of their knowledge, but serious ethical considerations inevitably come into play when researching human beings and applying the information gathered. In the 1960s, the U.S. Army commissioned anthropologists to study and explain how warfare was carried out in Central America. But many anthropologists objected that this information would be little more than intelligence used to better plot warfare in the interest of the U.S., and the ensuing Camelot Affair drove the American Anthropological Association to draft its first Statement on Ethics in 1967.

On the other hand, many anthropologists have been pivotal in using anthropology to better human life. You can find out more about these issues throughout Part IV of this book.

Part II
Physical Anthropology and Archaeology

The 5th Wave   By Rich Tennant

THE FIRST HOMO ERECTUS

"Is this so difficult? Just bend at the waist and lift with your legs."

In this part . . .

What is humanity's place in the natural world? How are we related to the rest of the primates, and how has our species changed over time? This part discusses how physical anthropology and archaeology investigate these profound questions. It also explores early human migration, farming, and the evolution of civilization.

Chapter 4

The Wildest Family Reunion: Meet the Primates

There are millions of kinds of living things (some estimate that millions more are undiscovered in the jungles and oceans), and making sense of them has been the labor biologists for centuries. (Check out the "Biological classification" sidebar in this chapter for more on this process.) Among these swimming, hopping, and crawling life forms are the primates, a group of about 200 kinds of animal that share some distinctive anatomical and behavioral characteristics. This is the Primate order, our home in the biological world.

To better understand the human species, anthropology has taken up the study of our closest relatives: Where do they come from? How long have they been living there? Why do they eat the things they eat? This chapter gives you an overview of what that family is like and how you fit in.

Monkey Business: Primate Origins

The earliest proto-primates have been traced from fossils of the *Palaeocene* epoch some 65 million years ago; most anthropologists agree that the Primate order was well underway by 60 million years ago. The number 65 million may ring a bell as the time of the extinction of the dinosaurs, and the rise of primates is related to the demise of the dinosaurs. Early mammals, from which the primates evolved, appear somewhat earlier, but when the dinosaurs became extinct, the way opened up for other life forms to flourish. Many more mammals show up after 65 million years ago, and among them are the first primates.

The fossils of the earliest primates show two main features:

- ✔ **Small body size,** averaging roughly 150 to 3,000 grams, or about ⅓ pound to about 6 pounds
- ✔ **Teeth,** indicating an *insectivorous* diet specializing in insects

So our earliest primate relatives were small, insect-eating mammals, in many ways physically similar to squirrels. You can see a reconstruction of one of these first primates in Figure 4-1). Skeletal analysis suggests that these early primates were *arboreal* (lived in trees) and that's very common in the living primates.

Most of the characteristics of the early primates are studied from fossils of their teeth and skulls (and a few limb bones). *Bone fossilization* is the process by which minerals slowly replace the organic content of the bones of a dead animal, resulting in a very detailed stone replica of the original bone. Fossils can be so detailed that they show scratches (on the teeth, for example, from chewing) under a microscope.

Figure 4-1:
An early
primate.

Biological classification

Scientists first began to systematically classify living things in the 1700s according to a system laid out by Swedish naturalist Carolus Linneaus, inventor of *Linnean Classification*. Linneaus noted (obviously enough) that many life forms had anatomical and (in the case of animals) behavioral similarities to other life forms, and he began grouping them according to those similarities. Dogs and horses, for example, shared the characteristic of having hair-covered skin and suckling their young; although dogs and horses are different in many other ways, those characteristics made dogs and horses more similar to each other than either was to some other life forms like fish. Despite their differences, dogs and horses are both mammals. Anatomical similarity is still the basis of life-form identification, but genetic data increasingly factor in as well.

The four main levels of the hierarchical classification system used today are significant to understanding primates:

- ✔ **The order:** All primates are in the Primate order, which is different from the order Canidae (the dogs and dog-like animals), the order Felidae (all the cats, from lion to Tom), and so on.

- ✔ **The family:** The Primate order contains several families of primates, including the Pongidae (chimpanzees, gorillas, and orangutans), the Hominidae (humans and our ancestors), and the Colobinae (the primates of South America).

- ✔ **The genus:** Several *genera* (plural of genus) are members of the Primate order, including the genus *Papio* (the baboons) and the genus *Homo* (humans and their ancestors).

- ✔ **The species:** About 200 species of primates exist. If two individuals are *sexually viable* (can interbreed and have healthy offspring that themselves can have healthy offspring), the two individuals are in the same species.

Humans, then, are in the order Primate, the family Hominidae, the genus *Homo,* and the species *sapiens.* Subspecies designations exist as well, and all humans today are in the subspecies *sapiens.* Therefore, humans are *Homo sapiens sapiens,* whereas Central African chimpanzees are in the family Pongidae, the genus *Pongo,* and the species *pygmaeus;* they're known as *Pongo pygmaeus.*

You Look Like an Ape: Primate Species

Biologically speaking, you're an ape. So am I, and so is everyone else in the world. It's true. This section shows you the general characteristics of all primates and then focuses in on the main groupings of primates, including the apes.

What's in a name? General primate characteristics

As primates evolved after 65 million years ago, they developed the more distinctive characteristics seen in the living species as well as their fossil ancestors. Today, although the many kinds of primates vary a great deal, they do share some basic traits:

- Wide range of body size, from 100 grams (⅓ pound) to 200 kilograms (more than 400 pounds). On average, primates are about 10 pounds, which is a little larger than most rodents and a little smaller than most hoofed animals.

- Large eyes with three-dimensional vision, allowing keen depth perception.

- Lack of emphasis on a snout. Primates focus on vision rather than sense of smell, which appears in other animals' snouts.

- Large brain case containing the largest brain — relative to body size — of any land animal.

- *Heterodont* (differentiated) teeth, indicating a varied diet. For example, the incisors can clip one kind of food, and the molars can crush another.

- Nails rather than claws, allowing more sensitive grasping of tree limbs.

Today, the primate order contains about 230 living primate species (give or take a few, depending on whom you ask). Although you could spend a lifetime studying them in all their diversity (not to mention the fossil record of the ancestry of each living species), for most purposes it's enough to recognize four main subgroups in the primate order: the prosimians, the Old World monkeys, the New World monkeys, and the apes. I take a closer look at these subgroups in the following sections. You can see how they relate to one another in Figure 4-2 (refer to the nearby sidebar for a refresher on biological classification), and Figure 4-3 shows how some of them appear. Regarding Figure 4-2, note that different physical anthropologists classify the primates in slightly different ways, and some don't even consider the loris — shown in this figure but not discussed in the text — a primate. Although variations like this exist, the classification shown here is widely used.

The primate *dental formula* is a notation of the number of various tooth types in the individual mouth, counting incisors, canines, premolars, and molars, in each quadrant of the mouth (upper left, upper right, lower left, and lower right). Different dental formulas can tell anthropologists about the relationships between species. For example, humans have two incisors, one canine, two premolars and three molars, for a dental formula of 2.1.2.3, whereas New World monkeys (a very different group) have an extra premolar, for a formula of 2.1.3.3. Figure 4-4 compares the dental formulas of an Old World ape and a New World monkey.

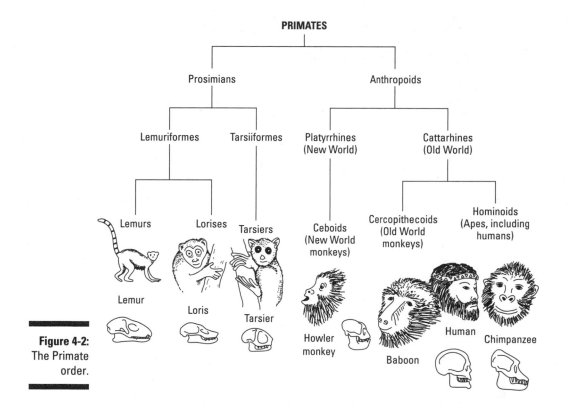

Figure 4-2:
The Primate
order.

Although you read lists of separate species characteristics, like body weight or diet, those characteristics always intertwine. Therefore, diet can have effects on body weight and vice versa, and exactly how one characteristic affects another isn't always easy to understand. In fact, I'd say that although anthropology today has very good lists of these characteristics and can very clearly describe the primate species, as a field anthropology doesn't always have a good explanation for how the characteristics interact. That doesn't mean that anthropology can't ever understand them, but at the moment I'd say that anthropologists are just now working out the interactions of the anatomical and behavioral characteristics.

Going ape (and prosimian): Primate subgroups

All the primates have the characteristics I mention in the preceding section, but even a quick look at the primates reveals some clear divisions. The following sections describe the four main kinds of primates.

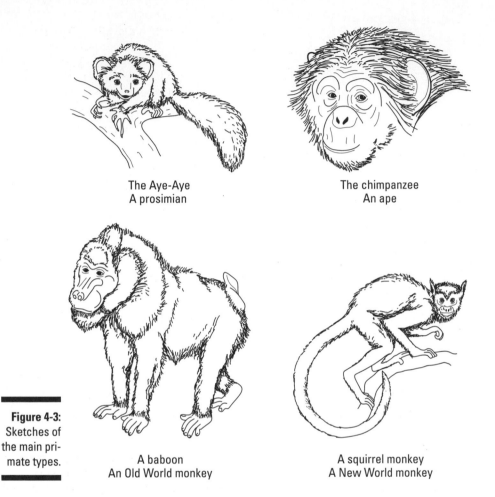

The Aye-Aye
A prosimian

The chimpanzee
An ape

Figure 4-3:
Sketches of
the main pri-
mate types.

A baboon
An Old World monkey

A squirrel monkey
A New World monkey

Squirrel-cats: The prosimians

One of the major divisions in the Primate order is that between the *Anthropoidea* (the people-like apes and monkeys) and the Prosimii (or prosimians, which are pretty different from people even though they're clearly primates). Baboons, chimpanzees, and gorillas — all in the *Anthropoidea* — are very obviously similar to humans, but connecting to, say, the ring-tailed lemur (a cat-like prosimian of Madagascar that has a long, striped tail) or the tiny, bug-eyed, shrew-like tarsier that can fit in the palm of your hand is a little more difficult. Still, these animals are primates — even though they can look like a cross between a squirrel and a cat — and they typically have the following distinctive traits:

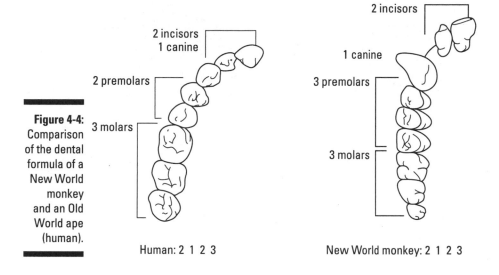

Figure 4-4:
Comparison
of the dental
formula of a
New World
monkey
and an Old
World ape
(human).

Human: 2 1 2 3

New World monkey: 2 1 2 3

✔ Relatively long snouts in some species (long for primates, anyway), although they may also have very large eyes

✔ A dental formula of 2.1.3.3

✔ Small body size compared to other primates; they range from mouse-size to cat-size, averaging about 5 kilograms or 10 pounds

✔ Some are nocturnal and have a diet that favors insects but includes tree saps, grubs, fruit, flowers, and leaves

Nocturnal animals are most active at night, whereas diurnal species are most active in daylight. Making a living in darkness or light has effects on what foods animals eat, how they avoid predators, how they move about their environment, and so on.

Probably the strangest primate is the aye-aye of Madagascar. About the size of a cat with enormous, hairless ears, the aye-aye climbs through trees by moonlight listening for larvae beneath tree bark. When it hears a squirming treat, it uses a thin, elongated finger to scoop the meal out of the bark. Even the driest textbooks of primatology can't help but marvel over this creature, which one author called the most "improbable" primate; another said that the aye-aye, though clearly a primate, displayed the most extreme specialization of anatomy in the order. This means that although most primates are somewhat general in their diet (many have a varied, omnivorous diet), the aye-aye is quite specialized and inflexible in its diet. Unfortunately, such specialization can prove disastrous if the prey species itself becomes extinct or somehow declines.

You can't go home again

An *adaptive radiation* is the adaptation of a species to a new environment. When new environments open up — for example, when a land bridge connects two previously separated continents or islands — life forms normally migrate into these new environments. If they survive, the colonists adapt to the new ecological conditions and, over evolutionary time, become adapted to those conditions. When the colonists are so different from their ancestral population (the ones who didn't cross the land bridge, for example) that they can no longer interbreed with those ancestral forms, *speciation* has occurred.

So if the prosimians are so strange, why are they considered primates? Well, they generally have nails rather than claws, focus on vision rather than smell for their sensory specialty, have relatively mobile wrists and ankles, and live mostly in the trees. For all these reasons (as well as connections shown to the rest of the primates in the genetic data), the prosimians are, in fact, relations (albeit some pretty strange ones; of course, they could say the same about us). Because the prosimians are very much like the earliest primates, understanding them and what they can reveal about primate origins is important; unfortunately, they're endangered.

Many of the prosimians live on the island of Madagascar, off East Africa, where they've been isolated, in an evolutionary sense, for millions of years. Today almost 50 known species exist (two new species were discovered as recently as 2005), and, unfortunately, they're all in danger of extinction. Humans first came to Madagascar just 1,500 years ago, and since that time many prosimian species have become extinct due to deforestation. You can keep up with these issues at http://www.wildmadagascar.org/.

The Old World monkeys

The monkeys of the Old World, members of the *parvorder* (a major division in the order) Catarrhini (meaning narrow-nosed) are distinct from the New World monkeys because they live on a different continent, distinct from the apes because the apes are generally larger, and different from the prosimians because they're generally larger and have evolved more ecological adaptations than the prosimians. They also have the following distinctive anatomical characteristics:

- ✔ Narrow nose with nostrils facing down (as opposed to wide-nosed, out-facing nostrils in New World monkeys)

- ✔ A dental formula of 2.1.2.3 (one premolar fewer than the New World monkeys,) with some species having molars shaped like knives for shearing vegetation

✔ Lack of a prehensile tail (see the next section for more on prehensile tails)

✔ Both arboreal and terrestrial lifestyles

The Old World monkeys are themselves split into at least two main groups: the subfamilies *Cercopithecinae* (including the terrestrial, brilliantly colored mandrill baboons) and *Colobinae*, which include the large-nosed proboscis monkey and the leaf-devouring colobus monkey, with its large, complex, leaf-digesting stomach. Old World monkeys live in diverse habitats, from dry African savanna to the snowy mountains of Japan. Africa's patas monkey, distributed south of the Sahara, is a consummate survivor, consuming fruit, bird eggs, roots, and leaves; it can also sprint at up to 88 kph (55 mph), making it the fastest primate. Japanese snow monkeys spend winter hours soaking in natural hot springs.

The New World monkeys

The New World (South America) is home to primates as well; they're members of the parvorder Platyrrhini, meaning "broad-nosed," as compared to their Old World counterparts discussed in the last section. Shortly after the origin of the primates around 40 million years ago, South America was already sliding away from its previous link with Africa, and riding on it (or perhaps drifting to it on natural rafts of vegetation, purely by accident) were the ancestors of the New World monkeys. They survive into the present and have the following distinctive characteristics:

✔ Wide nose (compared to the Old World monkeys)

✔ Dental formula of 2.1.3.3 (an extra premolar)

✔ Most have a prehensile tail used to grasp tree limbs

✔ A completely arboreal lifestyle

The New World monkeys include the very loud howler monkey (which scares tourists because the howl sounds like a Hollywood jaguar), the fruit-eating spider monkey (which has a very handy prehensile tail), and the strange little marmosets, which live high in the trees on a diverse diet of insects, fruits, and leaves. Generally speaking, the New World monkeys are somewhat smaller than those of the Old World, with most species averaging about 7 kilograms (about 15 pounds).

Our gang: The apes

The most human-esque group — the apes — are scientifically known as the Hominoidea, or "human-like" primates. Fossil evidence puts the origins of this group around 30 million years ago, in Africa's middle Oligocene epoch. By 6 million years ago, a new group appeared in the Hominoidea — the Hominidae; these are the apes that walked upright, and one of their kind eventually evolved into the genus *Homo*, which evolved into *Homo sapiens sapiens:* humans. So, modern human origins can be traced by fossil evidence to Africa, 6 to 30 million years ago, in the evolution of the Hominoidea. Remember, we're not the only member of the group, and our neighbor species, such as the chimpanzees and gorillas, have also survived all this time. (***Note:*** This classification is a bit of a gray area. Only recently have some anthropologists included chimps and gorillas in the same family as humans, as I do here; previously, Hominidae was reserved only for the bipedal primates.) The main anatomical characteristics of the Hominoidea are

- Dental formula of 2.1.2.3

- Lack of a tail

- Both arboreal and terrestrial lifestyles

- Relatively long arms (even with a terrestrial lifestyle) due to origins as tree-swingers

- Simple molars for crushing, rather than the Old World Monkey's shear-like molars

- Relatively large body size, averaging more than 10 kilograms (30 pounds)

The Hominoidea is easily divisible into two main families, which mainly separate the Hominoidea into the somewhat monkey-like gibbons of Southeast Asia and the African apes.

- The Hylobatidae contain the gibbons of Southeast Asia, who tear through the forest canopy like Tarzan and have complex vocalizations (also like Tarzan). They're the lightest of the Hominoidea and the least like humans: They spend a lot of time in the trees, they have relatively small brains, and they survive on a diet that, although somewhat varied, is predominantly fruit.

- Much more like humans are members of the *Hominidae*, the group containing the, chimpanzee and gorilla (according to the DNA and skeletal evidence), and humans themselves. Generally speaking, these primates are large (averaging over 40 kilograms or 80 pounds), may live much of their lives on the ground, and have a generalized rather than specialized diet. They include *Homo sapiens sapiens,* a relatively large primate (averaging 70 kilograms or 140 pounds) that possesses a very large brain compared to body size and uses extremely complex behavior and tools to adapt and survive. That should sound familiar because you're one of them.

When you think about the past, and the fossil record, and the many individual primates that lie in your own past (right back to the first primates more than 60 million years ago), remember that a lot of speciations and extinctions have occurred. Generally speaking, most species (defined in the "Biological classification" sidebar earlier in the chapter) survive only about 4 million years; most genera survive for about 20 million years. Our species, *Homo sapiens sapiens,* has been around for about 100,000 years. But, as I discuss throughout this book, humanity is so different from most other life forms — for an array of reasons — that this natural timescale doesn't necessarily apply to it. Humanity has invented many ways to prevent itself from falling prey to the circumstances that cause other species to become extinct (and at the same time has invented many means of committing suicide, such as nuclear and biological weapons).

Yes, We Have No Bananas: Primate Subsistence

The previous sections give you a good idea of the origins and main groups of the primates; now take a look at some details or characteristics that can help to clarify where humanity fits in as one of many primate species. I begin with subsistence in this section; later sections cover locomotion, social groups, and behavior.

Subsistence refers to how an organism fulfills its need for food, water, and nutrients. All kinds of subsistence have evolved in nature, including *carnivory* (eating prey animals) and *herbivory* (eating plant matter). Most primates basically practice *omnivory*, meaning that they eat wide variety of foods.

Many anthropologists today believe that the most important factor driving the diversity of subsistence behavior in primates is *food availability and distribution;* that is, what's the distribution of food in space, and how does that distribution vary with time? Because, like any species, primates have to eat, the extent to which their foods are available from season to season has important effects on their behavior and anatomy. Some common primate responses to seasonal changes in diet include switching to different food sources, increasing the time spent in search of food, and splitting the social group to spread out the resource demand. For example, studies show that in lean times, *spectral tarsiers* (tiny, giant-eyed, super-cute Southeast Asian primates) spend more time traveling in search of food than they do in better times. This change affects all kinds of behavior, including conflict resulting from territorial disputes.

The following sections take a closer look at the actual diets processed by primates.

The indiscriminate-eaters: Omnivores

Although the following sections show some exceptions, most primates are rather omnivorous, eating a variety of foods from bird eggs to leaves to seeds and even grasses, insects, tree gum, and flowers. This is in pretty stark contrast to, say crocodiles, who eat meat (fish and any vertebrate that falls into the water), or zebras, who eat only vegetation (grass and shrubs). Those animals are dietary *specialists*; primates, generally speaking, are *generalists*. Chimpanzees, for example, eat lots of fruit, snack on termites, and occasionally hunt down small monkeys; some monkeys savor bird eggs; and gorillas live in a giant salad bowl, eating just about whatever vegetation is in reach. This dietary diversity is reflected in the nature of our versatile mouth.

The average primate mouth reflects the order's tendency toward omnivory in the teeth. We have several kinds of teeth:

- ✔ **Incisors** are the thin, blade-like teeth at the front of the mouth for snipping and clipping.

- ✔ **Canines** are the pointed, conical teeth used for puncturing and light crushing; many primate species use these teeth to defend and threaten, so they're much larger than in our species.

- ✔ **Premolars** are the somewhat-pointed-but-somewhat-jagged teeth immediately before the molars, and they do the light crushing.

- ✔ **Molars** are the heavy, flattish teeth in the back of the mouth that do the heavy crushing.

You can see that this multitalented mouth can process just about any food, so primates generally fall into the category of *heterodont* (different-teeth) rather than *homodont* (same-teeth). Your dog and cat are homodont — both are carnivores (at least evolutionarily) — and omnivores, such as people and pigs, are heterodont.

Technically speaking, homodonty really means that all the teeth have the same form, as in crocodiles. Because dogs and cats (mentioned in the preceding paragraph) do have differences between their incisors and molars, for example, they're technically heterodont. However, relatively speaking, all their teeth are for processing a meat diet, so compared to primates (who eat a more varied diet), they're considered homodont.

A trained anthropologist can learn an enormous amount from a single fossil tooth. Under a microscope, scratches and polishing, called *dental microwear*, can reveal how the jaws worked and even whether the diet was moist or dry. Knowing that it was moist or dry, in turn, can tell you something about the general conditions in which the animal survived. Extrapolations like these are used to reconstruct the lives of ancient species.

The bug-eaters: Insectivores

Insectivores eat a diet heavy in insects; this is where the primates began: as small early mammals eating small insects. Today, many primates eat a few insects — like the chimpanzees who fish termites out of their mounds by using twigs — but few focus their diet on insects, and even those who do still eat other foods such as tree gum and leaves. But for mouse lemurs and some other prosimians, insects may compose close to half the diet. The characteristics of these insectivores include

- Generally very small size, normally under 100 grams (¼ pound)
- A nocturnal lifestyle
- Sharp teeth for processing insect bodies
- An arboreal lifestyle
- A short and simple digestive tract

The insectivorous primates include the African *bush baby* or *galago,* a prosimian that also eats tree gum. It has enormous ears and, unlike most primates, uses these rather than vision to locate its food sources. Weighing up to 5 kilograms (about 10 pounds), the bush baby can leap as far as 4 meters (12 feet) at a time.

The leaf-eaters: Folivores

Folivorous primates focus on eating leaves but still get plenty of variety in most of their diets — they also eat fruit and seeds if they're available. The red howler monkey of South America dines on nearly 200 different species of plants and apparently prefers eating younger rather than more mature leaves. The most folivorous primates are characterized by the following traits:

- Generally medium size (or large, compared to insectivores), averaging 5 kilograms (10 pounds)
- A nocturnal lifestyle
- Mixed sharp and flat teeth for processing vegetation (snipping it with the incisors, shearing it with the premolars, and then crushing it with the molars)
- A long and complex digestive tract used to process vegetation

Leaves are hard to digest, so folivores' guts are larger and more complex than those of many other primates; essentially, leaves ferment in primate stomachs. And because leaves don't have a very high caloric content (relative to a lot of other potential foods), folivores eat a lot of them. (It takes a lot of leaves to make up a pound, which is about what some captive lemurs eat each day.) How the food is dispersed in the trees, what season it is, and how the animals get around are all linked in complex ways.

Folivorous primates have very specialized and sensitive innards for their unique diet. Zoos often have difficulty keeping folivores healthy because they can't supply the proper kinds of leaves. Special feeding programs have to be established to properly care for folivores, such that keepers realize they're not just feeding the primate but also the bacterial colony in the primate's gut that ferments the leaves.

The fruit-eaters: Frugivores

The *frugivores* (fruit-eaters) focus on fruit, but they eat other things as well. Among the most frugivorous primates are the apes, and of these, the most fruit-obsessed are the orangutans, which devour large quantities of the custard-like durian fruit as well as the leaves, fruit, and seeds of nearly 400 other plant species. The frugivores have a sweet tooth, focusing on sugary plant products, and they display the following characteristics:

- ✔ Generally large size (compared to most primates), averaging over 10 kilograms (20 pounds)

- ✔ A diurnal lifestyle, being active mainly at day

- ✔ Mixed sharp and flat teeth for processing vegetation (but sometimes with particularly large incisors for opening up tough-skinned fruit)

Of the more striking characteristics of the frugivores is their good memory. They're very good about remembering just where good patches of fruit appear each year and therefore spend a little less time foraging in search of food than some other primates. This skill can have important (if currently unknown) effects on variables like the complexity of social interactions because they spend more time sitting, grooming, and feeding together than traveling in search of food.

Monkeying Around: Primate Locomotion

How primates *locomote* — get from place to place — is fascinating, and it can tell you a lot about how they live. Some leap from limb to limb, others swing like trapeze artists, and of course humans walk on two feet (unless you're a pirate or something). I discuss the main types of locomotion in the following sections; they're illustrated in Figure 4-5.

Arboreal quadrupedalism
(Spider monkey)

Brachiation
(Gibbon)

Vertical clinging
and leaping
(Lemur)

Figure 4-5:
The main
types of
locomotion.

Terrestrial quadrupedalism
(Knuckle-walking gorilla)

Bipedalism
(Human)

Stand back, Tarzan: The brachiators

Brachiation is swinging from one hold (like a tree limb) to another, and the speed champion species here is the gibbon. Southeast Asian gibbons can swing through forest canopy at more than 30 miles per hour, about ten times as fast as most humans walk. Slower brachiators are the big, heavy orangutans, who hang, reach, and shift their body weight instead of really smoking through the canopy like the gibbons. Brachiators have several main anatomical characteristics:

- ✔ **Long arms:** The longer the muscle, the greater its power, so evolution has selected for longer and more powerful arms over time.

- ✔ **Short, relatively weak legs:** These animals don't spend much time on the ground and really prefer to hang from their hands.

- ✔ **Very powerful hands:** These primates have strong, long fingers but very small thumbs; thumbs would get in the way of the hooking action used to grasp tree limbs and vines.

Bug-bashers: The vertical-clingers-and-leapers

The vertical-clingers-and-leapers (VCLs) do just that: They hug tight to a tree trunk, with their spine vertical, until they're ready to move, and then they twist at the waist and push off hard with their legs, leaping at their target. That target is often an insect, a juicy treat that makes up a large part of their diet. The VCLs include the tarsiers and the lemurs, both members of the prosimian group discussed earlier in the chapter. Their anatomical characteristics include

- ✔ Short, weak arms because they propel with their legs
- ✔ Strong legs for powerful leaping

In the trees: Arboreal quadrupeds

Moving *quadrupedally* means moving on four legs or feet, and it's how many monkey species get around. It involves using both the hands and feet to grasp relatively horizontal tree limbs, which they walk on with great skill and a seemingly daredevil attitude. But evolution has shaped their instincts and abilities, and although accidents happen, they're infrequent enough not to have extinguished this kind of locomotion. The arboreal quadrupeds have the following anatomical characteristics:

- ✔ Strong arms and legs.
- ✔ Relatively low body weight (most of them).

✔ A divergent big toe, such that their feet look much like our hands, with the big toe sticking off to the side; this allows the feet to be used like hands, to grasp tree limbs.

✔ A prominent tail (in most species) used as a balance; one kind of primate, the spider monkey, has a *prehensile tail* that can be carefully controlled to wrap around objects and hold them, just like a hand.

Soldiers beware: Terrestrial quadrupeds

The *terrestrial quadrupeds* get around on all fours, but on the ground rather than habitually in the trees. These animals include the baboons, which live in large, complex social groups *(troops)* and can be fearsome to humans. One troop in South Africa particularly disliked one turn-of-the-century British officer and regularly pelted him — and only him — whenever they saw him marching his own troops! The terrestrial quadrupeds have the following attributes:

✔ Moderately strong arms and legs

✔ Lack of massive upper- or lower-body build for either brachiating or clinging-and-leaping

✔ Calloused feet, hands, and buttocks from spending so much time on the ground

Technically, the chimps and gorillas mix things up a little: They spend a lot of time on the ground, so they're officially terrestrial quadrupeds, but they have the bodies of arboreal quadrupeds because they've only recently (in evolutionary time) come down from the trees in a substantial way. They have one important distinguishing characteristic: heavily built, locking knuckles that allow the heavy upper body to be supported with the knuckles of the hands by pressing down on the ground.

Other primates do some locomotor mixing as well. Bonobos, a kind of West African chimpanzee, are terrestrial quadrupeds, but they also spend some time brachiating and even walking on two legs. This walking is different than human walking, though, because the bonobos only do it on occasion, which is called *opportunistic* locomotion. Humans walk *habitually*, meaning their anatomy is adapted for this kind of locomotion.

The great women of great ape studies

A great deal of what anthropology currently knows about the apes has come from long-term field studies carried out by some remarkable women. Jane Goodall began as a student of anthropologist Louis Leakey, who encouraged her to study the chimpanzees to better understand humanity. She did and for 45 years has observed these primates in great detail at a research station at Gombe, Tanzania. Recently Goodall has shifted from studying the chimpanzees to advocating for protection of chimpanzee habitat; like the other apes, the chimpanzee is endangered.

Another great ape, the orangutan of Borneo, has been studied for more than 30 years by Biruté Galdikas of Canada's Simon Fraser University. Like Goodall, today Galdikas argues forcefully for protection of orangutan habitat, which is being deforested at an alarming rate; some estimate that the orangutan will be extinct by 2012. Dian Fossey (who, like Galdikas and Goodall, was also inspired by Louis Leakey) studied gorillas for nearly three decades, but she was murdered under mysterious circumstances in 1985, and today the gorilla is also becoming extinct, facing the deforestation of its habitat as well as a threat from the Ebola virus. For more on the extinction of primates, see the section "Primates Today (But For How Long?)" later in the chapter.

One of the most important things these women did was to study apes in the wild — not in zoos; you can imagine how different ape behavior would be in these situations. Remember, though, that even the observer's presence would effect ape behavior, so rather than saying they were observing *wild* apes, anthropologists say they were studying *habituated* apes, apes that were accustomed to seeing human observers. Exactly what effects the observers have on ape behavior in non-zoo settings is debatable, but it's very likely to be more "natural" than zoo behavior.

A group of one: Bipeds

Although many primates occasionally stand up to walk on two feet (and one gorilla in West Africa has even been observed to use a walking stick to cross a swampy patch of ground), they do so on occasion rather than habitually. Of the living primates, only *Homo sapiens sapiens* walks on two legs; I discuss why that's a fascinating question in Chapter 6. For the moment, take a look at the main anatomical characteristics of bipedal primates:

- Relatively long, strong legs
- An *S*-shaped spinal column that acts as a spring to absorb stresses
- A wide pelvis that keeps the thighs somewhat apart, helping balance
- A parallel big toe lined up with the rest of the toes (rather than the divergent big toe used by other primates to grasp tree limbs)

> ✔ Thighs that angle inward toward the knees and down from the pelvis, also assisting balance
>
> ✔ Lateral and transverse arches built into the foot so that we aren't flat-footed but supported by three main points of contact (the heel and under the big and small toes) in a stable, tripod-like structure

Humans aren't the only species ever to evolve bipedalism; kangaroos are another, and, given enough time and the right circumstances, bipedalism could easily evolve again, perhaps in the African meerkats, who spend a lot of time standing on their hind legs. But among the primates, humans are the only *living* habitual bipeds. As Chapter 6 shows, though, other primates did evolve bipedalism and used to be quite numerous between about six million and two million years ago.

Monkey See, Monkey Do: Primate Social Groups and Behavior

Primates are very social creatures, and although other social mammals (like zebras) live in groups, primate social groups are extremely complex, with elaborate rank hierarchies and codes of conduct. Anthropologist Franz de Waal even called one book about chimpanzee behavior *Chimpanzee Politics*. Primate groups are also usually (but not always) quite large; baboon troops can have up to 300 members.

Keep in mind that social behavior can depend on group size, which can in turn depend on variables such as whether the species is nocturnal or diurnal, what kind of foods it focuses on, what its local environment is like, and so on. The complex interplay between these variables is, I think, just being understood by anthropologists, who have spent much of the last few decades simply observing, understanding, and then describing (rather than comprehensively explaining) the variety of primate social behaviors.

Primates live in large, complex groups for three main reasons:

> ✔ **Protection from predators (protection in numbers):** Predators can be put off by large, noisy, and dangerous groups of primates (like troops of baboons), and in a large group, one individual member is less likely to become lunch for a big snake or eagle.

Is that a threat?

Primate social behavior isn't always sweetness and light. Like many animals, primates often threaten one another, but coming to actual physical blows is rare; it's just too risky. A better tactic is to bluff, and plenty of that goes on: chimpanzees scream, throw sticks, beat on their chests, and bare their teeth all in an effort to intimidate — and it works. Over the eons, intense competition among primates has favored those with large, intimidating canines; the baboons' teeth can be knife-like and particularly scary. Among humans, most threats and displays of prowess are accomplished verbally or with objects that show our rank, and so the pressure for especially big canines has lifted. This pattern seems to go back at least 2 million years, where fossil evidence indicates that our early ancestors' canines aren't as large as they are in most primate species.

- **Greater access to food:** Larger groups who inhabit areas where food is distributed unevenly in the forest are more likely to find food patches because they have more eyes looking.

- **Raising offspring:** Primates reproduce not by having vast numbers of offspring (like fish or frogs) but by having relatively few offspring that require a lot of care, both to protect them from predators and to teach the babies to socialize.

The following list describes the four main kinds of primate social groups:

- **Loners:** This kind of social organization is called *noyau*. Only the nocturnal primates (like some of the prosimians discussed earlier in the chapter) and the orangutan have evolved noyau, in which males wander alone, staying with mates only long enough to mate. Females are also solitary, unless they have young, which they carry as they move around.

- **Families:** Humans love families (or the idea of families) so much that we've been watching the Simpsons — Marge, Homer, Bart, Lisa, and Maggie — for 20 years (and they're only one of a gazillion fictional families shown on television for the past 50 years); we've probably been telling stories about human families as far back as anyone can remember.

In the primate order, *monogamous* families of a mated male and female with their offspring pop up among some gibbons and other kinds, but monogamy is actually quite rare in the primate order outside the human species.

✔ **Troops:** *Troops* are multi-male, multi-female groups that contain no stable, long-term male-female mating relationships; males and females each have several mates. This situation is most common among the semi-terrestrial primates, whose groups may number into the low hundreds. These troops' large numbers protect them from the big, terrestrial predators like leopards and lions and can help in finding food by sending scouts out on reconnaissance treks.

✔ **Harems:** Groups that contain a single male, several females, and their offspring are known as *polygynous* groups or *harems*. Gorillas live this way; silverbacks, the dominant males, typically kick out male youngsters that are starting to come up in the ranks. They sometimes tolerate powerful young males for a while, but in the end the young guys normally have to leave. When they do, they have to find another group, defeat its silverback, and live to be the dominant male. It's not an easy life.

Just when you have a handle on primate characteristics and behavior, another unusual situation arises. In this case, it's *polyandry*, the social pattern among nonhuman primates in which a single female has several male mates. This tendency is only found among the tiny, nocturnal, insect-eating marmosets and tamarinds.

Primates Today (But For How Long?)

The living primates — anywhere between 233 and 290 species, depending on whom you talk to — are widely distributed from South America to Africa to Japan. (Figure 4-6 shows this distribution.) Most are found in the tropics or semi-tropics (within 1,500 miles north or south of the equator). New species still occasionally surface — for example, the sideburn-sporting *titi* monkeys of South America (found in 2002) and two new lemur species found in 2005 in Madagascar. Some species are flourishing in large wilderness areas, but development is steadily reducing and fragmenting these regions.

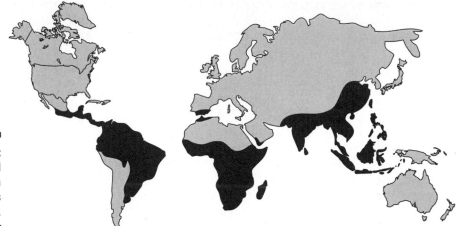

Figure 4-6:
Global
distribution
of primates
today.

In 1996, the World Conservation Union reported on the many threats to primate species, and in 2003 they revealed that about half of the more than 200 primate species were under severe threat. The situation hasn't gotten any better since that report. In October 2007, the International Primatological Society and Conservation International copublished a list of the 25 most threatened and endangered primate species. Astonishingly, these groups include chimpanzees, gorillas, orangutans, and some kinds of gibbons; essentially, aside from humans, *all the great apes are facing extinction.* Maybe we should be more ashamed than astonished, though; conservationists have been telling us for 30 years that these and other species were in trouble. But even pointing out that we share at least 95 percent of our DNA with most of these species hasn't reduced the threats to our closest living relatives. These threats include

- ✔ Habitat destruction from logging, particularly in Southeast Asia and Borneo, home of the orangutan

- ✔ Habitat destruction from agriculture, particularly in the African Congo, where farms are encroaching on gorilla habitat

- ✔ Poaching, much of it for meat, some of which sells for spectacular prices on the African "bush meat" market

Any conscientious anthropologist today will tell you that for the threatened and endangered species, right now research priorities must include conservation effort. If the species aren't preserved, how can you find out about our species from them? And if humans let our closest living relatives go extinct without a real fight, what does that say about us?

Chimpanzees and people

One reason people may feel ambivalent about the fate of chimpanzees — and, by extension, other endangered primates — is that for a long time Western civilization has looked on the chimpanzee with suspicion, hatred, fear, and disgust. Medieval sculptures depict chimpanzees as gargoyle-like winged devils; in the Victorian era, captive chimpanzees disgusted many Londoners, who believed that the chimpanzee was a species locked in time, a throwback to a disgusting, primordial past. Of course, the Victorians were wrong: Chimpanzees are here in the present and have evolved for as long as we have. That they didn't evolve the kinds of language and culture of modern humans is neither here nor there; each species adapts in its own way, and cross-species comparisons of this kind are pointless. Today, despite knowing that most of our DNA is identical to that of the chimpanzee, chimps are still dressed up for commercials and movies and essentially looked on as comical quasi-humans. But some scientists feel that, due to chimpanzees' genetic and anatomical similarities to humanity, the chimpanzee genus — *Pan* — should be dissolved, and chimpanzees brought into our genus, *Homo*.

Chapter 5

My Career Is in Ruins: How Anthropologists Learn about the Past

• •

• •

Humanity, like any other form of life, didn't just pop up out of nowhere. Our species evolved from earlier forms of life over vast stretches of time. Just as you ask a new acquaintance where they come from, how long they've lived in a certain city, or about their family history, anthropologists recognize that things in the world today have roots — a past — and that knowing about that past is important to understanding the present. To learn about the human past, anthropologists invented a specialized field of study, archaeology: the study (-ology) of the ancient (archae-).

Archaeology is one of the four main subdivisions of the larger field of anthropology. Archaeologists, therefore, are anthropologists, even if they humanity they study is ancient. Chapter 3 introduces all four of the main fields of anthropology.

Everyone's favorite archaeologist, of course, is Indiana Jones; whether he's in tweeds at his university office or crashing through a jungle with loot under his arm, everyone thinks, "There, that's archaeology." But the truth is that archaeology is a slow and meticulous business — so slow, in fact, that to all but the professionals, watching either field excavations or lab analyses can be boring with a capital *B*.

What's archaeology really about, then? Why do archaeologists go so slowly, meticulously flicking dirt from a broken, thousand-year-old pot? Why do they get excited when they find ancient garbage heaps or even ancient outhouses? How can something as fascinating as investigating our species' family history be turned into something as boring as sieving dirt through a mesh filter? The answer, of course, is that it's *not* boring; it's just slower than a Hollywood blockbuster.

In this chapter, you discover why archaeologists obsess about knowing how old artifacts are and precisely where they come from, and you see how archaeologists think and classify what they find to rebuild humanity's past from a million artifacts — like chips of stone, glass, pottery — lost or discarded by our ancestors. All this information will give you a good appreciation for understanding how archaeologists piece together the human past.

What, How Old, and Where: It's All You Need to Know

Somewhere near the end of my four-hour oral PhD examination, something clicked in my mind. It was something I'd been learning for years, and it finally crystallized in a single statement. All I'd done, over eight years of PhD research and five years for my master's, was document *how many (of certain kinds of artifacts) were found in certain places, at certain times*. That was it! Of course, I'd gone on to analyze what was found where, to try to answer questions about how people lived in the past, but really the most important goal for archaeologists was to know *what kinds of artifacts* (objects made by ancient people) *were found in certain places at certain times*. That's the essence of archaeology.

 Artifacts are objects used or made by humans; *fossils* are relics of ancient bones, described in more detail in Chapter 6. Artifacts are often assigned to time periods in the same way as fossils, but — as you discover in this chapter — some techniques of dating artifacts don't work for fossils.

The significance of where

Archaeologists have to dig carefully if they want a good representation of what people did in the ancient world. They have to keep track of where they find artifacts. Why is *where* so important? Because humans do different tasks in different places. They use some places for ritual (like churches), some places for commerce (markets and malls), some for privacy (the home and areas within it), and so on. And because they make and use so many objects to survive, those objects tend to reflect what's going on in those different spaces. If a terrible calamity flattened my home this instant, the archaeologist of 5,000 AD would find my computer by my window, my SCUBA gear over in a closest, my subsistence items over by the kitchen, and so on. Careful excavation could reveal a lot about my life. Digging haphazardly, though, may mix the things from my apartment with items from next door (making my occupation difficult to discern from my neighbors'); it may mix my cookbooks with my research library, even though in my life the two kinds of books have very different purposes. I don't research cooking, I research the ancient world, and that's reflected in my keeping different kinds of books in different places.

The places where archaeologists find artifacts are *archaeological sites* (not *sights*). A site can be as simple as a scatter of stone chips by the remains of a campfire — where a hunter resharpened a stone tool and had a bite to eat 9,000 years ago — or as complex as the whole ancient city of Tenochtitlan, the Aztec capital now largely buried by Mexico City.

The significance of when

When is important because humanity has changed through time: Our bodies have changed, but so have our behaviors, the things we do. And because humans survive by using artifacts like spears or dog sleds, those objects reveal what ancient people were doing across time. For example, consumers used to receive music on vinyl discs, then on cassette tapes, then on CDs, and now as MP3 files on electronic players. The change in these music-delivery artifacts will someday tell a future archaeologist a lot about how our society changed through time. In the same way, today's archaeologists carefully investigate how ancient cultures' artifacts changed through time.

The significance of artifacts

So, how do archaeologists reassemble the artifacts that reflect ancient lives? Very carefully. Archaeology studies three main kinds of traces of life in the past:

- ✔ **Artifacts** are items that humanity has moved, used, or made. (In this context, *humanity* applies to modern humans as well as all our ancestors back to around 2 million years ago.)

- ✔ **Features** are traces of human activity that you can't easily transport to a laboratory, such as a stain in the ground where a wooden post once stood.

- ✔ **Sites** are clusters of artifacts and/or features, ranging in size from a cave dwelling as big as a two-car garage to the entire ancient city of Babylon.

Archaeologists also study a wide range of other topics related to life in the ancient world; for instance, *archaeozoologists* study animal bones (such as the remains of ancient meals), and *archaeobotanists* study ancient plant remains (such as core samples of ancient pollen), to see how plant life, and therefore ancient climates, changed through time. These professions are special sub-fields of archaeology, and at most archaeological sites, excavators collect and document bones and plant matter in addition to artifacts and features.

The Pompeii premise and the study of taphonomy

The first hundred years of archaeology mainly dealt with documenting obvious traces of ancient human life, like the Parthenon or Maya temples. But as it became clear that humanity had a vast, 2-million-year history, archaeologists started to look for (and find) less-visible traces of prehistoric humanity. By digging very carefully, prehistorians found ancient campsites and even cave dwellings. Many times, they found these sites in layers, one stacked on another as one hunting band moved on and another later camped in the same place. By studying how the artifacts changed through time, archaeologists reasoned, they could understand how human behavior changed over time.

This conclusion was correct in theory, but researchers started to discover complications. At some sites, for example, rodents or flowing water had disturbed the ancient campsite remains, moving artifacts *after* ancient people left them behind but *before* archaeologists excavated them. This deviation was a problem because if artifacts were moved vertically, for

example, from one layer to another, archaeologists may assign them to very different time periods. The *Pompeii premise* — the idea that archaeological sites were perfect, unchanged reflections of the past (like at the well-preserved Roman town of Pompeii, buried in ash that captured the bodies of fleeing people in 79 AD) — was rejected. Now archaeologists had to prove that their sites were well-preserved and undisturbed rather than assume it.

To establish this proof, archaeologists started a new research field: the study of *taphonomy,* or how archaeological sites are formed in the past and transformed by water, wind, rodent activity, frost action on soil, and every other conceivable factor. Only after understanding how an archaeological site has been formed and transformed before excavators arrived can archaeologists really learn about the past. Many sites have been so severely transformed that archaeologists pass them up in favor of less-disturbed sites.

Artifacts, then, are concrete items that people used in the past. Archaeologists excavate them carefully to keep from breaking them and note exactly where they came from. The artifacts are then typically bagged up, given a catalog number, and transported back to a lab for future analysis. Examples of artifacts include stone tools such as arrowheads or hand axes; these are very common because humanity has used stone for millions of years, and it doesn't decay quickly. Archaeologists document features in the field by using drawings and photography, but features are nearly impossible to take back to the lab. In fact, after the archaeologists document features, they typically just continue to excavate through them. Examples of features include *hearths* — piles of ash, burnt rock, and perhaps some charred bone or other remains of ancient cooking.

By keeping careful track of where artifacts and features are found at archaeological sites, archaeologists can identify patterns of life in the ancient world. Comparing the food refuse (like cast-aside bones from cuts of meat) associated with slave owners' houses, for example, with the food refuse associated with slave dwellings, archaeologists can reconstruct how these peoples' diets differed. Of course, circumstances change through time, so archaeologists also keep careful track of how old certain artifacts and features are.

Keeping Time: How Archaeologists Date Finds

Archaeologist Sir Mortimer Wheeler once said that *chronology* — the study of time — is the backbone of archaeology. Not the whole skeleton, but nothing less than the backbone. He was right. A pile of artifacts haphazardly dug from a cave — where 10,000 years of continuous occupation left behind hundreds of thousands of artifacts and features — would be little use to anyone; without knowing whether certain artifacts came from the oldest layers or the most recent, archaeologists are at a loss to understand how the ancient society changed through time. So the study of time is the backbone of archaeology, and archaeologists keep track of time with a number of methods.

The deeper, the older: Stratigraphy

Almost every place ancient people lived has been covered by some kind of geological layer. For example, the city of Pompeii was buried by dozens of feet of volcanic ash; the Pacific Northwest Coast native village of Ozette was buried by a mudslide; and remnants of Harappan civilization were buried by sediments laid down by thousands of years of Indus River overflow.

This constant process of burial is very handy for archaeologists because it preserves archaeological sites. Two principles help understand why it's so important:

- ✔ **Uniformitarianism** indicates that the geological phenomena burying landscapes today (like landslides or ash layers) operated in the same way in the past. The laws of physics haven't changed appreciably since the formation of the Earth.

- ✔ **Superposition** shows that, all other factors being equal, items found deeper in a series of geological layers were *deposited* (laid down in that layer) before items found shallower in the series of layer, simply because layers stack up over time. These stacks of layers are *stratigraphic sequences,* the individual layers of which are *strata*.

Basically, the principle of superposition is the deeper, the older. Remember, though, that not all archaeological sites are pristine; tomb-raiders, burrowing rodents, and even earthworms and other factors can and do move artifacts from one layer to another. (See the sidebar "The Pompeii premise and the study of taphonomy" for more information.) Still, archaeologists are trained to spot the signs of such disturbance and usually focus their studies on undisturbed sites, where deeper really does mean older. Considering that (stop me if you've heard this one) human behavior has changed through time and that change is of great interest to archaeologists, you can see just how important understanding stratification is. Figure 5-1 shows a student standing with over 3 meters (12 feet) of strata at one of my excavation sites in the Pacific Northwest.

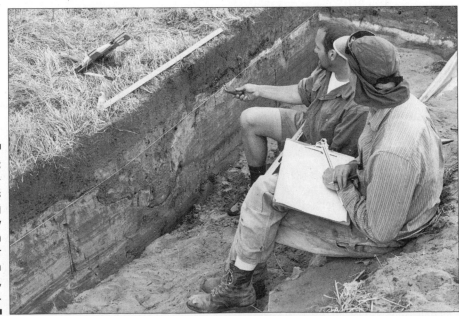

Figure 5-1: Archaeologists examining stratigraphy at a site on the lower Columbia River, Washington.

Before or after? Relative dating

Although today archaeologists can date artifacts and features with a wide array of methods (which I discuss later), for a long time it was only possible to do *relative dating*, or identifying whether artifacts or features were older or younger than other artifacts. That's because archaeologists didn't have the technical methods to date individual artifacts; they could only identify whether artifacts came from lower or higher strata in a stratigraphic sequence. Remember, in an undisturbed stratigraphic sequence, lower strata are older, and higher strata are more recent.

Relative dating allowed archaeologists to sketch out basic sequences, but not date them very precisely. For example, the 19th-century Danish prehistorian Christian Thompsen noted that in the prehistoric strata of Europe, stone tools were found at the lowest (earliest) strata, bronze tools above these, and iron tools above these. He devised the *three-age system* in which the ancient world was divided into the Stone Age, the Bronze Age, and the Iron Age. This division was very useful but a little incomplete: No one could say just how long the Stone Age lasted, for example; prehistorians knew only that it came first, because it was lowest in the strata.

European prehistorians still use the Stone, Bronze, and Iron Ages to some extent, but these designations serve more for general discussion than detailed understanding. For example, subsequent ages continued to use stone, and although the Iron Age began in southeastern Europe around 2,500 years ago, it took centuries to reach northern Europe. Also, these ages focus on the raw materials from which artifacts were made but don't reflect other, important aspects of ancient life like subsistence, symbolism, or religion. So although they're a part of the story, they don't tell everything.

Absolutely probably 6,344 years old (plus or minus): Radiometric absolute dating

By the 1950s, methods to date individual artifacts based on radioactive decay began to give precise dates for such time periods as Thompsen's ages (see the preceding section). These dates are termed *absolute* because they specify when a certain event occurred (such as the death of a tree or animal, or the solidification of lava into rock) as opposed to the *relative* dates of prior archaeologists, which only indicated that an item was older or younger than some event.

Radiometric dates are based on the decay of certain elements contained in artifacts and features. Many different radiometric methods can date various materials to different date ranges. The following list shows two of the most important techniques for archaeology:

- ✔ **Radiocarbon dating** dates the remains of most living things, including bone, plant matter, and wood; it's useful to about 50,000 years ago.

- ✔ **K-Ar dating** calculates the age of basaltic rocks starting about 100,000 years old and reaching back into the billions of years; it's particularly important to the dating of early hominid sites, such as Olduvai Gorge.

The most commonly used method in archaeology is *radiocarbon* or *carbon 14 dating* (also known as *14C dating*).

Radiocarbon dating

By measuring how much carbon is in the remains of a once-living thing, scientists can know how long it's been since the original 14C began to decay — in other words, when the living thing died. All living things ingest the element carbon in the form of its isotope carbon 14 (14C), which floats freely in the atmosphere and is present in all foods. When a life form stops ingesting 14C (when it, you know, dies), no new 14C enters the body, and the 14C in the body begins to radioactively decay into 14N (nitrogen isotope 14). Importantly, 14C decays into 14N at a known and pretty stable rate: After about 5,600 years, only half of the original 14C remains because the rest has decayed into 14N.

Archaeologists mark the passage of time in many different ways. *BP* stands for *before present,* which basically means "years ago." *BC (before Christ)* is more commonly used in Europe and other areas that have historical records going back thousands of years, to around the time of Christ. So as not to favor the Christian religion, some archaeologists say *BCE (before the Common Era)* rather than BC. But this designation still points back to the time of Christ and is a little over the top in my view. Just because I use the term *BC* doesn't mean I'm pushing religion. Other common terms are *kya* (thousands of years ago) and *mya* (millions of years ago).

K-Ar dating

Another kind of radiometric dating works on objects that never lived, such as lava. The rock called basalt is, basically, cooled lava. As a liquid, the lava contains potassium (K), which, when the rock cools and hardens, begins to decay into argon (Ar). Thus, K-Ar dating measures how much Ar an object has in relation to K, indicating how long ago the lava cooled (because Ar is able to escape liquid lava as gas bubbles until the lava cools and traps it in the rock).

Dating rock layers allows the sediments between them to be *bracketed* in age. For example, if a lava flow solidifies at 2.2 million years ago, and then a lake forms over it and deposits many layers of silt before it dries up and is capped by another flow of lava at 1.7 million years ago, geologists could reasonably state that the silty lake layers bracketed between the lavas were deposited between 2.2 and 1.7 million years ago. Artifacts or fossils found in these silty strata, for example from a band of hominids that camped on the lakeshore, would be dated to the same general period.

Issues with radiometric dating

One minor hitch with radiometric dates: Although the radioactive decay rates are well known and pretty stable, lab observation reveals that decay is a little faster at some times than at others. Because of this discrepancy, a date of, say, 6,344 years since a piece of wood stopped taking on 14C has an attached error factor. Therefore, a radiometric date of 6,344 years may be followed by "+/- 650 years." This variation is why the title of this section is "Absolutely probably 6,344 years old."

The need for an error factor doesn't mean that radiometric methods don't work, only that archaeologists need to get several dates from each sample to be sure all dates point at about the same time range. The best way to ensure that your dates are good is to get multiple 14C dates and then back them up through independent means, such as relative dating or other radiometric methods, to be sure all is in order. Still, you can't get around the fact that radiometric dates always come with an error margin. The fact that this, and some other, corrections and adjustments need to be considered with radiometric dates doesn't undermine their use. They've been central to giving archaeologists a better understanding of the past, and each method continues to be refined. For example, labs often date items of a known age, such as bone from a burial of a known date, to be sure of their methods and equipment.

Don't worry — radiometric dating is very secure. And archaeologists themselves are the first to point out any problems with the method; their studies demand a good understanding of the passage of time.

Many people, having heard about error factors associated with radiometric dates, think they shouldn't trust the methods. But certainty of dates can come from many sources. One way is to send your radiocarbon samples to different labs; I may send samples to radiocarbon labs in Canberra, Australia; Davis, California; and Oxford, England. For about $500 per sample date, each lab will send me their radiocarbon date of the sample. Now, remember, I haven't told them what date I expect (the dated material could be 500 or 5,000 or 50,000 years old), and I haven't told the different labs who else I'm sending the material to, so I don't get some conspiracy to send me a particular date. What happens? Normally — barring some kind of contamination or other problem — the dates come back essentially the same, and I know the method is secure.

Saving Space: How Archaeologists Keep Track of Where Artifacts Are Found

The preceding section discusses how archaeologists keep track of time, the backbone of archaeology; now you need to understand how they keep track of where artifacts come from. Together, these two variables tell archaeologists much of what they need to know: *how much, of what kinds of artifacts, are found in certain places at certain times?*

Be there: Provenience

Every year or so a well-meaning person arrives at my office with artifacts he or she has found outdoors — stone arrowheads, bits of pottery, and so on — and wants to know what these pieces represent, how old they are, and who used them in the ancient world. My first question is always to ask where the artifacts came from, but unfortunately the answer is normally too vague. As I discuss earlier in the chapter, knowing which layer an item came from is vitally important because layers stack up over time; a few centimeters may mean a difference of thousands of years. If the item was dug from the ground without carefully recording the various strata, I have no way of knowing whether it came from layers 10,000 years old or 1,000 years old. And where it came from in the site horizontally is also critical: If the site was a cemetery, for example, I need to know whether it came from a peasant's burial or a royal burial. That distinction could tell archaeologists about the differences between the lives of peasants and royalty. However well-meaning my visitors are, I often have to tell them that without such detailed information the item is just a curio and can't tell us nearly as much as we'd learn if we had precise records.

When the importance of location began to sink in for archaeologists in the late 19th century, they invented methods to keep very careful track of *provenience*, which is a precise record of where artifacts are found. Archaeologists measure provenience in two dimensions: vertical (basically, indicating time) and horizontal. Provenience is tracked in relation to a *datum*, or a known point established at the beginning of the excavation. The datum is normally a known, immovable spot, such as a surveyor's *benchmark* (like a metal stud drilled into a rock so it won't budge over time) that has a precisely known elevation, latitude, and longitude.

Be square: Site grids

Knowing exactly where an artifact comes from down to the centimeter allows archaeologists to make precise three-dimensional maps of the distribution of artifacts and features at an archaeological site. This mapping is very easy; archaeology may take a long time, but it's not that technically difficult. Essentially, archaeologists excavate in square holes and regular trenches, not because they look better than shoveled potholes but because by laying out a datum — and from it a *site grid* (a grid of reference points and lines superimposed on the site) — they can keep better track of just where artifacts were found, right down to the centimeter. (***Note:*** Like most scientists, archaeologists normally use the metric system [centimeters, meters, grams, and kilograms] for all measurements; only the oldest records report their findings in imperial measures [feet, inches, pounds and ounces].) Figure 5-2 shows excavators working with a site grid.

Figure 5-2:
A site grid in use on a burial mound in northern Kenya.

How do archaeologists find sites in the first place? Many sites are discovered accidentally by the kind of interested, well-meaning people who bring fascinating curios to my office. After the initial find, though, the person needs to lay out a grid and excavate carefully. Sometimes archaeologists find sites by going into the field with a research question in mind; for example, "Where was the first farming practiced?" This is a big question, but it still allows excavators to narrow down the field somewhat by eliminating some possibilities.

Archaeologists largely find sites by systematically searching vast areas in order to answer certain specific questions and then excavate them with the care described in this chapter.

Type Casting: How Archaeologists Classify Their Finds

After archaeologists slowly, tediously, and delicately excavate artifacts from sites with tools like whisk brooms, toothbrushes, and even chopsticks when they're appropriate, the artifacts go to a lab for cleaning, preservation, and further study. Because archaeologists are trying to reconstruct ancient worlds and ways of life with only fragments to work with, they're very careful to extract every possible shred of information from any given find. Personally, I've lost count of the hundreds of hours I've spent peering down a microscope to document the tiny chips, abrasions, and polishes found on the edges of ancient stone tools that can tell me exactly what the tools were used for.

Types of types: The theory of classification

One of the first tasks is to *classify* artifacts — that is, to order them into *types* that reflect something of interest. Archaeologists classify objects according to their *research paradigm*, or research framework; the research paradigm depends on the questions the archaeologist is trying to answer. At the core of classification theory is the fact that you can classify nearly any object in many different ways. You can classify a Greek wine jar as "large" if your interest is in the history of the volume of Greek wine jars (maybe because it can tell you about wine consumption in ancient Greece). But if you were interested in the evolution of Greek jar-painting, you may classify the same jar as "decorated with animal figures" as opposed to "decorated with human figures"; in this case, volume may be irrelevant. If your interest is in the evolution of projectile point size through time, you focus on size measurements rather than other possible variables, such as the color of the stone used to make the arrowheads.

Just because research questions differ among archaeologists doesn't mean that they use absolutely no standardization; to make cross-site comparisons possible, for example, archaeologists of various regions do to an extent standardize their artifact classes and measurements. And, in some cases, worldwide standards are accepted. This global standardization is especially true of many kinds of stone tools or pottery because different cultures worldwide have in fact devised the same methods, across time, to make the same kinds of tools (like stone scrapers or pottery jugs).

The illusion of finished tools

The moment you pick up an artifact like a stone tool, it's easy to start wondering what its purpose was. Sometimes that seems obvious; it fits nicely in the hand and seems the right size and weight for some task you may imagine, like whittling wood or butchering an animal.

But you have to remember that appearances may be deceptive; what if the item you're looking at isn't a finished tool after all, but just a chunk of rock that's only been flaked a few times without being completed? Or what if the item has been used so much that its working edge has been worn away, so that you can never really understand the original function?

Archaeologist Harold Dibble pointed this concept out in a famous study of tools from Stone Age Europe. He showed that as large knives were sharpened over time (their *uselife*), their shape changed dramatically; what most people considered two different kinds of tools were actually pieces of the same kind of tool that changed shape through its uselife. Food for thought.

Unearthing the most common artifact types

Luckily for archaeologists, people of the ancient world left traces of their passing across the globe. From massive garbage mounds to entire buried libraries, ancient battlefields, hunting camps, and cave dwellings, traces of our ancestors are just about anywhere you care to look. Of course, not everything has survived the eons; fragile items, like papyrus scrolls or wooden boxes, don't normally preserve. So if archaeologists are trying to rebuild a puzzle of life in the past, remember that in most cases, archaeologists aren't even equipped with every piece of the puzzle from the start.

But many pieces do remain — enough to tell a lot about the human past. They include items made from the three most common materials used in the ancient world: stone, bone and/or antler, and pottery. The following sections deal with each of these materials in more detail

The nature of an artifact's composition and environment determine its preservation. Wooden ship beams sunk in the Mediterranean, for example, are eaten up by woodworms so that only ballast stones and cargo remain. On the other hand, at some *wet sites*, where the oxygen is so scarce that bacteria can't survive, even delicate tissues can survive for thousands of years. In the bogs (wetlands) of northern Europe, for example, bodies dating over two thousand years seem to turn up every few years. My personal hope is to find a frozen Neanderthal somewhere in the Siberian tundra!

Stone

Humans and their earliest ancestors have shaped stone into tools for millions of years. Different kinds of stone have different properties, and our species has long known and exploited the various properties of the basic rock types:

- ✔ **Igneous rocks** (volcanic in origin) range from coarse (like pumice) to razor-sharp (like *obsidian,* or volcanic glass).

- ✔ **Sedimentary rocks** (bits of other rocks concreted into new forms) include sandstone (good for scraping or rubbing) and flint (a dense stone that can be as sharp as obsidian but is far less brittle).

- ✔ **Metamorphic rocks** (any kind of rock that has itself been altered by heat or pressure) include quartzite (compressed sandstone), which is extremely hard and dense.

Mastering the most advanced techniques of stone toolmaking can take years; the toolmaking process normally proceeds through three main stages:

- ✔ **Core selection,** in which the toolmaker chooses a chunk or block of stone (the core) because of its properties

- ✔ **Initial reduction,** in which the toolmaker uses a hammerstone to break away unwanted parts of the core or flakes of stone he plans to work further

- ✔ **Secondary reduction,** in which the toolmaker continues to shape the core into the desired tool or refine the flake knocked off during initial reduction; this may be done by *pressure flaking,* or using a bone or antler tip to snap fine flakes off the stone edge to make something like an arrowhead

These basic methods shaped stone into a wide array of artifacts; the most common artifacts in the ancient world included

- ✔ **Projectile armatures** (such as arrowheads) that were fixed to projectiles (such as arrows) used to hunt animals from a distance

- ✔ **Cutting implements** (from razor-blade-sized fine tools to hand axes) used for heavier work such as shaving wood or butchering very large animals

- ✔ **Scraping implements** used for working wood or even removing unwanted tissues from animal hides

- ✔ **Perforating implements** such as drills, which were often inserted into a *haft* (a handle) and used to make small holes in bone, wood, and other dense matter

These tools had many variations; on the Pacific Northwest coast, slate was worked into daggers by abrasion or broken into slats fitted into leather vests as body armor.

The earliest stone tools date to more than 2.5 million years ago, but very complex tools such as symmetrical hand axes weren't formed until about 1.8 million years ago. The earliest traces, like the earliest traces of the earliest hominid fossils, are all found in Africa.

Stone tools can reveal information about ancient activities, such as whether people were working wood or butchering animals, at a given campsite. But they can also tell you about ancient human movement. *Sourcing analysis* identifies the outcrop of rock a given stone tool came from based on its chemical fingerprint. Where I work in the Pacific Northwest, we've found that obsidian at some lower-Columbia River villages came from outcrops in Southern Oregon hundreds of miles away. In Europe, archaeologists have used sourcing to identify that Neanderthals normally moved their stone no more than about 20 kilometers (12.5 miles) from their quarry sites.

Bone and antler

Bone and antler were the plastics of the ancient world. They could be scraped or rubbed into shapes — such as barbed harpoon points — that didn't shatter as easily as stone. Toolmakers often soaked them in water or some other liquid before working with them; they often manipulated bone by using the following methods:

- **Groove-and-splinter:** Workers cut two parallel grooves into a dense piece of bone or antler and then pried out the splinter between them for further work.

- **Abrasion:** Toolmakers used any number of materials — from sandpapery shark skin to rough pumice — to hone a point or blade. Bone knives, effective for butchering large animals, were made this way.

- **Sawing:** This technique was more difficult with stone blades but much easier with metal blades (for those cultures that possessed them).

With these basic methods, bone and antler became a wide array of impressive and efficient artifacts, including

- **Snow goggles** (consisting of a slab of bone with two narrow slits cut in as eyelets) made by Arctic peoples to allow vision but prevent snow blindness (caused by the sun reflecting off the snow)
- **Fish hooks** for catching fish of all sizes
- **Needles** for sewing everything from tent skins to clothing

The earliest bone and antler tools, including digging implements, date to over a million years ago, but the more complex working of bone and antler are much more recent, beginning around 100,000 years ago.

Pottery

Pottery is clay that's been heated so that the minerals recrystallize; it's common in all cultures that practiced farming because pottery can be reheated without breaking when cooking food. Nonfarmers also heated clay into solid tablets and some small containers, but large-scale use of pottery really originated with farming peoples.

Basically, people form pottery in three stages:

- ✓ **Preparation of the clay,** such as the removal of dry chunks or the addition of material such as sand or straw, makes the clay keep its shape.

- ✓ **Shaping of the item,** often with slabs of clay grafted together, rolled cylinders of it stacked up to make a vessel, or the use of a potter's wheel, makes the item useful.

- ✓ **Firing of the formed item** to drive out water and harden it requires temperatures over about 1,000 degrees Celsius (1,832 degrees Fahrenheit), which is hotter than a normal campfire and requires special preparation (such as the use of a *kiln,* a housing in which fire is carefully controlled).

Dozens of variations on each of these manufacturing stages exist from culture to culture.

Although baked clay figurines date to more than 20,000 years ago, the first substantial use of clay for containers occurs around 10,000 years ago with the invention of a farming lifestyle.

Billions of pottery vessels were used in the ancient world; in Roman times, *amphorae* (storage jars ranging in size from bottles to barrels) were as common as jars and bottles today. After pottery breaks down to pieces about 3 centimeters (1 inch) in size, little in the natural world breaks them down further. Many archaeologists have spent entire careers fitting together pieces of ancient pottery to understand commerce, food preparation and storage, and other aspects of life in the ancient world.

Chapter 6

Bones of Contention: The Fossil Evidence for Early Human Evolution

In This Chapter

▶ Tracing the rise of hominids in Africa

▶ Understanding the impact of bipedalism on early humans

▶ Tracking the evolution of humanity from the australopithecines through early *Homo* and *Homo erectus*

When Darwin first published *On the Origin of Species* in 1859, only a few early human fossils had been discovered, and nobody really knew what to do with them. (Here I use the term human loosely — more on that soon.) A century and a half later, anthropologists have a collection of hundreds of early human fossils as well as Darwin's theory of evolution to make sense of them. So what do they have to say?

In short, they tell the story of human evolution, or at least parts of it. They tell us how our ancestors got around their landscapes, how they hunted or scavenged their food and processed it with stone tools, as well as how they eventually controlled fire, crossed open bodies of water — and all the while carried brains of ever-increasing size.

No wonder these fossils are normally kept in high-security vaults in their countries of origin. They're priceless windows onto our species' distant past. In this chapter, you find out what early human fossils reveal about the human past.

For this book, I'm using the traditional term *hominid* to refer to the large, bipedal primates, which include humans, our fossil ancestors, and some of their relatives; generally these can all be called early humans, though in Chapter 7 you can find a more precise definition of what it is to be human. You may see the term "hominin" in some anthropological works these days, but this is a new term that's not universally used and, for reasons I lay out in the Introduction, I'm sticking with the more widely used "hominid."

Great Africa: The Earliest Hominids

One of the main discoveries of anthropology has been that the roots of the human species are in Africa; go far enough back in the family tree and your ancestors — be they South Asian, Inuit, or Danish — all originate on the great continent of Africa. That's where archaeologists find fossils of early humans time and again, such that today no serious anthropologist doubts that early hominid evolution occurred exclusively in Africa. (For more on what a fossil is, see Chapter 4.)

A *hominid* is a large primate that walks upright. Today *Homo sapiens sapiens* (that's you, me, and everyone we know) is the only living hominid species, but the following sections describe the many others that have come before us. Compared with the rest of the primates, the most distinctive trait of the hominids (living and extinct) is that hominids walk (or walked) upright.

Another characteristic of the hominids is that they generally have a smaller canine tooth than the other primates. The fact that early hominids had smaller canines is interesting because primates with large canines normally use them in threat displays to intimidate other primates. Social behavior may have been a little different in the early hominids, with smaller canines perhaps reflecting less inter-hominid competition. Unfortunately, anthropologists just can't be sure, even though the canine info presents a pretty good argument.

The earliest fossils displaying bipedal anatomy include

- **Fossils of thighbones from the Tungen Hills, Kenya,** dated to about 6 million years ago

- **Footprints preserved in volcanic ash at Laetoli, Tanzania,** dated to just less than 4 million years ago

- **Pelvic, thigh, shin, and foot bones from various large primates,** dated after about 3 million years ago and including the Lucy specimen (more about Lucy later) from Ethiopia

Clearly, some large primates were walking upright after about 6 million years ago in the same general area (Africa) where you can later see evidence of our own lineage, *Homo*.

So what happened? Why would our primate ancestors evolve a new way to get around, a new form of locomotion? Read on!

Stand and Deliver: The Riddles of Bipedalism

Over 20 years ago, when I was an undergraduate at the University of London, I heard a pretty simple story about the origins of bipedalism: around 3 million years ago, early hominids moved into a savanna ecosystem and rose on hind legs to adapt to it. Today, we anthropologists know a little different. Our knowledge is improving, though it's still not making explanations any clearer. Anthropologists can say for sure that

- Bipedalism has origins over 5 million years ago.
- Bipedalism originated in forested environments, not savanna, though hominids did move onto the savanna by 3 million years ago.
- The advantages of bipedalism apparently outweighed the disadvantages.

To make sense of these facts, you need to understand early hominids not as actors on a stage with the landscape as a backdrop but as fully involved members of ancient ecosystems. In the sections that follow, I explain how the advantages of bipedalism overcame its disadvantages to early humans, and I give you a look at the complexity of early hominid evolution.

Walking upright: Pros and cons

Most anthropologists recognize the following likely advantages of bipedalism for primates likely to have been the immediate predecessors of habitual bipeds:

- **Efficiency:** Walking bipedally is efficient for animals of early hominid size.
- **Carrying capacity:** Bipedal movement would also allow the hands to be free to carry objects.
- **Improved scouting:** Walking bipedally would enable hominids to see over tall vegetation.
- **Body cooling:** Switching to bipedalism would allow more efficient cooling of the body in tropical and subtropical Africa.

You can pretty easily look at any anatomical characteristic and say, "Well, I can see why that would be useful," but remember, every evolutionary adaptation is a compromise. Most anthropologists would also agree that bipedalism has its downsides as well:

- ✓ **Climbing ability:** Bipedal anatomy would make hominids less capable climbers (for example, making escape from predation more difficult).

- ✓ **Speed and agility:** Bipedal anatomy would make hominids slower and less agile than equally sized *quadrupeds* (animals moving on four limbs).

Remember, any theory that purports to explain the origins of bipedalism has to account for both the pros and cons. Beware of any theory that attempts to explain too much with just one factor, like the aquatic ape theory. Evolution is complex, and single factors usually don't account for everything.

The complexities of early hominid evolution

Sorting out what was involved in early hominid evolution has preoccupied hundreds of anthropologists for decades. Today I think anthropology has a pretty good handle on some of the most important factors involved, and I sketch them out in this section.

Trophic levels

Early hominid evolution didn't take place in a vacuum — our ancestors lived out their lives as active members of a variety of African ecosystems. Environmental changes that affected other species ended up affecting early hominids, and vice versa.

The *Pliocene* geological epoch from about 5 to 1.8 million years ago is particularly important for early hominid studies because it's the period in which bipedalism really took off as a hominid adaptation. The Pliocene was marked by global cooling and pretty severe ecosystem changes in Africa. The *Pleistocene* begins at about 1.8 million years ago and is a period marked by the ice ages (which ended around 10,000 years ago). Many anthropologists term the archaeology of the early hominids *Plio-Pleistocene archaeology*.

One major global environmental change began around 2 million years ago as global cooling began to fragment the massive, steamy forests that dominated Africa (instead of straddling the equator as they do today). As some of those forests were replaced by open grassland, many dense-forest ape species became extinct because they were unable to adapt to the changing environment; however, the ancestors of today's wildebeest, zebras, and other savanna species began to flourish. Some form of hominid also flourished — or at least survived — as it moved from fragmented forest onto more open savanna. There, the species interacted in the classic savanna ecosystem of several *trophic* (nutrition) levels:

- ✓ **Primary biomass:** Consists of grasses, roots, seeds, and other plant matter

- ✓ **Herbivore:** Subsists mainly on primary biomass; includes grazing herd species such as zebra, gazelle, and elephant

✔ **Carnivore:** Subsists mainly on herbivores; includes the big cats such as lions, leopards, and cheetahs

✔ **Scavenger:** Subsists mainly on the remains of carnivore kills; includes hyenas, foxes, and vultures

Like any plant or animal, all early hominids fit somewhere in this hierarchy — and the hierarchy itself could change. For example, consider that over time, one kind of early hominid — early *Homo* (our first relative of this period) — moved up the trophic "ladder," directly competing first with other scavengers (for the scraps left behind by the carnivores) but later competing directly with the big cats (for prey species such as zebras and wildebeest). To get their hands on these species, hominid groups had to be agile, numerous, intelligent and — I imagine — very proactive. You don't try to drive a lioness and her cubs away from a fresh kill with anything other than total commitment!

Factors and interactions

Considering that early hominid evolution was part of larger ecosystem evolution, you can be sure that it was very complex; single-factor models explaining just about anything never seem to pan out.

Having said that, I do think that anthropology has identified some very important *factors* of early hominid evolution, but how those factors interacted — how one may have promoted another but dampened others — is still poorly understood. The following are all important factors in early hominid evolution:

✔ **Territoriality:** How animals keep track of and note their territories; chimpanzees occasionally go on patrol, attacking interlopers, and presumably early hominids had similar concerns.

✔ **Sexual behavior:** Was sexual activity seasonal? If so, what was the mating season, and how did this affect hominid behavior and ecology?

✔ **Offspring-rearing behavior:** How long did offspring have to be protected? Were males kicked out of the group when they became a threat to the alpha male, like in gorilla society?

✔ **Resource distribution:** How are the species' (both the hominids and the animals that hominids interacted with) food, water, and other resources distributed on the landscape? Do they turn on and off on a seasonal basis? How does this cycle affect territoriality?

✔ **Tool use:** Did the species use tools, like the sharp chips of stone early hominids used or the probe sticks chimpanzees use to investigate termite mounds? And if so, what effect did those tools have on subsistence mode? For example, finding good stone to make tools may be included in travel decisions or even territorial behavior.

✔ **Subsistence mode:** Did the species eat a restricted or general diet? What were the constituents of that diet, and how did this make-up affect territoriality and/or competition with other animals, including, perhaps, other groups of hominids?

✔ **Social behavior:** All primates have complex social interactions; what were these interactions for the early hominids? Can anthropologists draw useful parallels with the modern chimpanzees and gorillas, or is such comparison inappropriate?

✔ **Communication and language:** Primates handle the intensity and complexity of their social interactions through communication, ranging from physical grooming to bodily postures, vocalizations, and — in humans and some of our ancestors — language. So, what was the nature of communication among the early hominids?

✔ **Anatomy:** What limits did the anatomy impose on behavior related to subsistence, tool use, sexual behavior, or any other factor? At the same time, what options did early hominid anatomy allow?

Although other factors were certainly involved in early hominid evolution, the preceding list is an excellent summary of the most important ones, and it's plenty of food for thought.

The aquatic ape theory

Unfortunately, I need to dispel the common myth that the aquatic ape theory (AAT) is a legitimate scientific theory on the origins of bipedalism.

In short, AAT supporters suggest that early hominids developed bipedalism by spending a lot of their time in bodies of water. To be able to breathe, they would have to keep their heads above water, which they accomplished by standing on two legs. The problems with AAT are many, but you can boil them down to the fact that AAT supporters' so-called evidence typically involves lists of human anatomical characteristics that are similar to those of aquatic mammals (such as whales). But the biologists and physical anthropologists who've reviewed these lists find little compelling evidence; the similarities are trivial or misleading and have better explanations than AAT.

AAT is well known because it's often publicized as a groundbreaking alternative to mainstream anthropology. It's an alternative, all right, but so is the space alien theory that extraterrestrials were responsible for bipedalism. Possible, but with precious little evidence for it.

My own experience of AAT came during my work at Kenya's Leakey Research Station on the shore of Lake Turkana. The lakeshore where we waded while fishing wasn't a good place for bipeds (including me) because the lake was home to thousands of Nile crocodiles. I can't fathom how small, lightweight early hominids could have survived crocodiles' ambush attacks in the murky water. This area was a spectacularly dangerous place, much more so than even the open savanna.

Clearly, early hominid evolution was no simple matter and can't be easy to reconstruct. But anthropologists and archaeologists are ingenious in their ability to extract as much as possible from any fragment that can reveal something about the past. In the following sections, I show you just what the fossils have to say about early hominid evolution.

All the Same from the Neck Down: The Australopithecines

For years, palaeoanthropologists have been obsessed with finding and interpreting the fossils and (sometimes) stone tools these hominids used. Many of the fossil discoveries have been of the genus *Australopithecus* (*austral* referring to South Africa, where they were first found, and *pithecus* referring to their ape-like nature). As a group, they're referred to as australopithecines.

Fossil discoveries have made it clear that between about 4 million and 1 million years ago, two main groups of African hominids — the *robusts* and the *graciles* — existed. In many ways these creatures were similar to humans: They walked on two legs, probably lived in social groups of roughly the same size as chimpanzees or gorillas, probably had some complex vocalizations (though anthropology doesn't have good evidence to support the existence of modern language this early), and probably lived lives you would recognize as similar to that of other primates today, or even other social mammals, such as wolves or big cats. The sections that follow describe these two groups in more detail.

Keep in mind that although some preaustralopithecine hominid fossils exist, the time of the australopithecines is when the fossil record really becomes rich and well known, so I'm focusing on them in this book.

The basic differences and similarities

The robust and gracile australopithecines share the following anatomical characteristics:

- **Bipedal locomotion:** Walking habitually on two legs
- **Encephalization:** Having brains *slightly* larger than expected for their body size as compared to other primates, such as the chimpanzee
- **Canine reduction:** Having smaller canine teeth than other primates

> ✔ **Moderate degree of sexual dimorphism:** Different body sizes for males and females; this is common in nonhuman primates — gorilla males can be about 50 percent larger than females — but is less pronounced in humans, where males are only about 10 percent larger than females
>
> ✔ **Moderate body size:** Standing between 4 and 4.5 feet (about 1.2 meters to about 1.4 meters) and weighing from 65 to 100 pounds (about 30 kilograms to about 45 kilograms)

For some anthropologists, the real differences in the robusts and graciles are in their heads — that is, in their diets as reflected by their teeth. In the next sections I explain why some anthropologists say the australopithecines were all the same from the neck down.

In other words, the australopithecines were somewhat larger than chimpanzees but smaller than modern humans, had largish brains (more on this later) and smaller, more human-like teeth than other primates, and walked upright. These creatures are what Hollywood calls ape-men (of course, things would have gotten pretty boring pretty quickly without some ape-women), and in a way Hollywood is right. Good evidence shows that the gracile australopithecines were direct ancestors of the earliest members of the genus *Homo*, the originator of all humans today. Figure 6-1 shows the crania (braincase and face) of the main early hominid species (and some others discussed in Chapters 7 and 8), including their facial bones and teeth and the relative sizes of their brains. Figure 6-2 shows you how these species were related and when they existed. In both figures, you can see commonalities and differences that I discuss in the following sections.

One way to think of the robust and gracile australopithecines is in the same way you think of lions and cheetahs; both have the same essential body plan, live in similar environments, may go after some similar food sources, and have a common evolutionary ancestor, but each has developed its own way to live, diverging evolutionarily to become a different animal. The evidence suggests the same about the australopithecines.

Classifying fossil material means deciding which biological group it belongs in; anthropologists often do this classification on the basis of shape, which reveals a lot about the animal. For example, nobody is going to place a fish skull into the rabbit category. But when it comes to our own ancestors — early hominids — things aren't so easy; anthropology can get personal (anthropologists are human, of course), and things can get sticky. Remember that some anthropologists are *lumpers* (people who overlook details in order to focus on common patterns and place new finds in existing groups), and others are *splitters*, who focus on details and tend to create new groups rather than place new fossils into old groups. Personally, I'm a lumper, and you can bet that this tendency has affected my interpretations of the material. Still, on a broad scale, most anthropologists would agree with the gist of the early hominid evolution narrative I give in this book.

Homo

  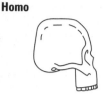

Homo habilis   *Homo erectus*   *Homo sapiens sapiens*   *Homo sapiens neanderthalensis*

Robust australopithecines

Australopithecus robustus   *Australopithecus boisei*   *Australopithecus aetheopicus*

Figure 6-1:
The main
hominid
species'
crania.

Gracile australopithecines

Australopithecus africanas   *Australopithecus afarensis*

The crusher: Robust australopithecines

The *robusts* were a heavily built kind of australopithecine. Their anatomical characteristics included

- **Massive, flat grinding molars** for processing a relatively dry diet (see more on the diet later in this section)

- **Massively buttressed and fortified facial structure** to absorb enormous chewing stresses

- **Sagittal crest,** or a flare of bone atop the skull — like a mohawk — that served as an attachment point for massive chewing muscles

- **Moderate brain volume,** about 550 cubic centimeters (about 19 fluid ounces or about 1.5 typical soda cans)

Robusts, then, were robust in the head (their molars were four times the size of your own), and that had to do with massive chewing pressures. What were they chewing? Analysis of the microscopic wear on their tooth fossils indicates a diet very much like the modern rhinoceros (yes, rhinoceros), which subsists on leaves and grasses on the African savanna. The rhino crushes the vegetation with flat teeth that are scratched and worn down by dust that adheres to the leaves. The robust, then, is evidence of a vegetarian hominid whose massive teeth weren't used to sink into the flesh of prey animals but to snip, crush, and grind leaves and other plant matter.

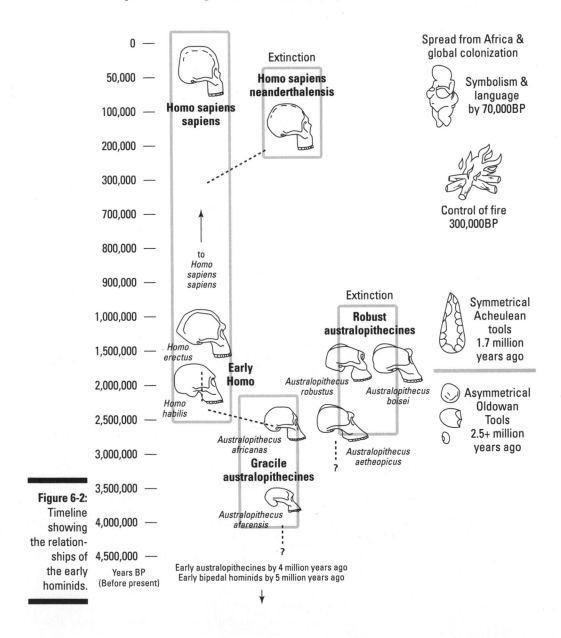

Figure 6-2: Timeline showing the relationships of the early hominids.

The earliest robusts (*Australopithecus aethiopicus*) are known from around 2.5 million years ago, and the most recent from about 1 million years ago. Robusts are variously classified as *Australopithecus robustus* or *Australopithecus boisei,* and some classify them in a different genus altogether: *Paranthropus.* Because I'm a lumper, though, I'm putting them all in the generic "robust australopithecine" group.

Some interesting robust specimens include

- **The Black Skull,** a 2.5-million-year-old robust from northern Kenya

- **Olduvai Hominid 5**, a later robust (about 1.7 million years old) discovered in 1959 by Mary Leakey at Olduvai Gorge, Tanzania

- **The Peninj Mandible,** the lower jawbone of a robust dated to about 1.5 million years ago — one of the last known robusts

After 1 million years ago, no more robust fossils appear at all; in fact, it looks like the robusts became extinct. That's not unusual; most species do become extinct after a few million years (the average is about 4 million years) for all kinds of reasons. One reason species become extinct is that they overspecialize on a food source that suddenly becomes extinct itself. Unable to react quickly enough to this change in food source (biologically, of course; they can't *will* their bodies to adapt), the species dies out. This scenario may well be the case with the robusts — they had a pretty specialized diet. Whatever the case, after 1 million years ago the robusts are gone, and no species after them, including *Homo,* bears any trace of them.

The omnivore: Gracile australopithecines

The *graciles* were a lightly built kind of australopithecine. Their anatomical characteristics include

- **Moderate tooth size** is smaller than the robusts' massive teeth but larger than modern humans'.

- **Moderately built facial structure** absorbs more chewing stress than modern human skulls but far less than that of the robusts or even chimpanzees or gorillas.

- **Lack of a sagittal crest** means they're missing the robusts' massive bony flare for massive chewing muscles.

- **Moderate brain size** is about 480 cubic centimeters (about 16 ounces or just over one typical soda can).

Graciles, then, seem to be intermediate between the characteristics of the chimpanzees and gorillas (our closest living relatives) and modern humans. They lack the massive grinding teeth of the robusts (and their microscopic tooth wear indicates a varied or omnivorous diet), but they're not like the chimpanzees or gorillas, either; compared to them, graciles are much more like humans.

For these reasons, many have called the graciles the *missing link* between *Homo* and the rest of the primate order. Although some anthropologists say the origins of *Homo* are still unknown, many (perhaps most) anthropologists believe that the graciles are the immediate ancestor of *Homo*. I agree with this theory, though science always allows room for new discoveries and reinterpretation of the matter at hand.

The earliest graciles are known from around 4 million years ago, and the most recent from about 2 million years ago. Graciles are a little better known than the robusts, and this group contains significant variations within it that I just don't have room to cover here. As a lumper, I'm putting them all in the generic "gracile australopithecine" group; this classification isn't misleading for my purposes here. Some interesting gracile specimens and species include

- *Australopithecus ramidus.* The earliest known australopithecine — robust or gracile — about 4 to 6 million years old.

- *Australopithecus afarensis.* The most famous specimen is Lucy, the 3.2-million-year-old partial skeleton discovered in Ethiopia in 1972 by palaeoanthropologists listening to the Beatles' song *Lucy in the Sky With Diamonds*. (Lucy is actually only one of 33 known individuals of *Australopithecus afarensis*, but she's the most famous.)

- *Australopithecus africanus,* a very well-known species found from South to East Africa and dated to about 3 to 2 million years ago; one, the Taung Baby discovered in South Africa, was only a few years old at death, and marks on the skull suggest it may have been killed and snatched up by a large bird of prey!

After about 2 million years ago, gracile fossils disappear; instead, you find only robusts and members of a new group, *Homo* (which you can read about in the next section). Although robusts' disappearance was complete — no later hominid carried characteristics of the robusts — that's not the case here. Early members of the genus *Homo* did carry characteristics of late graciles. This evidence strongly suggests that the graciles aren't only a link to the other primates but also to the origins of our own lineage as well. Gracile australopithecines, then, are a missing link.

The Cracked Mirror: Early Homo

By about 2 million years ago. The savanna was home to at least two kinds of hominid: the robust australopithecine and members of a new biological group, the genus *Homo*. This creature, at the root of each person today, also originated in Africa. Gazing at the fossils of early *Homo,* I feel that I'm looking into an ancient, cracked mirror: *That's me, isn't it?*

Exploring characteristics of early Homo

Early *Homo* possessed some very distinctive anatomical characteristics:

- **Very large brain,** about 700+ cubic centimeters, which is around 24 fluid ounces (or 2 soda cans), compared to about four soda cans (48 fluid ounces) for modern humans and around a single can —12 fluid ounces — for chimpanzees and gorillas)
- **Relatively light facial structure,** absorbing less chewing stress than any australopithecine
- **No sagittal crest,** also indicating a lack of emphasis on heavy chewing
- **Fully modern hand** with opposable thumb, making for relatively extreme dexterity

In contrast to the australopithecines, though, the distinctive characteristics of early *Homo* weren't just anatomical; they also included the first traces of some important behavioral characteristics that continued throughout the lineage, right up to the present day. One trait is a heavier reliance on tools like the stone ones used increasingly after 2 million years ago; by 1.8 million years ago, you may begin to wonder how *Homo* survived without tools. Early *Homo* also placed a greater emphasis on animal tissues in the diet, a feature indicated by an increase in the number of animal bones bearing marks from stone butchering tools and/or hammerstones used to get at nutritious marrow.

So early *Homo* was a pretty new creature, indeed. It had a brain almost twice the size of the gracile australopithecine, was lighter-built (though perhaps a little taller) than any australopithecine, and had some radical new behaviors. Though australopithecines may have made and used some simple tools fashioned from sticks, bones, antlers, and even chunks of stone, early *Homo* is when tool use goes from being a part of life to a necessity of life.

For example, consider that brain tissue is extremely expensive from a caloric perspective, consuming more than 20 times as many calories as muscle tissue does. It has its uses (such as increasing the potential for intelligence), but that calorie-hog brain has to be fed! And of all the foods on the hominid savanna, the most calories came from the bodies of other animals — from their fat, blood, and meat. Early *Homo* foraged for just about any food it could find, but it also began to eat more animal tissues than any other hominid did, and that was only possible with tools created to butcher those animals and get at the calories.

The earliest specimens of *Homo* are known from around 2.5 million years ago and the most recent from about 1.5 million years ago. Recent discoveries have shown that several varieties of early *Homo* probably existed, including *Homo habilis, Homo rudolfensis,* and *Homo ergaster.* However, as a lumper I'm putting them all in the generic "early *Homo*" group.

Some interesting early *Homo* specimens (the catalog numbers are included here so you can find them easily on the Web or in other texts) include

- Skull 1470, a beautifully preserved skull and face of early *Homo* that some assign to *H. rudolfensis* and some to *H. habilis*

- Skull 1813, another well-preserved full skull and face with lots of teeth; it's so similar to both late graciles and early *Homo* that for as long as I've been studying the matter, nobody has made a final decision on which species it is

After 1.8 million years ago, early *Homo* evolved into *Homo erectus*, a species I discuss later in the chapter

Dalmatians and cigar smoke: Finds at Olduvai Gorge

Smoking cigars, quaffing whisky, and herding her pet Dalmatians every day for decades, Mary Leakey was a force of nature dedicated to understanding the life of early humans. With her husband Louis, she made incredible discoveries about the life of early *Homo* in Tanzania's Olduvai Gorge, where geological layers have preserved a long record of human evolution from over 2 million years ago to the present day. The Leakeys' finds include

- Many *stone-and-bone scatters* of stone tools and bits of fossil bone; the stones include tools as well as toolmaking debris, and the bones sometimes bear nicks and scratches from stone butchering tools

- Many hominid fossils, including the remains of robust australopithecines and early *Homo;* in fact, the Leakeys showed that these two species lived in the same area at the same time, but because they were after different kinds of food, some argue, they would have had little friction between them

A force of nature: The life of Mary Leakey

Mary Douglas Nicol was born in London, England in 1913. She married Louis S. B. Leakey in 1937, and soon thereafter began her African research into early human origins. In 1948, she discovered the nearly complete fossil remains of *Proconsul africanus,* an important extinct primate species dating to roughly 20 million years ago.

In the 1950s, the Leakeys began their excavations at Tanzania's Olduvai Gorge, where they worked for decades. In 1959, Mary discovered the beautifully preserved fossil remains of an extinct early hominid, *Australopithecus boisei* (named in part for Boise State University, which was funding part of the excavation). Unfortunately, overnight the fossil skull was crushed by wandering cattle, and Leakey had to spend weeks fitting the pieces back together. The find was so spectacular, though, that the National Geographic Society took an interest and began to both fund the Leakeys' excavations and publicize their findings.

Through the 1960s, the excavations and tremendous discoveries continued. Mary excavated the fossil bones and stone tools of early *Homo,* finding evidence sometimes for hominids butchering other animals, and sometimes for other animals gnawing on hominid bones. By the early 1970s, a number of methods allowed for very precise dating of the layers at Olduvai, which has sites going back more than 2 million years. Excavations continue at Olduvai today.

Although Louis Leakey passed away in 1972, Mary Leakey kept working. Her most spectacular discovery came in 1976, when she found a track of fossilized footprints at Laetoli, Tanzania. Dated to nearly 4 million years ago, the footprints proved that early hominids were walking by this time.

In later years Mary Leakey focused her research on the rock art of Africa, compiling detailed records of thousands of sites across the continent. She died in December 1996, having spent nearly half a century giving humanity a look at its roots.

Out of Africa: Early dispersals of early Homo

Not too long ago, the general consensus was that hominids first left Africa around 1 million years ago in the form of *Homo erectus*, the hominid that early *Homo* evolved into by 1.8 million years ago. But recent discoveries show that *Homo* left nearly twice that long ago, or even earlier:

- The 1.8-million-year-old Dmanisi site on the east shore of the Black Sea has recently revealed stone tools (of the Oldowan type; see the next section) and the spectacular fossils of a new-to-science hominid that's certainly within *Homo* but of a debatable species; some say it's late *H. rudolfensis*, some that it's early *H. erectus*.

- At the Wushan Cave site in China, fossils of early *Homo* are dated to 1.9 million years ago; for a long time, many doubted the dates for this site (published in the mid-1990s), but the fact that Dmanisi is securely dated to 1.8 million years ago has inspired more confidence in the Wushan Cave dates, which may well be a second line of evidence showing a dispersal of *Homo* far earlier than once believed.

Tool time: The decoupling of behavior from anatomy

After you begin to study *Homo*, you're in the world of *tools*, artifacts made or used by hominids. Because stone decays more slowly than the bone, wood, or antler used to make other tools, the best-known of the early tools are the stone tools. So archaeologists have spent a lot of time classifying and studying stone tools. For early hominid studies, two types of tools are most important to remember. *Oldowan* tools are dated from about 2.5 million years ago and persist until about 1.8 million years ago; they're largely asymmetrical and consist of battered stones or chips of stone (often choppers or cutting flakes). But by 1.8 million years ago hominids had invented and/or learned to apply the concept of symmetry to their tools, and carefully chipped, often teardrop-shaped hand axes are common.

Starting with early *Homo*, hominid behavior began to detach or decouple from its anatomy; that is, the body was no longer the factor that really set the boundaries of behavior for the species. With tools, hominids could do things that the body alone couldn't do. For example, they could use stone tools to smash open bones to get at marrow — fresh bone is extremely tough to break with anything but a heavy hammerstone — or open the hide on carcasses of sun-baked dead animals. (Ready for lunch yet?)

So for humans, tools take the place of other bodily characteristics of other species, such as the hyena's bone-crushing jaws and the big cats' sharp, slashing teeth. And through time the tools of *Homo* become even more complex, eventually including artifacts made from several raw materials like bone and wood lashed or glued together and increasing the behavioral range of the hominids. And it all started with stone tools — simple chips of stone.

The Traveler: The Accomplishments of Homo erectus

In my classes, I often refer to the world of *Homo erectus* as shadowy because although the species has some resemblance to modern humans and was definitely more human-like than any other ape, many facets of its life have been mysteries for a long time. But today archaeologists know quite a bit more about *H. erectus* than they did even 20 years ago, so I also say new light is shining on the subject. In this section I sketch out what archaeologists have discovered about this fascinating early hominid.

Characteristics of Homo erectus

By 1.8 million years ago — well after the appearance of early *Homo* around 2.5 million years ago — two main hominids were on the scene: the robust australopithecines and *Homo erectus*. When first discovered in the late 19th century, people though the fossils of *H. erectus* represented the first bipedal primate, but that was quite wrong; evidence now puts bipedalism at close to 6 million years ago. Still, the name *Homo erectus* (from the erect nature of the bipedal spine) stuck. Like its ancestor early *Homo*, *Homo erectus* possessed some very distinctive anatomical characteristics:

- **Very large brain:** About 1,000+ cubic centimeters — about 33 fluid ounces (or nearly 3 soda cans, compared to about 4 cans for modern human brains).

- **Very small teeth:** Compared to any hominid so far they indicate even less chewing stress, because *Homo erectus* more commonly processed food with tools rather than just the mouth.

- **Larger body size:** The Turkana Boy specimen, a 5-foot-3-inch teen at death, would have been close to 6 feet tall at adulthood).

Like early *Homo*, though, the adaptations of *H. erectus* weren't just anatomical; they included some important behavioral characteristics:

- **Even heavier reliance on tools:** By 1.8 million years ago, anthropologists can hardly imagine *H. erectus* surviving without tools.

- **More complex stone tools:** These tools include the symmetrical, multipurpose hand axes used to butcher large animals and work pieces of wood.

- **Wide geographical distribution:** *H. erectus* migrated into the cool mountains of Northeast Asia, survived in the jungles of Southeast Asia, and hunted in the forests of mainland Europe.

In short, *Homo erectus* continued all the trends seen since the origins of the genus *Homo*; therefore, society and even communication presumably became more complex. I discuss the evolution of language further in Chapter 13; for the moment, remember that *Homo erectus* didn't have what you would consider fully modern language. This doesn't mean *H. erectus* was a dumb, knuckle-dragging brute. The following sections look at some of its accomplishments.

From confrontational scavenging to ambush hunting

Homo erectus probably began as a confrontational scavenger like its ancestor early *Homo*. *Confrontational scavengers* (like hyenas) confront big cats and drive them away from carcasses, which the confrontational scavengers then eat. Now imagine a troop of smart, confrontational, 6-foot *H. erectus,* and you can imagine how they survived. Later, though, *H. erectus* began to compete directly with the top carnivores such as the lion and, perhaps a little more often, the slightly less-intimidating cheetah. Discoveries like that of seven 400,000-year-old spears at Schoeningen, Germany help illustrate this progression. These artifacts, up to six feet long and shaped with a pointed tip, show that *H. erectus* was going after big game, and not in any half-hearted way; these tools are evidence of ambush predation, taking on species like horses and wooly rhinoceros with the fierceness of a big cat.

The use of fire

By 300,000 years ago, *H. erectus* clearly had control of fire; sites in China (Zhoukoutien Cave, near Beijing) and Spain (Torralba and Ambrona) show burnt patches that appear to be hearths used to cook animal food. Fire would have been useful to hominids for several reasons. It could have provided protection from fireless animals (such as big cats). It also offered several food processing benefits like preventing dehydration, killing off harmful bacteria, and denaturing protein, which increases digestibility. Fire could also keep hominids warm at night.

Symmetry, watercraft, and the "15-minute culture"

H. erectus also made symmetrical stone tools; if that doesn't impress you, you try to do it! Modern humans need months to master this skill, and not even all moderns are good at it. But *H. erectus* banged out these tools by the score, using them for a variety of tasks from digging to butchery to woodworking. This practice also reveals that *H. erectus* was capable of some kind of abstraction — it imposed the concept of a symmetrical form on a chunk of stone. This act isn't the fully developed symbolism present in modern humans, but it's no simple trick, either. Chapters 7 and 13 of this book further discuss the significance of symbols.

Recent excavations have revealed that *H. erectus* arrived on the island of Flores, Indonesia, somewhere after 800,000 years ago. (***Note:*** These *aren't* the recently discovered "Flores man" or "Hobbit" fossils, which are of a different species dated to only 18,000 years ago.) Reconstruction of sea levels at that time indicates that some kind of watercraft would have been necessary for such a voyage of up to 20 miles across the open sea. This development is so unexpected, so far out from what I've known and thought about *H. erectus,* that its significance hasn't really hit me yet. Trust me, it's astonishing.

Finally, southern England's Boxgrove site has revealed that *H. erectus'* stone tools may have taken hours to make (rather than just minutes, as some archaeologists had previously thought), and that archaeologists may well be underestimating its abilities. This discovery seems to counteract the common consensus that *H. erectus* had a relatively short attention span — what one archaeologist has called a *15-minute culture.*

Underestimation of early peoples' abilities wouldn't be a new mistake in archaeology. In my opinion and experience, archaeology, consistently underestimates both how long ago events first happened and how far people traveled in the ancient world. We archaeologists are forever pushing back the dates for the earliest occurrence of some development (like the wheel, writing, stone tools, and so on) and being surprised at how far ancient travel really reached, either on foot or by water.

Chapter 7

It's Good to Be Home: Homo sapiens sapiens, Our Biological Species

. . . .

In This Chapter

▶ Discover what makes humans anatomically and behaviorally modern

▶ Review fossil evidence for the first traces of anatomically modern humans

▶ Find out what happened to man's close relatives, the Neanderthals

▶ Understand the full complexity of modern human thought and the evolution of consciousness

. . . .

*B*eing really human, it turns out, is a relatively recent pleasure (and occasional annoyance). It's also complicated; to understand what humans are, you have to recognize the difference between being anatomically modern and behaviorally modern, something physical anthropologists and archaeologists base entire careers on. In the last 100 or so years they've completely overturned widely accepted ideas of what humans are as a species. How? Well, they've shown that humans didn't descend from European Neanderthals as early anthropologists thought, but rather from Africans of 100,000 years ago. And they've shown that cave art isn't just crude decoration; it's the hallmark of a spectacularly new, essentially modern human mind. These and other discoveries help you understand just who humans are — just what makes up Homo sapiens sapiens.

Because anthropology is the study of humanity at large, defining humanity is a good beginning; in this chapter I give you a better understanding of how anthropologists define humanity.

Distinguishing Modern Homo sapiens sapiens (That's You!)

How did humanity *become* human from some proto-human ancestor? What does it mean to be human, anyway? Anthropology has been struggling with these questions for decades. Today people can say a lot about when and where modern humanity first happened, but exactly *why* or *how* — well, that's always the hard part. Start with what anthropologists know for sure.

First, you have to consider each of the two ways to be a modern human separately. *Anatomical modernity* is having an anatomical structure that's indistinguishable from that of modern populations. *Behavioral modernity,* on the other hand, is displaying cultural behavior that's indistinguishable from the behavior of modern populations. Why consider these distinctions separately? I address that topic later in this chapter. First, check out the following sections, which explain when anatomical and behavioral modernity first appear. Understanding modernity's origins may help a lot in explaining them — at the very least, it's necessary as a background to explaining modern humanity today.

This chapter deals with a lot of evolutionary concepts; for a refresher on evolution, head to Chapter 3.

Anatomical modernity

In the previous section, I mention that anatomical modernity means having anatomy — a body — that's entirely modern; you can't distinguish it from modern, living human bodies. These physical characteristics are what define *Anatomically Modern Homo sapiens sapiens,* widely known as AMHss; they're what separate the AMHss from their ancestors, known as the *pre-moderns* or *Archaic Homo sapiens* (AHs). These characteristics include traits of the *cranium* (the head) and the *postcrania* (the skeleton below the head).

In the cranium:

- The teeth, brow ridges, and face of AMHss are smaller overall than those of the AHs, reflecting less chewing stress (probably related to increased tool use for processing food).

- The AMHss' brain case is larger (containing a brain almost the volume of a six-pack of soda cans — about 1,450 cubic centimeters or 50 ounces), almost certainly indicating a more complex culture.

- A distinct chin is present in AMHss. Nobody has ever convincingly explained the chin, but it may also be related to reduced chewing stresses.

Brain matter matters

Big brains are one of the most distinctive traits of anatomically modern humans, but cranial volume doesn't necessarily directly correlate with intelligence (and intelligence is tough to measure anyway). Still, scientists today often gauge intelligence by an individual's capacity to deal with changing circumstances. This guideline is okay for today's times, but it's pretty tough to measure in ancient hominids. Nevertheless, anthropologists do know that through time

✔ Hominid cranial volume increased.

✔ Hominid behavior became more complex.

✔ Hominid geographical range became more expansive.

These three points prove that hominids were gradually able to adapt to new or changing ecological circumstances. Over time, they gained intelligence!

No matter how you measure, then, hominids clearly became more intelligent over time — more capable, for example, of modifying their behavior based on past experiences. This adaptability was very helpful in survival. So, even though anthropologists know that intelligence and brain volume aren't perfectly correlative, studying hominid cranial volume and comparing it to migration and behavior as a crude measure of hominid intelligence is a fascinating pursuit.

The postcranial bones of AMHss also are distinctive from those of their ancestral AHs:

✔ AMHss bones are basically longer and thinner.

✔ The AMHss body is lankier and a little less robust.

Like the cranial differences, these differences in body build probably reflect increased tool use; the AMHss used tools rather than brute strength and physical fitness to adapt to their constant outdoor life, camping, traveling, hunting, and gathering every single day.

This, then, is humankind, at least anatomically. Of course, basic "humandom" has its variations, such as differences in height or skin color (which you can read more about in Chapter 14), but they all occur within the human species, among anatomically modern humans.

Behavioral modernity

Being human isn't just anatomical; it's also behavioral. If *anatomical* modernity is being physically indistinguishable from modern humans, you can easily deduce that *behavioral* modernity is acting in a way that's indistinguishable from modern humans. Behavioral modernity also implies that these actions are clearly different from all other animals — they're unique to humans. Two main behavioral characteristics are unique to the human species:

- **The use of symbolism** (using one object or sign to mean something else)
- **The use of complex language** (communicating by stringing together audio and visual messages according to complex rules, syntax, and grammar)

Although other animals communicate — anyone knows that a cat's meow is different from its hiss — human communication is distinctively rich, employing metaphors and communicating massive amounts of information accurately, quickly, and according to complex rules (syntax and grammar). Just think of the difference in complexity and subtlety between the sound "HISS!" and the very short phrase, "I think, therefore I am."

Africa: The Cradle of Humanity

In the 19th and early 20th centuries, it wasn't clear just where modern humanity first appeared; some suggested central Asia, and others thought it must have been in central Europe. Today, though, anthropologists have dozens of fossil finds and archaeological sites that clearly show modern humans first evolved in Africa. In this section, I discuss this fossil material as well as introduce you to when early modern humans migrated out of the great continent; in Chapter 8, you can read more about how modern humans spread across the globe.

Discovering the first AMHss

The best early AMHss fossils are from Herto in Ethiopia, dated to around 150,000 years ago. By 100,000 years ago, the Near East (including countries like Israel and Syria) was also home to populations of AMHss.

The AMHss populations that appeared first in Africa moved out of that continent quickly and spread widely, colonizing the globe in roughly the following order:

- By 50,000 years ago, AMHss were in China and (shortly thereafter) Australia.
- By 40,000 years ago, they were in southeastern Europe, and by 20,000 years ago, they'd made it to Western Europe.

- By 14,000 years ago, they reached North and South America, colonizing these continents after crossing the Bering land bridge connecting Siberia and Alaska.

- By 3,000 years ago, they'd colonized parts of the Pacific and the Arctic.

For a long time, hominids didn't migrate with the concept of discovery in mind; instead, they migrated for two main reasons. First, they followed prey animals like herds of wild horses or mammoths across vast landscapes, following the grazers as they moved from one natural pasture to another. Second, early hominids migrated into new areas as new areas became available. That is, like any life form, they tended to move into areas that could support them. Nature, it turns out, really does abhor a vacuum.

Exploring behavioral modernity

After humanity became anatomically modern and emerged from Africa 100,000 years ago, the story of human evolution gets a little simpler than it's been so far. That's mainly because one main hominid dominates the scene: AMHss. The Neanderthals were also around, but I discuss them in the next section. For the moment, have a look at the other way of being human: behavioral modernity.

Earlier in this chapter, I explain that the two primary benchmarks for discovering behavioral modernity are symbolism and language. Because language is ultimately symbolic, and early humans evidently made symbols such as cave art, or notches on bone or antler tablets with their artifacts, anthropologists can reasonably infer that early humans used (or could have used) language. So archaeologists have focused their search for behavioral modernity on the search for the earliest symbols and symbolic artifacts.

The archaeology of the origins of modern human consciousness (*cognitive archaeology*) is at the cutting edge of a lot of archaeology today. This newness doesn't mean cognitive archaeology isn't valuable or that its proponents aren't making fantastic new discoveries, but as in the beginning of any new research effort, the public should be careful to demand very good evidence for radical new interpretations. Having said that, I think the archaeology of the evolution of consciousness is some of the most interesting ever attempted, and it's well worth considering.

The best archaeological evidence for behavioral modernity comes from two main sites:

- **South Africa's 70,000-year-old Blombos Cave** has yielded dozens of stone tablets bearing scratched *x's*, some divots that look like *o's*, parallel lines carved into their surfaces and rows of notches suggesting counts of something; these markings are clearly the products of symbol-using minds (and perhaps the world's first tic-tac-toe fiends).

✔ **Israel's Skhul Cave,** where ten AMHss were buried about 100,000 years ago, contains handfuls of perforated snail shells which proved under the microscope to be worn down a little, apparently from being suspended on a necklace. Wearing jewelry certainly reveals a symbolic mind (and the burials themselves are decent evidence for this argument as well).

In both cases, symbolism is clear. An *x* carved in rock doesn't just mean two crossed lines: in contemporary culture, it can indicate Christianity (if arranged in one way) or the plus sign (if arranged another way). Nobody knows what Blombos Cave's people meant with their *x's* and *o's*, but anthropologists do know they were communicating symbolically, which means they were behaviorally modern. And the Skhul Cave necklace evidence is also compelling because a necklace — just like the jewelry humans wear today — tells a story. For example, people today often wear rings to say much more than simply, "I own this band of metal"; rings can indicate that a person is married or attended a particular school — the possibilities are endless but almost always meaningful. And when you say things with objects, you're acting in a distinctively modern human way by using complex symbols. You're behaviorally modern.

South African archaeologists have told me, informally, that they've found many more such sites as Blombos Cave and that in the next decades they'll reveal more evidence of early symbolism in South Africa. Archaeology is a slow business, but it produces amazing results. Anthropologists are some of the most patient people on earth.

Out of Africa: An Epic Migration

Earlier in this chapter, I mention that after 30,000 years ago AMHss was the only hominid left in the world with the exception of the Neanderthals. Neanderthals now can tell anthropologists a lot about modernity.

Anthropologists agree that AMHss emerged from Africa after about 100,000 years ago in a global migration of epic proportions. These beings were humankind's ancestors, and the proof is in man's very genes. This multimillennium story of survival and long-distance travel in the ancient world eclipses anything ever cranked out of Hollywood. It begins with an exodus from Africa and ends with people colonizing the Arctic and Polynesia. Figure 8-1 in Chapter 8 shows the main routes of migration.

What do Neanderthals have to do with it? Well, as behaviorally and anatomically modern humans migrated across the globe, they found that not every possible path was new. Emerging from Africa, AMHss found hominids already occupying the various ecosystems of the Old World (basically the world excluding

North and South America, which weren't reached by humans until around 15,000 years ago), from Europe all the way east to China. Equally strange is that these hominids weren't anatomically or behaviorally modern; they were proto-humans, ancestors of the *first* hominids to move out of Africa almost two million years before AMHss did. (See Chapter 6 for more on proto-humans.)

Taking a closer look at Neanderthals

Although *Neanderthals* (hominids that lived in Europe and the Near East from about 300,000 to 30,000 years ago) behaved and looked a lot like folks today, they were also different. Anthropologist Trenton W. Holliday has written that they were a "hyper-polar" hominid, adapted for the cold of ice-age Europe. Their anatomical and behavioral characteristics include

- A heavily built, stocky, heat-conserving body
- Cranial capacity meeting or even exceeding that of AMHss (but remember, brain volume doesn't necessarily indicate intelligence; see the "Brain matter matters" sidebar for more info)
- Heavily stressed teeth and bones indicating use of the body as a tool, periodic starvation, and frequent injury
- Simple stone tools with no compelling evidence for complex symbolism

You can see that the Neanderthals had brains as big as modern man's but little symbolism; they had stone tools more complex than any other creature — you'd need about a decade to figure out how to make Neanderthal tools from stone — but the tools were simple compared to those of AMHss. Neanderthals are an enigma because they're so much like humans today, yet so different.

Figure 7-1 compares a typical Neanderthal skull with a typical AMHss skull.

Figure 7-1:
Typical Neanderthal (a) and anatomically modern human (b) skulls.

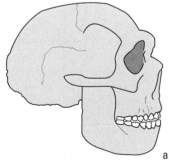

a

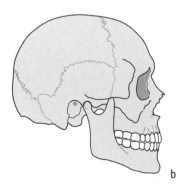

b

Getting Neanderthals and AMHss together

What happened when AMHss bands met indigenous folk like the Neanderthals? Were their interactions peaceful or violent? Did they interbreed or kill one another? Do humans carry Neanderthal DNA in their bodies today? The best answers come from examining two competing theories about the interaction of AMHss and the species (such as the Neanderthals of Europe) they encountered: *Multiregional Continuity Theory* and *Replacement Theory*.

Multiregional Continuity Theory

The Multiregional Continuity Theory states that in each of the regions occupied by the first hominids to move out of Africa, Archaic populations — which preceded AMHss by almost two million years — evolved into AMHss somewhat independently. That is, from China to the Near East, populations of Archaics all independently evolved toward the characteristics of AMHss.

To support this theory, proponents provide one main piece of evidence: According to them, hominid populations in each area occupied by the first Archaic *Homo sapiens* out of Africa developed unique physical traits that humans still exhibit today.

That is, Archaics settled into their respective regions, such as the Far East, India and Pakistan, the Near East, and Europe and then *independently* developed into AMHss in each of those areas. Multiregional Continuity theorists contend that regional characteristics, like Neanderthal characteristics in modern Europeans and Archaic features in East Asians, support this hypothesis.

The major problem with this theory is that few biologists (or physical anthropologists) buy the idea that these separate populations would all evolve toward the same ultimate AMHss form. This is such a serious flaw in the argument that some Multiregional Continuity theorists have proposed what they call *Soft Replacement,* the idea that, yes, AMHss evolved first in Africa and spread into already-inhabited regions, but then mated with the indigenous Archaics, producing the regional variants you see today.

Well, maybe. This scenario is possible, but many anthropologists believe they have a much better theory, one that's supported by many — and many different — lines of evidence: Replacement Theory.

Replacement Theory

In contrast to Multiregional Continuity Theory, *Replacement Theory* (also known as the *Out of Africa model*) says that AMHss first evolved in Africa and then spread out from it after 100,000 years ago, replacing the Archaic populations that they encountered from Europe to China. Most Replacement theorists don't care whether AMHss engaged in a little "soft replacement" with the Archaics they encountered. For these anthropologists, the fact that AMHss *replaced* the Archaics in every way is what's most important.

The evidence for Replacement is pretty good and based on multiple, independent lines of evidence:

- ✔ In the fossil record, most physical anthropologists don't see the ancient, regional variations that the Continuity model demands.

- ✔ In the fossil record, archaic skeleton traits disappear rapidly after the introduction of AMHss. In Europe, for example, only 10,000 years after AMHss appears, the Neanderthals go extinct after 170,000 years of Neanderthal survival in Europe!

- ✔ Archaic tool types disappear rapidly and are replaced with AMHss tool types.

- ✔ Symbolism first appears in Africa and spreads, also replacing the distinctly nonsymbolic archaeological traces of Archaic life.

- ✔ Genetic studies show that modern populations outside Africa are very similar to one another, indicating that everyone outside Africa emerged from the continent (and then diverged into regional groups) relatively recently.

- ✔ Studies show that humans carry very little Neanderthal DNA, if any, so even if Neanderthals and AMHss did interbreed, it didn't matter in the long run.

Evidence for what some call the *mitochondrial Eve* also supports Replacement Theory. Because the DNA of any life form accumulates changes over time at a rather predictable and known rate, comparing the DNA of two closely related but different species can show how far back in time they diverged in time; species like wolves and dogs, for example, have pretty similar DNA, but species like whales and hippos, which share a common ancestor many millions of years ago, have very different DNA. In humans, the study of *mitochondrial DNA* (or mtDNA, a kind of DNA passed from mother to offspring) has allowed some researchers to estimate when modern humans outside Africa began to diverge from African populations — from a founding Mitochondrial Eve population. Not surprisingly, that date comes in around 100,000 years ago. This is just one more line of evidence suggesting that some very fundamental changes for humanity happened in Africa about 100,000 years ago.

In short, the bulk of the most recent data strongly supports Replacement Theory. No one really knows how most of the AMHss/Archaic interactions went, but in the long run, the anatomically and behaviorally modern AMHss simply out-competed the Archaics.

A Portuguese half-human? Neanderthals and you

Are you part Neanderthal? Some anthropologists say yes, but for most, the answer is no: The Neanderthals were an evolutionary dead end.

At the Portuguese site of Lagar Velho, a 25,000-year-old skeleton shows characteristics of both Neanderthals and Modern humans. Some say it's just a stocky Modern. Others believe that it's the smoking-gun evidence for Neanderthal-Modern interbreeding, putting Neanderthal blood into every European today.

But although Lagar Velho is an interesting case, most researchers agree the bulk of the archaeological, genetic, and fossil evidence doesn't support a significant amount of Neanderthal/Modern interbreeding. One of the most respected authorities, British archaeologist Clive Gamble, has said that for him the case is closed and the mystery solved: Moderns out-competed and replaced the Neanderthals. Lagar Velho is, at the most, a very late, last flicker of Neanderthal genes in Europe.

A theoretical compromise?

As always in anthropology, just as things look simple they get complicated. Basically, some anthropologists feel that the either/or choice between the Multiregional Continuity and Replacement theories is a false choice — that both can be accommodated to a degree with a subtler model of modern human origins. They suggest that although AMHss did move out of Africa around 100,000 years ago, significant interbreeding between these colonists and the people they encountered could have occurred and led to AMHss in each region. My opinion is that the Replacement model is more compelling, but there's plenty of room for debate. The essence of good science is a willingness to be open to reinterpretation when the evidence doesn't convince everyone of the same thing.

The Origins of Language: The Social Grooming Theory

Anatomically, humans have been about the same creature for something like 100,000 years. But in that time human culture has changed a great deal. In part, the changes had to do with adapting to new environments as human bands migrated across the globe. (See Chapter 8 for details on these migrations). Because culture, as I define it in Chapters 3 and 12, is socially *transmitted* (rather than biologically; it doesn't ride on the genes, but passes through language from one generation to the next), you need to look at the origins of language.

So much has been written about the origins of language that, back in the '50s, one prominent journal of prehistory actually refused to take any more papers on the subject; it was all speculation, the editors reasoned, and anthropology needed more time to study the matter. That time has passed now, and I think anthropology has come a long, long way. Today the most compelling theory of the origins of language is based on an evolutionary model, and I think it's the best around; to tell the truth, I'm not even going to mention the others because I don't think they carry the weight of this one. This very persuasive model is anthropologist Robin Dunbar's *social grooming hypothesis.*

The social grooming hypothesis is that social primates maintain their connections and relationships largely through grooming: picking insects and debris out of other primates' hair and generally showing them consideration. That grooming, Dunbar argues, became more complex through time as hominid social group sizes increased. Noting that primate brain size is larger in larger primate social groups, Dunbar reconstructed the following hominid group sizes through time (I discuss these hominid types in more detail in Chapter 6):

- ✔ **Australopithecines** (from about 6 million years ago to about two million years ago) lived in groups of about 60 individuals.

- ✔ **Early *Homo*** (about 2 million years ago) lived in groups of about 80 individuals.

- ✔ ***Homo erectus*** (from about 2 million years ago to about 300,000 years ago) lived in groups of about 110 individuals.

- ✔ **Early Modern *Homo sapiens*** (after about 100,000 years ago) lived, and traditionally continue to live, in groups of about 150 individuals.

Dunbar's hypothesis is that as these group sizes increased for various reasons, language increasingly replaced physical grooming. Language, Dunbar argues, can convey a lot more information more rapidly than physical grooming, and it can address more than one individual at a time.

Dunbar hasn't convinced everyone in anthropology that he's entirely right, and of course talking doesn't leave much of an archaeological trace, so the hypothesis is hard to prove one way or the other. But many anthropologists, me included, think that he's onto something and that this concept may be the strongest candidate theory of the origins of language so far.

Humans aren't the only animals that can evolve language; one primate species (*Homo*) has done it, so why not others? In 2004, German anthropologists reported a case of commenting among macaques (a kind of monkey) in which one macaque appeared to observe social interactions in a distant group and then make an utterance, a sort of comment about that group to its own group. This noise was different from an alarm call or other common communications;

it really seemed to be one macaque talking about what the other group was doing. As in many cases, anthropology will have to study this occurrence closely to verify it, but if it's true, it's a fascinating reminder that humans aren't so different from all other animals.

The Origins of the Modern Mind

According to the Stanford Encyclopedia of Philosophy, "Perhaps no aspect of mind is more familiar or more puzzling than consciousness and our conscious experience of self and world." So consciousness is a concept that should be handled carefully. Still, a clear difference exists between being conscious and unconscious, and even though science hasn't completely delineated what consciousness is, it's clearly important.

For my purposes in this book, *consciousness* is the uniquely human capacity for self-contemplation. The question is how did this come to be? The answer is rooted in evolution.

The evolution of consciousness: Two models

Consciousness — basically, self-awareness — is clearly a major part of being human. Losing consciousness robs you of many distinctly human qualities, like the ability to respond to a question in detail with all the nuances of human language. Humans may be the most self-aware and self-conscious living things — so self-conscious, in fact, that they sometimes drive themselves crazy with the continual rehashing of memories and ideas that other animals are, perhaps, blissfully free of. Of course, many animals have some self-awareness, and chimpanzees can recognize themselves in mirrors, but it's in humanity that this self-awareness is most radically developed.

So how did this consciousness, this obsessive self-awareness, come about? Archaeologists have two models for the evolution of modern consciousness, which I summarize in the following sections. Just remember, these models are the cutting edge of thought on the origins and evolution of modern consciousness. I see good in both of them, but they're so different that I don't think they can both be entirely correct, and I'm excited to see how they pan out over the next few decades.

From episodic to theoretic consciousness: the Donald model

Psychologist Merlin Donald produced the first truly evolutionary model for the origins of modern consciousness in his 1991 book, *Origins of the Modern Mind.* Basically, Donald's model says that the evolution of consciousness came in a series of drastic changes in the mind's way of storing and representing its experiences, with each of these revolutions yielding a new state of consciousness. Donald proposed four types of consciousness in hominid evolution:

- *Episodic* consciousness (that of all primates before the genus *Homo*) was the original primate state, characterized by short-term and small-space memory. Such limited memory prevented this kind of consciousness from shuffling ideas, which limited deep contemplation and innovation, resulting in a *bubble of consciousness.*

- *Mimetic* consciousness (originating around 2 million years ago with the appearance of the genus *Homo*), was characterized by longer and finer-grained memories and communication based on bodily gestures (such as miming) and simple vocalizations. These changes allowed for slightly more complex culture and deeper contemplation and idea innovation.

- *Mythic* consciousness (originating with rich symbol use more than 100,000 years ago) was characterized by the use of myths and long narratives to organize the increasingly complex volume and diversity of ideas in the mind.

- *Theoretic* consciousness (originating with the invention of objective science in Greece about 2,000 years ago) was characterized by seeking natural rather than supernatural explanations for the world.

Cognitive fluidity: the Mithen model

Archaeologist Steven Mithen produced the second truly evolutionary model for the origins of modern consciousness in his 1996 book, *The Prehistory of the Mind.* Basically, Mithen's model says that the evolution of modern consciousness came about as the mind forged new links between previously isolated *intelligence modules,* or kinds of thinking. The four intelligences, according to Mithen, were

- Social intelligence, used to manage complex interpersonal primate relationships

- Technical intelligence, used to manipulate tools

- Linguistic intelligence, used to manage complex communication

- Natural history intelligence, used to understand cause-and-effect relationships

Mithen's model goes like this: By 4 million years ago, our African proto-human ancestors (the Australopithecines, which I cover in Chapter 4) possessed the well-developed social intelligence expected in groups of large social primates. By 2 million years ago, hominid life changed significantly as early *Homo* began using stone tools to butcher carcasses scavenged from big-cat kill sites, significantly sharpening their technical intelligence (by making tools) and natural-history intelligence (by finding carcasses). Fully fluid communication between intelligences began in the last 200,000 years only, promoted by language, which became more complex as social groups became larger and more complex. Bits of information about one kind of intelligence, Mithen argues, began to include communication about other kinds of intelligence, and the cross-pollination of ideas sparked a massive revolution of creativity that eventually led to the modern mind.

The roots of myth

Myths, according to Merlin Donald's theory (see "From episodic to theoretic consciousness: the Donald model" earlier in this chapter), arose as a way of organizing the contents of humans' increasingly complex and memory-crowded minds. Narrative in structure, myths typically tell what the universe is like and what to do about it, often with cautionary tales. Unfortunately for archaeologists, spoken myths don't leave much of an archaeological trace, and no one can be sure when they first arose. But anthropologists can be reasonably sure that humans were using myths at the time of cave art, which flourished in Europe around 30,000 years ago. Many archaeologists believe that, apart from being decorative, cave art depicts at least four main concepts:

- **Shamanic voyages,** wherein *shamans* (traditional healers) traveled to a spirit world to fix problems such as poor health in the material world. Traditional shamans continue to do this today, recording their voyages in rock shelters. (See Chapter 16 for more on shamans.)

- **Hunting magic** depicting scenes people wanted to see, such as large herds of fat, vulnerable animals.

- **Myths or narrative parables** instructing people how to live properly.

- **Rites of passage,** which ritually ushered people into various stages of life. These ceremonies were then recorded on cave walls.

Although this cave art dates to 30,000 or so years ago in Europe, remember that it probably originated 100,000 years ago and in Africa; anthropologists rely on the European evidence because it's been studied for so long.

The roots of ritual

According to the late anthropologist Roy Rappaport, rituals evolved as a kind of social glue meant to remind humans of their shared basic core beliefs, or *ultimate sacred postulates*. Exactly when ritual first appeared is also hard to pin down; many rituals in the present leave little material trace, and you can assume the same was possible in prehistory. But at least two archaeological traces seem to clearly indicate ritual:

- **Complex burials,** in which people were prepared and maybe even equipped for an afterlife with tools, food, and other items placed into the grave. These rituals first appear around 30,000 years ago but may well predate this period.
- **Organized religion,** in which civilizations clearly organized religious ritual with temples, pyramids, and public displays meant to unite the citizenry.

The roots of symbolism

You have to remember just how complex and important symbols really are. At least two kinds of symbolism are critical to the issue of behavioral modernity:

- **Shallow symbols,** which can only stand for one other thing — for example, a monkey's aerial-predator-warning screech, as opposed to its ground-predator-warning screech.
- **Deep symbols,** which can stand for many different things, perhaps even simultaneously — for example, humans can say "That guy is a real snake," and other humans understand that he's not a physical snake, but that he has snakelike characteristics.

Shallow symbols are pretty common in animal communication, and their real significance isn't clear until you consider how different they are from the deep symbols that can stand for several different ideas. What these deep symbols really reveal is the capacity for metaphor; however complex any other animal communication system is, none of them use metaphor. But humans can't seem to get away from it; even saying I can't "get away from it" is a metaphor. Metaphor is ingrained in our language, and its power to foster complex and cross-pollinated thoughts is tremendous. See Chapter 13 for more on symbolism.

Chapter 8

Hunting, Fishing, Sailing, and Sledding: The Spread of Humanity Worldwide

*W*here do you come from? I mean way back, centuries ago? Your family names may help a bit, but most people can only point at a vague blob on a map, a country that may not even exist anymore. But how about the people who came from there? Where did they come from? And how did they get there? Ultimately, everyone's roots reach back thousands of years to Africa; Chapter 7 tells you that. This chapter tells you about what happened next: how humans (officially, anatomically modern Homo sapiens sapiens, or AMHss) adapted to the multitude of new ecosystems they encountered, how they survived them by inventing everything from igloos to dogsleds and sailing canoes to fishing nets, and a little about how and when they migrated into and colonized such forbidding places as the islands of the open Pacific and the Arctic

Migration and Survival: The Decoupling of Behavior from Biology

Pay attention here; I'm giving a quiz later. Just kidding. But really, this is one of the main lessons of anthropology and of this entire book!

The first thing to keep in mind is that for a long time — from at least 100,000 years ago to about 10,000 years ago — most human beings were *foragers*, or people who moved from place to place to gather and hunt for their daily food and water. Sedentary farm life just wasn't an option until farming was invented around 10,000 years ago. And even then, not everyone took up farming; for thousands of years, many people continued to forage, trekking thousands of miles across the Arctic or voyaging on the open Pacific.

But why? Prehistoric humans moved for lots of reasons, including

- **Resource exploration:** Foragers are always interested in what other resources may be available just out of sight.

- **Social fission:** Some foragers move to get away from neighbors with whom they have bad blood; others travel to disperse a population that's getting too high for the resources in the immediate environment to support.

- **Incidental migration:** Foragers often migrate in pursuit of their prey animals — like herds of mammoth — who are also moving across landscapes to take advantage of new resources like expanding grassland in a changing ecosystem.

For these reasons (and others people may never know), humanity spread far and wide after 100,000 years ago.

Human migration required adaptation to survive in new environments. As a noun, an *adaptation* is an object that allows survival in that new environment, such as warm fur clothing for a cold environment or a new kind of sail for your sailing vessel. All other animals adapt unconsciously and with their bodies (which either do or do not have traits that allow survival in new environments); on the other hand, human bodies are biologically frail and could hardly survive the Arctic or the Sahara.

But humans have invented ways to live in both places, for thousands of years and in fine health; humanity has invented adaptations to places that our biology couldn't withstand. In fact, this is one of the most distinctive characteristics about humanity: It proactively chooses to make and invent new adaptations. Humanity, then, adapts not only with its body but also with its inventions, be they artifacts or social customs. This is one of the most important lessons anthropology has learned about humanity: For good or ill, humanity has evolved ways of adapting that have decoupled behavior from biology.

The rest of this chapter is really here to give you some examples of the diversity of these two main types of fascinating adaptations:

- **Artifacts:** Physical adaptations, like a warm coat or a sun-deflecting hat

- **Behaviors:** Cultural adaptations, like the practice of committing suicide when one can no longer support the foraging group and is a burden on the already-meager resources

One way to begin imagining the staggering history of early human global migration is to consider the environments people were moving into and what material and social adaptations could have made those new environments survivable. You can do this fascinating thought-exercise by considering the variety of environments humanity was exploring and adapting to in Figure 8-1, which generally sketches out the various dispersals of humanity around the world after about 100,000 years ago. The routes shown are pretty general, but keep in mind some major barriers, such as the Himalayan mountain chain. A couple of other things to keep in mind: By 100,000 years ago, the continents were in their present positions, so you don't need to wonder about South America shifting around or anything. Also, during ice ages ocean water was locked up in glaciers, so water levels were about 300 feet lower than they are today, thus making coastlines extend out farther. If you need a visual of this extension, you can check out sahultime.monash.edu.au/explore.html for a series of maps showing these changes in the coastlines of Australia.

Considering the principles of why and how humanity emerged from Africa, take a closer look at some of our species' thrillingly ingenious methods of survival in this epic of epics: the colonization of the globe by our prehistoric ancestors.

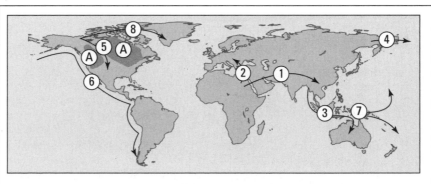

Figure 8-1:
Overview of the spread of AMHss after 100,000 years ago.

1. AMHss emerges from Africa c.100,000 BP, moving East across Sub-Himalayan Asia.
2. AMHss colonizes Europe after 42,000 BP, replacing Neanderthals.
3. AMHss colonizes Australasia after 50,000 years ago.
4. AMHss crosses Bering Land Bridge and enters Americas over 15,000 years ago.
5. AMHss enters North America by the Ice-Free Corridor route.
6. AMHss enters North and South America by Coastal Migration.
7. AMHss colonizes the Pacific Islands after 3,000 years ago.
8. AMHss colonizes the High Arctic after 1,500 years ago.
A= Cordilleran and Laurentide ice sheets.

The Colonization of Australasia

The initial colonization of Australia is a mind-boggling odyssey of hunting and foraging among the island chains of Southeast Asia toward the open ocean leading to Australia. Somehow, people invented some kind of watercraft and used them to hop from island to island, until they reached The Big One: Australia itself. Then, they trekked into the desert interior of this immense continent.

The mysteries of Australian colonization

Something's up Down Under. When humanity first came to the continent of Australia is one of the great mysteries of archaeology. Many sites date earlier than 30,000 years old, but none seem to be definitively dateable because the strata have been disturbed a little or the method being used to date the site is at the edge of its useful range — something's always a little off. Still, anthropologists are confident that Australia was colonized well over 40,000 years ago. Main finds that make that clear:

- The Lake Mungo skeleton, found in 1974, has recently been redated to just over 60,000 years ago.

- In 2002, rock art at the Nauwalabila I site in Northern Australia was dated to more than 50,000 years ago.

- Rock art at the Carpenter's Gap site is securely dated to about 40,000 years ago.

Whatever the ambiguities with some of the data from these sites, they all point in the same direction: to occupation of Australia at least by 40,000 years ago, and maybe much earlier. How much earlier? One claim, published in 1996, was for a site dated to more than 175,000 years ago. That would be even earlier than AMHss, and few people — myself included — buy it. I want much better evidence (and multiple lines of it) all pointing in the same direction before I accept such an early date.

Only 50 years ago, many thought Australia was colonized no earlier than 8,700 years ago, but today data indicate it was colonized at least three times earlier than that. This is a pattern in archaeology; dates for the earliest circumstance of something — like the colonization of a region or the invention of an artifact — constantly get pushed back as new sites surface. This pattern doesn't mean that archaeology is rudderless and constantly rewriting its books, however. What it does do, like any good science, is update what it knows and move on. In this case, the update is pretty major, but it's still just an update, not a condemnation of all archaeology.

What anthropologists know for sure

Despite the mysteries of Australian colonization, a few facts are certain:

- ✔ Australia was colonized by 40,000 years ago.
- ✔ Australia was colonized by AMHss, as evidenced by their skeletons.
- ✔ Australia was colonized by behaviorally modern *Homo sapiens sapiens*, as evidenced by their cave art, which indicates symbolism.

Reconstruction of sea levels reveals that at the time Australia was colonized, it was already an island; therefore, the colonizers must have used some kind of watercraft, such as rafts or canoes. No such artifacts have been found (though that doesn't mean they don't exist), but water crossings beyond the sight of land would have been necessary, so archaeologists infer that early Australians used watercraft.

Another Grand Exploration: The Colonization of the New World

Yet another wild, hair-raising, and unlikely story of prehistoric migration and colonization is that of the colonization of the New World (North and South America). Combined, this region opened up more than 40 million square kilometers (more than 15 million square miles) to humanity, who swiftly spread to inhabit every conceivable ecological niche — the grassy Great Plains, the icy Arctic, the windswept coast of Peru, the steaming jungles of Central America, the hardwood forests of Appalachia, the Mississippi basin, the blustery Pacific Northwest, the arid Great Basin, and just about everywhere in-between. How people survived to become today's Native Americans is a staggering tale this section can only begin to cover; however, it can give you an idea of what was involved.

Dueling hypotheses: A couple of migration theories

The real mysteries about the colonization of the Americas lie in the timing and circumstances of the earliest occupants. At one time, a book like this would have delved deeply into the question of where the first Americans came from, but today that mystery is solved. Dental, genetic, linguistic, and archaeological data all clearly link the native peoples of the Americas with the native peoples of Northeast Asia: specifically, Siberia.

Although this link was first proposed as early as the 16th century, as people made the obvious connections between native people of these areas, the many lines of evidence have come together only in the last century to support this common-sense notion. A recent widely published hypothesis — that Native Americans came across the sea ice from Europe (about 18,000 years ago) — relies on the scantest evidence and isn't convincing any archaeologists I know or know of. Right now, all lines of evidence point to Northeast Asia. From there, humans moved toward North America by crossing a land bridge (between eastern Siberia and Western Alaska) called Beringia. During the ice ages (which didn't end until about 10,000 years ago), Beringia was an expansive vegetated tundra grazed by herds of *megafauna* (large animals), such as the wooly mammoth. After crossing into Alaska, however, the question is where he colonists went next, as we'll see in the following sections.

Ice-Free Corridor hypothesis

The *Ice-Free Corridor hypothesis* suggests that migrants entered the Americas between two great ice sheets that covered Canada until about 12,000 years ago. The Ice-Free Corridor model proposes that as the ice sheets melted due to the end of the ice age, a broad corridor opened between them, allowing plants to colonize this strip of land connecting today's western Canada with the United States' Great Plains. Large grazing animals such as bison and mammoths migrated south to feed upon these plants, and bands of human foragers followed.

According to some geographers and glaciologists, the big problem with the Ice-Free Corridor hypothesis is that so much water would have poured off the mile-thick ice sheets that the newly exposed ground between them couldn't have stabilized quickly enough for the plants to take root, let alone support grazers. Rather, the corridor would have been a no man's land of glacial outwash, blasted by roaring rivers that changed course unpredictably. These folks maintain that nobody came through the corridor until many thousands of years after the ice melted, the water drained off, soil stabilized, and plants took root.

The Ice-Free Corridor model is usually proposed by the Clovis-First theorists, who believe that the first people into the Americas bore distinctive stone tools called *Clovis Points*. For a long time, this theory was generally accepted among archaeologists, but in the last two decades new data (see the following two sections) have strongly suggested that Clovis wasn't first at all.

Coastal migration hypothesis

In contrast to the Ice-Free Corridor hypothesis, the coastal migration hypothesis proposes that migrants traveled ever southward down the coasts of Alaska, British Columbia, Washington, Oregon, and then California. At least at first; eventually, they also headed east further into the North American continent by following the big rivers that empty into the Pacific from north to south: the Fraser (near Vancouver, British Columbia), the Columbia, the Sacramento (at San Francisco Bay), and others.

The first evidence for this hypothesis is a coastal route that many people used to rule out simply because they thought the great ice sheets extended far out to sea, creating a 300-foot ice-wall barrier that no humans could migrate along and survive. But recently, *glacial refugia* (islands that weren't iced over) have come to light; scientists have confirmed these islands were actually forested, serving as refuges from the worst conditions. Alaska's On Your Knees Cave (yes, that's its real name) contained bear remains more than 15,000 years old; people argue that if the refuges could have supported bears, they could have supported equally omnivorous humans.

Although the tide of opinion currently favors the coastal migration hypothesis, keep in mind that it's going to be tough to prove. When the ice sheets melted by 10,000 years ago, the runoff poured into the oceans, raising the sea level. Today the water is 300 feet deeper than it was when the coastal migrants presumably made their way south, so remains of their campsites are underwater. Diving more than about 100 feet starts to get really complicated, so SCUBA survey is a tough proposition.

Just the facts, ma'am

I personally strongly favor the coastal migration hypothesis, but whatever the case, people were definitely in the Americas well over 10,000 years ago. Three archaeological sites make that clear:

- The Monte Verde site in Chile is securely radiocarbon dated to more than 12,000 years ago. (See Chapter 5 for more on radiocarbon dating.)
- Idaho's Buhl skeleton is securely dated to 10,600 years ago.
- The Kennewick Man is securely dated to 9,400 years ago; though this date isn't actually more than 10,000 years ago, it's pointing in the right direction. If people reached southern Washington by 9,400 years ago, you can pretty safely bet they were into North America just 600 years before that. (See the nearby sidebar "The Kennewick controversy.")

And the story keeps changing. A site in Oregon currently shows radiocarbon dates for human occupation spanning back to 14,300 years ago. If the dates pan out and the research holds up under the thorough scrutiny that's the hallmark of good science, this will be the oldest well-accepted date for human occupation in North or South America. This find is exciting to say the least, but as anthropologists we'll will have to wait for all the evidence to be reviewed by the scientific method before we begin rewriting the textbooks.

The Kennewick controversy

In 1996, anthropologists found the partial skeleton of a human male eroding from the bank of the Columbia River in southwestern Washington state. Radiocarbon dated to about 9,400 years ago, these bones were some of the oldest human remains in North America (the oldest are from Buhl, Idaho, dated to almost 11,000 years ago) and excited immediate interest. The skeleton had a stone point imbedded in its hip, indicating an interesting life history, but something else brought the media. The anthropologist who first examined the bones said that they had "Caucasian" features. Because all prior evidence suggested that Native Americans ultimately came from Asia, the word *Caucasian* — used in common speech to mean white — ignited a tremendous legal battle.

Scientists wanted to study the DNA; Native Americans (who didn't believe the skeleton was white) wanted the remains for proper reburial; and other groups (including white supremacist organizations) tried to lay claim to the remains for their own proper burial and fixed on the skeleton as proof that the Americas belonged to whites and not to the Native Americans, who clearly derived from Northeast Asia. The initial characterization of the remains as Caucasian stirred up a lot of bad blood. In the strictest terms, people of the mountainous Caucasus region of central Russia (Caucasians) may in fact be related to the Northeast Asian ancestors of the Native Americans. In fact, later studies showed that the skeleton was of Asian descent. Undeterred, the white supremacists still want the skeleton. The Native American tribal coalition still wants the bones for reburial, and some scientists still want the material for analysis.

One reason Native Americans are so set on getting the remains is that they have endured archaeologists digging up their ancestors' skeletons for more than a century; imagine if someone went to your ancestors' graveyards in, say, Scotland or Germany and started digging up your ancestors out of sheer interest without even asking permission! My impression is that anthropologists should turn the bones over to the Native Americans as a sign of goodwill. This gesture could lead to better collaboration between Native Americans and archaeologists, which would be good for everyone. Many Native Americans support archaeology but, of course, want to be involved in it and not studied like museum specimens.

Igloos, Dogs, and Whalebone Knives: The Colonization of the Arctic

I love the Arctic. I've spent several winters there, taking in the harsh beauty while traveling on foot. I have always found it hard to survive even with my modern equipment and wondered how people with simpler gear did it thousands of years ago. The archaeological record indicates that they did it like people worldwide have accomplished colonization time and again: with ingenuity, fortitude, and the ability to adapt.

First arrivals

By 5,000 years ago, hardy humans had taken up life in the North American Arctic, hunting, fishing, and foraging as their predecessors had all the way from Siberia and across Beringia. Like all Arctic peoples, they were hunters, and they survived on seals, caribou, birds (and bird eggs, in the right season), and just about anything else the human body could metabolize. They also made distinctive artifacts, including

- ✔ Ivory carvings of animals, including polar bears
- ✔ Wooden figurines from driftwood
- ✔ Harpoons — heavy and simple but effective — for catching seals
- ✔ Ice cleats for strapping to sealskin boots

By 1,000 years ago, however, new inventions and artifacts appear in the western Arctic just before their rapid and wide spread all the way east across thousands of miles of ice and snow to Greenland. This was the origin of the Thule expansion.

The Thule expansion

The *Thule expansion* was an active migration of humans from the western to the eastern Arctic after about 1,500 years ago. The name comes from an archaeological site in Greenland, where these people's artifacts were first found. Their migration was characterized and made possible by a number of distinctive inventions:

- ✔ **Dog sleds,** sometimes with runners made of frozen fish
- ✔ **Effective watercraft**, including the *kayak*, a boat made of hide stretched over a framework of animal bones and/or driftwood
- ✔ **Specialized whale-hunting harpoons** for taking the largest sea mammals, which may feed a whole village for a whole winter
- ✔ **Igloos,** snow houses that could be built in a few hours by using a long, distinctive whalebone knife

Imagining the northern lights, the cracking ice, and the strange new creatures, fish, and foxes the Thule folk would have met on their treks, I think their eastward expansion must have been one of humankind's greatest and most audacious adventures.

A native Alaskan winter feast

In February 2007, I was privileged to attend a Winter Feast on Alaska's North Slope, 300 miles north of the Arctic Circle. The three-day festival called Kivgiq, hosted by Inupiat natives of North Alaska, centered on dances performed by members of many communities across Arctic Canada and Alaska. As I watched, I learned that the feast and the dances were much more than just a big party: They were reminders of an ancient code, an ancient way of life that was important to get right because it kept people alive.

Fifteen drums at a time beat slowly, directing the subtle movements of dancers' bodies, a shoulder shrug, an arm or wrist gently turned. The slow beat was the invitation to let go, to be taken by the spirit of the dance. After a time the pace and volume increased — BOOM BOOM BOOM . . . BOOM BOOM BOOM — accompanied by wailing and chanting, as the dancers stamped their boots and locked their bodies in stiff postures of shock or terror. Sometimes they used syncopated paddling motions — the communal pursuit of a whale. Sometimes they hauled their arms joyfully toward their chests, pulling in a whale that would provide sustenance for a whole village and stave off starvation off for another season. The dances included pantomimes of hunger and plenty and respect for the land and its animals, the gravitational center of this culture around which all else revolved.

These performances were as important to Inupiat survival as any harpoon or kayak; they were instructions for a proper life. I'd asked, "How did they survive here?" It was a question only a wholly urbanized person could ask. How did they survive here? Easy. Keep your population low. Don't mow down your resources. Manage the plants and animals so their populations will be healthy for your descendants, as your ancestors did for you. Be respectful of the land. It's not rocket science.

And have a sense of humor! Some of the greatest applause at Kivgiq came for "Eskimo Elvis," a dancer outfitted in a caped jumpsuit, sunglasses, and pompadour. "E" rocked the crowd with a fusion of Inupiat and Elvis moves complete with a karate-kick ending that sent the crowd through the roof. Kivgiq ended with solemnity, but laughing was just as important. Life is short, after all.

The Voyage of Ru and Hina: The Colonization of the Pacific

Between 3,000 years ago and 1,500 years ago, the ancient Polynesians voyaged throughout the Pacific, building a habit of exploration typified by the legend of the exploring siblings Ru and Hina (who, having discovered every scrap of land in the Pacific, looked to the moon, saw a new place to tread, and built a magical ship to take them there). The ancient Polynesians eventually colonized Tahiti, Easter Island, New Zealand, and Hawaii; just like everywhere else, this colonization effort was a masterpiece of adaptation. These peoples carefully shaped both technologies and cultures to make exploration and survival in the

Pacific possible. The technologies included the double-hulled voyaging canoes and special methods of navigation (see more on this in the following section). The following section describes some more examples of human adaptation to the Pacific.

In 1947, the Norwegian adventurer Thor Heyerdahl and his crew drifted from Peru to Polynesia on a 40-foot log raft named *Kon-Tiki* to show that Polynesia could have been colonized by ancient South Americans. Though Heyerdahl's feat was a bold adventure, no solid evidence suggests he was right; linguistic, DNA, and archaeological evidence all clearly show that the colonists of the Pacific originated in Southeast Asia, not South America.

The tools of the explorers

The earliest explorers of the Pacific were inventive people determined to survive their explorations. They didn't sail haphazardly or simply drift with the currents; on the contrary, they planned their expeditions and carried artifacts to enable them to survive at sea and start a new life after they found land. Among their inventions were

- Double-hulled *voyaging canoes* up to 60 feet long and carrying up to 100 people
- Pottery used to contain and cook foods on board
- Stone *adzes*, tools used to clear land for horticulture when the explorers found land
- Fish hooks made from shell and used to catch fish while underway

The society of the explorers

The Pacific explorers also invented cultural traditions to survive, which were just as important as any artifact. These traditions included

- **An acceptance of risk:** Although the explorers felt that life was precious, they acknowledged that bravery was often necessary at sea and that life could be unpredictable.
- **A mythology of divine intervention:** This system reassured voyagers that the gods did sometimes take pity, that every storm would eventually end, and that life would be good when they found land.
- **A glorification of exploration:** The greatest glory went to those who explored and found new land in which to raise the next generation. The tale of Ru and Hina exemplifies this belief.

Kavenga star path navigation

When the European explorers arrived in the Pacific in the 1700s, they marveled — if grudgingly — at the accuracy of native Polynesian navigators. Despite lacking (as the Europeans saw it) any instruments, charts, or knowledge of mathematics, native navigators were so competent that the Europeans took them aboard their own ships. The Europeans discovered that the natives navigated mainly by memory. Polynesian navigators, by rote memorization, knew when and where certain stars would come up and when and where they would go down, and that gave them a sort of clock as well as pointers to various directions on the horizon. A sailor would remember a trip from one island to another, not in the standard European measurement course degrees per leg of the voyage but as a series of stars to follow as they appeared and set — the *star path,* or "kavenga." Native navigators also used the following methods to keep on course:

✓ **Island location by swell direction:** Just as a radar signal bounces off an airplane, ocean swells bounce off islands and come back against the prevailing currents in distinctive angles.

✓ **Island location by flora and fauna:** Natives knew that certain fish stayed nearer to islands than others, as did certain birds, flying insects, and types of seaweed. Even the water tasted different nearer islands than it did at high sea, and Polynesian navigators were keen to all of these clues.

✓ **Island location by steering for a screen rather than a speck:** A single island in the vast Pacific really is a speck, but any island has a number of effects on the water that surrounds it, making it detectable by a number of means. A chain of islands, whose effects on the water run together, may make a 100-mile wide screen of island-affected water; instead of aiming for any one island, navigators just had to hit the screen and then fine-tune their course for their ultimate destination.

Chapter 9

Old, Old McDonald: The Origins of Farming

After two and a half million years of foraging, hunting, and gathering for their daily subsistence across the globe, about 10,000 years ago humans made a momentous discovery that would change nearly everything. It would lead to the establishment of cities, where once people had trekked across vast landscapes in search of food; it would lead to the development of armies and protracted warfare, where once conflicts were limited in duration and distance; and it would lead to the multifaceted evolution of civilization itself. This development was farming: growing food rather than pursuing it.

Because farming changed nearly everything and happened relatively recently in human prehistory (and because anthropologists have a good archaeological record reflecting the origins of farming), I'm giving it a whole chapter in this book. Understanding the agricultural roots of today's civilization is necessary if you want to understand how quite a bit of humanity lives today; in this chapter, I explain just what farming is and when and where it was first invented, as well as review some ideas about why it was invented and how it changed humanity for better and worse.

The Principle of Domestication

Farming is the domestication of plants and animals for human purposes. It's based on the principle of domestication (defined in the next section), which essentially allows humans to control food by *producing* it as farmers rather than *pursuing* it as hunter–gatherers. As the following sections show, this shift in how humans get their food has had major consequences for the human species.

Cultural selection

Farming is better described as *domestication*, which is basically the control of plant and animal species for human benefit. The important concept in this definition is *control;* at some point in the evolution of certain plants and animals (like corn, sheep, cattle, or sweet potatoes), these species came to be under total control of humans. In evolutionary terms, humans became the ultimate *selective agent* on these species, determining which plant seeds would be sown to grow the next crop, for example, and what animals would be slaughtered for meat or kept alive as the parents of the next generation.

What's important here is that the natural environment no longer determined which seeds would survive or which sheep would be selected against; humans did, and for their own purposes. In this way, the selective pressures on these plant and animal species shifted from natural selection to cultural selection. If Old McDonald liked his sheep to have long, curly fleece, he picked those with long, curly fleece to sire the next generation and perhaps slaughtered the others. If his wife preferred really large pumpkins to natu-rally-occurring small ones, she'd be sure to plant the seeds of the larger ones rather than the smaller ones.

And that's it. Domestication is basically selective breeding of plants and animals. It's humanity becoming some species' ultimate selective agent. It's taking advantage of the fact that some species can't do anything about it if humans want to put an animal in a pen or control which seeds they use in the next planting.

Of course, not all species are amenable to domestication. Nobody has ever really succeeded in domesticating the big cats, for example (Siegfried and Roy notwithstanding); humanity tended to focus — for staple foods anyway — on easily domesticable species, like sheep. You may think wrangling the first wild mountain sheep would have been a sketchy affair, but surely even early people were smart enough to simply capture youngsters.

Effects of farming on society

A farming lifestyle has some major ramifications for human societies:

✔ Farming requires a degree of *residential sedentism,* or settlement. Plants and animals require tending, and crops need harvesting and processing.

This sedentism has many ripple effects — houses have to be more substantial to withstand use for years or generations at a time, and so on.

✔ Farming normally requires more intense food-processing technologies and processes than foraging; seeds require separation from chaff, crops need sowing and harvesting with special tools, grain has to be ground into flour, and so on.

✔ Farming requires more investment in a landscape than foraging. Irrigation ditches and fences are often necessary, and soil needs tilling, fertilizing, and so on.

✔ Finally, farming leads to a more developed sense of property than foraging; when people invest so much blood, sweat, and tears in a particular patch of ground, changes occur in the principle of sharing. This shift doesn't mean that sharing ceases, but the concept of personal property becomes more developed and ingrained among farmers than among foragers.

These are general characteristics, and, as always, you can find exceptions. For example, not all foragers are highly mobile. On North America's Pacific Northwest Coast, Native American foragers lived as sedentarily as some farmers and at least as sedentarily as most horticulturalists for at least the last 3,000 years, not because they were farmers but because they were able to subsist on the area's plentiful salmon and sea mammals. Their environment was rich enough to support residential sedentism, so they quit moving around as much.

Plant domestication

In his book *Guns, Germs and Steel*, geographer/anthropologist Jared Diamond summarizes two unique features worth thinking about as you consider the origins of domestication, because the first domesticators would have needed to think about them as well:

✔ Plant domestication requires focus on very specific species because only some plants provide products — like fruit, seeds, or fibers — useful for human purposes.

✔ Plant domestication would require careful attention to dietary balance because plants are missing some nutritional elements found in a more varied diet.

Plant domestication normally has two main effects on the way plant species change through time:

✔ For most domesticated plant species, the plants being harvested are bigger than their wild predecessors; cultivators simply use the seeds from the biggest, best plants to grow the next crop. For example, domesticated limes are much bigger than the wild limes originally cultivated around 2,500 years ago in Southeast Asia; in the same way, modern corncobs are huge compared to the original, finger-sized wild corncobs.

✔ Most domesticated plant species are easier to harvest than their wild brethren; cultivators chose to plant the species that require less effort to reap. For example, the seeds of ancient, wild wheat (first domesticated more than 10,000 years ago in the Near East) were hard to knock off the plant, but over time early domesticators selected for strains in which the seed was more easily separated from the plant.

Plant species that don't naturally occur in a given landscape are called *exotics* and are often evidence of human introduction. This represents at least human intervention or interaction with the species, if not necessarily indicating domestication.

Plant domesticates can also be selected for taste, preservability, transportability, or other characteristics that might be hard to detect archaeologically.

Plant domestication can be labor-intensive because living plants need protection from pests (both plant pests such as weeds and animal pests such as crows), and harvested foods need storage (like grain, which must be kept dry and free of mold and relatively free of rats and mice).

Check out Table 9-2 later in the chapter for more on the origins of some common domesticated plants.

Animal domestication

Animals aren't all that easy to domesticate, either; Jared Diamond also points out that domestication-candidate animals must have

✔ A relatively good disposition toward humans (which is why big-cat and grizzly-bear taming haven't really worked)

✔ A relatively short life span (so the animals have plenty of offspring — for example, rabbits or chickens) if the human investment into the species is going to pay off. If our food species lived as long as we did before they could be slaughtered and eaten, it would be tough to keep up the food supply. Luckily, most of the animal species we eat reproduce quickly, providing lots of offspring at the same time.

✔ A flexible diet, because in captivity the animal must be able to eat whatever the humans provide, which won't necessarily be what it would eat in nature

Also, animal domestication normally has at least two main effects on the actual bodies of species under domestication:

> ✓ If the animals bear horns, people normally select for smaller and/or differently shaped horns, so the animal will be a little less dangerous.
>
> ✓ Most domesticated animals are a little smaller than their wild counterparts because humans tend to select for offspring that are a little easier to handle.

Domesticated animal populations normally have an age/sex profile different than a wild age/sex profile; for example, domesticated herds may have only a handful of adult males (for use as studs — other males are slaughtered), but most females are kept alive to bear the next generation and to provide milk and other secondary products. This setup is a population profile very different than what occurs naturally (where there are more than a handful of males, for example.) See Table 9-1 later in the chapter for a list of some common domesticated animals and their origins.

Principles of Horticulture

Keep in mind that farming was often preceded by a kind of low-intensity form of domestication called horticulture. *Horticulture* is hard to define — a recent paper discusses at least ten definitions, which I won't go into here — but generally refers to farming on a smaller scale than full-scale farmers, with simpler technologies and less overall emphasis on farming. (That is, some foraging — more than in farming societies — provides staple foods.) I discuss the details of horticulture a little more closely in the sections that follow.

Distinctive characteristics of horticulture

Although horticulture did precede farming in some areas, in others horticulture continues to thrive. In New Guinea, people have been living as horticulturalists for at least 6,000 years. Horticulture doesn't automatically lead to full-on farming.

Think of horticulture as a kind of gardening in which you congregate plants in a patch to protect them and promote their health by weeding and so on. This procedure is different from the intensive soil-tilling, seeding, and harvesting involved in farming.

Generally speaking, horticulturalists differ from famers in three distinctive ways:

✔ Horticulturalists use digging sticks rather than plows or other implements hauled by draft animals.

✔ Compared to farmers, horticulturalists farm small plots that have relatively simple irrigation. A typical horticulture irrigation system consists of simple earthen mounds that are breached to allow water through and then piled up again to prevent further water breach.

✔ Horticulturalists normally domesticate plants that aren't conducive to the same large-scale or long-term *storage* practiced in farming societies.

Garden horticulture

Horticultural plots often look more like gardens than farmed fields, and they often have some common characteristics. They're typically small (less than one acre) and utilize simple erosion-control measures such as using logs to divert running water. Horticulturalists embrace sloping land more readily than farmers do; because they have less investment in the farming lifestyle, horticulturalists simply live with the slope instead of exerting the time and energy required to cut notches out of the hillsides.

Among horticulturalists, women normally plant and harvest food, and men typically clear the land. On the other hand, women in farming societies generally deal more with processing harvested foods (grinding seeds, cooking vegetables, and so on) indoors, and men do outdoor activities involving the fields and agricultural implements.

Slashing and burning

Slashing and burning, also known as *shifting horticulture*, is the practice of clearing heavily vegetated land to make an agricultural field; this field is then used for some time — often from one to five years — before making a final harvest and then burning off the stubble to let it lie for several years as you move on to another, previously used field. This technique keeps horticulturalists moving from one plot to the next, and it has two main ramifications. It dampens any impulse to invest too heavily in one landscape, but at the same time it requires landowners to have a strong enough concept of property to protect their investment in that plot.

Maori horticulture

In 1924, New Zealander Elsdon Best published a description of Maori horticulture as they practiced it around the turn of the century. Although this horticulture certainly differed from what the Maori practiced prehistorically, it could have been pretty similar to what was practiced at the time Best wrote. The following paragraphs are excerpts from his 1924 work *The Maori as He Was: A Brief Account of Maori Life as it was in Pre-European Days;* check out the accompanying figure for a look at a traditional 19th-century Maori village supported by horticulture.

"Early visitors to these shores remarked on the careful tending of crops performed by the natives, and the extremely neat appearance of the fields, in which weeds were carefully eradicated. From [Captain] Cook downwards they emphasize the peculiar regularity of the sweet-potato fields, with each plant occupying a small mound, and the mounds arranged carefully and precisely in quincunx order [five plants, one at each corner and a fifth in the center, as on dice]. These labours were deemed to be of great importance, and the growing crops were rendered *tapu* [taboo] and placed under the protection of the gods."

"When the season arrived for the preparation of the ground for planting, then all the people of a village turned to work with a will. Chief, commoner, and slave, men and women, all joined in the work, which moved briskly until the ground was ready for planting. In pre-European times there were no predatory animals in the land, no quadruped that had to be fenced against; but in some places light barriers were put round the crops to protect them from the meddlesome *pukeko*, or swamphen. The introduction of the pig greatly increased the labours of the Maori husbandman, for that creature keenly appreciated kumara and was most persistent in his attempts to reach them."

"Different kinds of soil could be described by Maori terms, as he was provided with about fifty soil-names, and he was naturally a good judge of soils. Much care was displayed in selecting ground for cultivation, inasmuch as certain stiff, unkindly soils called for much extra labour. This consisted of carrying, perchance for a considerable distance, great quantities of gravel to be placed round the plants of *kumara* [sweet potato]. In some districts are seen pits of great size from which gravel has been taken for *kumara* crops."

Limited storage

Another characteristic of horticulture is that it normally doesn't involve as much storage as intensive farming situations do. Most of the places that feature horticulture are tropical or semitropical, and the hot, humid conditions make food storage difficult. This lack of storage has two main ramifications:

 ✓ **It reduces the distance to which horticulturalists can carry out warlike expeditions.** Unlike horticulturalists, farmers can store up literally tons of grain, which makes it easier for them to carry war to distant places for long periods of time. Without this storage luxury, horticulturalists can only leave for so long before they must return home to work in the fields.

✔ **It reduces the potential for self-aggrandizement (at least in relation to that in farming societies).** In farming societies, farmers on particularly productive plots of land can build up social status *(self-aggrandize)* by throwing feasts or assisting others in times of resource stress. In many horticultural societies, competitive feasting and self-aggrandizement are very important and common; because of their lack of storage, horticulturalists just don't have as many opportunities to show off in this way.

Principles of Farming

Farming is more intensive than horticulture. It's a larger-scale undertaking with different purposes than horticulture, and it includes the domestication of both plants and animals. It's practiced by people living in *civilizations* (large, populous social organizations; for more on what constitutes a civilization, check out Chapter 10). For these reasons, I'm going to call the type of farming that I describe in the sections that follow *state farming*.

Distinguishing state farming from horticulture

State farming is very distinct from horticulture, and it has some very significant differences:

✔ **State farming is intensified.** Farmers grow more crops on larger plots (which are now fields) in a shorter time with more technically intensive methods (such as plowing, intense fertilization, and irrigation).

✔ **State farming is systematized.** The state regulates units of measure, approves of crops, and takes a cut of farmed products in the form of taxes.

✔ **State farming is economically integrated.** The activities of the state and its citizens adjust to accommodate the farming schedule. For example, ancient Egyptian military service was carefully scheduled in accordance with the (state-mandated) planting and harvesting schedules.

✔ **State farming is commodified.** Farmers not only grow staple foods but also grow cash crops for export; in fact, farmers may or may not actually subsist on what they themselves grow.

Obviously, these conditions are very different from those of horticultural societies.

State farming, which some call *agriculture* to distinguish from less-intensive forms of domestication, has two main technical characteristics. It tills the ground with an animal-drawn plow rather than a simple human-held digging stick, and it also involves the intensive use of fertilization.

Water control

Control of water is obviously necessary for farming. Farmers in different areas achieved this control in different ways, including

- **Dyke-and-canal irrigation:** The use of dykes to channel water in canals; these systems could be massive works many miles long, as were those in ancient Assyria (Northern Iraq) more than 2,700 years ago

- **Chinampas:** A method of creating artificial islands in a lake (rather than bringing the lake water to land), as the Aztec civilization did around 1400 AD

- **Hill terracing:** The practice of cutting notches in the sides of hills to catch water on the flat terraces instead of letting it simply run down the hillside, as in Incan civilization around 1400 AD

- **Flood control:** The practice of managing floodwaters that overflow the banks of rivers, as in the ancient Egyptian technique of trapping the water on the fields immediately flanking the Nile by using simple earth mounds

- **Dams:** The collection of water in basins that were then strategically drained, as was the practice in ancient Iran more than 2,500 years ago

Animal domestication, farming-style

In addition to animals bred for all manner of secondary products, state farming promotes the raising of animals (sometimes known as *animal husbandry*) for use in warfare (as mounts for soldiers and pack animals for moving supplies), as pets (historically only available to the elite class), and as exotic novelties. These unusual animals were sometimes kept in zoos for public entertainment, but they also often served to show the prestige of a leader. One Chinese emperor reportedly brought a giraffe all the way from Africa for his own amusement.

Table 9-1 shows when and where some common domesticated animals first popped up. The *Fertile Crescent* refers to a region of Southwest Asia including parts of Turkey, Syria, Iraq and Iran.

Table 9-1	Origins of Some Common Domesticated Animals	
Animal	*Where Domesticated*	*Date*
Dog	East Asia	Around 15,000 BP
Sheep	Western Asia & the Near East	Around 10,000 BP
Cat	Fertile Crescent	Before 9,000 BP
Goat	Western Asia & the Near East	10,000 BP
Pig	Western Asia & the Near East	By 9,000 BP
Cattle	Western Asia/Near East/ possibly North Africa	By 8,000 BP
Guinea pig	Peru	By 3,000 BP
Chicken	South Asia	By 3,000 BP
Horse	Central Asia	By 5,000 BP
Llama	Peru	By 5,000 BP
Ass	Egypt	By 5,000 BP
Bactrian camel (two-humped)	Central Asia	By 5,000 BP
Dromedary camel (one-humped)	Saudi Arabian peninsula	By 3,000 BP
Yak	East-central Asia	By 3,000 BP
Reindeer	Northwest Asia (Siberia) and North Scandinavia	By 3,000 BP
Turkey	Mexico	By 2,500 BP

Table 9-2 shows you the origins of several common domesticated plants.

Table 9-2	Origins of Some Common Domesticated Plants	
Plant	*Where Domesticated*	*Date*
Rice	East Asia (China)	By 9,000 BP
Barley	Fertile Crescent	By 10,500 BP
Bread wheat	Near East	By 10,000 BP

Plant	Where Domesticated	Date
Chickpea	Southern Turkey	By 10,000 BP
Bottle gourd	Southeast Asia or Central America (unknown)	By 10,000 BP
Pumpkin squash	Mexico	By 9,000 BP
Corn (maize)	Mexico or Central America	By 9,000 BP
Manioc	South America	By 7,000 BP
Potato	South America	By 7,000 BP
Avocado	Central America	By 7,000 BP
Chili pepper	Central America	By 6,000 BP
Hemp	East Asia	By 5,000 BP
Sorghum	Africa	By 4,000 BP
Sunflower	North America	By 4,000 BP

Massive storage

State farming requires massive storage of farmed goods for several reasons. All early farming states had armies, and armies need to be fed while they train and while they're away on military expeditions. Farming states also had cobblers, bricklayers, masons, priests, scribes — in short, all manner of folk who had specialized trades outside of food production; each of these folk needed to be fed, and some of their food came from state-controlled coffers of stored agricultural products. Finally, most states had some means of redistributing food during drought or other calamity, and they had to store that food in massive, state-administered storage facilities.

I discuss the characteristics of civilization as though they're separate, but they're really all deeply interconnected. You can read more about these connections in Chapter 10.

Farming facilities and tools

Farming is technologically and materially intensive, in that it requires permanent facilities where products are processed and stored, as well as tools.

Obviously, facilities vary from farm to farm, but the following list describes some common ones found on early farms:

- ✔ **Granaries** for sorting harvested vegetal matter, such as dried grain.

- ✔ **Ovens** for cooking vegetal foods. These ovens are often substantial structures with chimneys, complex doors for putting in firewood, and vents; they're different from simply campfires and were normally built as part of the house.

- ✔ **Food-production yards,** which normally contain *threshing floors,* areas specially prepared for separating seeds from plant stems and *chaff* (unwanted plant matter).

Because farmers have to plant, tend, harvest, process, and store their crops, they require distinctive tools. Some implements that show up as artifacts in early-farming sites include

- ✔ **Sickles** for harvesting plant matter. Before the invention of metal scythes thousands of years after the earliest domesticators, early sickles were made of stone blades hafted into bone, antler, and/or horn handles; the blades bear very distinctive "sickle gloss" from rubbing against the vegetal matter, a clear sign to archaeologists that early farmers collected a lot of plant matter.

- ✔ **Pottery** for storage and cooking of vegetal foods. Pottery is basically clay hardened by heating (you can read more about it in Chapter 4) and appears in all farming societies. It's good as a container for dry foods, but also as a durable container for cooking, one of the ways that plant foods are often processed (because many need to be cooked to make them easier to chew or otherwise digest).

- ✔ **Mortar and pestle** for grinding/pounding vegetal foods to small pieces or even powder. The *mortar* (the open vessel) can vary in size and shape, but is essentially the receptacle for the grains to be processed, and the *pestle* is the instrument used to pound or pulverize the grains. Though nonfarming societies occasionally used mortar and pestle, when these tools are accompanied by other evidence for farming they're very distinctive.

- ✔ **Threshing tools** for separating seeds from plant stems and chaff. These tools may include threshing boards, batons, flails, baskets, and other instruments.

- ✔ **Axes** for clearing forested areas to convert into farmland. These items typically consisted of a stone ground and polished into shape over many hours. Early stone axes have been tested and found to be as effective as any steel axe when fitted into a handle; they are one of the most distinctive tools of the early farmer.

Farmers also have to birth, tend, feed, water, and harvest primary or secondary products from their domesticated animals. (More on these products in the next section.) These activities include distinctive tools:

- ✔ **Pens or other enclosures** to contain the animals being domesticated

- ✔ **Bridles, saddles, and other riding gear** to control animals ridden by a human

- ✔ **Yokes or other harnesses** to connect animals to items to be pulled

Secondary products

After (or sometimes at the same as) people began domesticating plants and animals as food, they domesticated them for secondary products as well. *Secondary products* are nonfood resources such as skins obtained from domestic plants or animals. In many cases, these products (or the goods created from them) can be just as valuable as the meat from animals or seeds from plants. They include

- ✔ **Fibers:** Animals and plants produce fibers such as wool and cotton that people can spin into yarn or thread and sew or weave to make textiles.

- ✔ **Machine-pulling and transportation:** Farmers can use their animals to pull implements like plows and carry people and goods along paths.

- ✔ **Milk:** Animals produce milk, which can be consumed or turned to butter or cheese. Technically, milk is a food source, but it qualifies as a secondary product because it's renewable — you can live on the "interest" of the animal without killing the "capital," as it were.

- ✔ **Blood:** People can consume animal blood for nutritive value. The pastoralist Maasai of Eastern Africa mix it with milk to make a rich froth. Of course, this practice also technically makes blood a food source, but, like milk, blood is renewable and therefore a secondary product.

- ✔ **Plant tissue:** Plant tissues such as papyrus stalks could be converted to writing sheets as in ancient Egypt (or to a little thing called paper that you use today).

- ✔ **Plant extracts:** Plant extracts are often ingredients in medicines, adhesives, pigments, and so on.

Of course, domesticated animals can simply serve as pets and assistants; some of the earliest domesticates were probably wolf puppies bred over time into hunting dogs, from which all of today's pooches are descended.

Palaeolithic to Neolithic: An adventure in confusing terminology

As archaeologists were laying out the foundations of archaeology in the 19th century, they arranged artifacts into several main time-specific periods. *-Lithic* means "stone;" the *Palaeolithic* was the period — of unknown origin or duration — reflected by old-type stone tools such as simple scrapers, hand axes, and so on. The *Mesolithic* came next (though no one is certain when it started, either) and was characterized by new stone tools, including stone spear points and *microliths,* razor-blade sized tools used for many purposes. The *Neolithic* was characterized by a single main tool type: the stone axe. Archaeologists knew that people in each of these periods used artifacts made from other raw materials such as bone and antler; however, the stone was best preserved, so the stone-based names stuck.

Defining these time periods as hard-and-fast eras can create some problems, though. For example, although new stone tools (particularly sickles for harvesting and axes for clearing land to farm) did appear, not all the old kinds of stone tools were abandoned. The bottom line is that the beginning of each period doesn't necessarily signal the definitive end of the previous one.

Looking Back on the Origins of Farming

Clearly, farming and horticulture are very different, and each clearly had significant effects on human cultures worldwide. In the rest of this chapter, I introduce you to what anthropology knows about when and where domestication began worldwide. In some places, you see that it was rather quickly followed by farming, though this sequence isn't universal.

Why farm in the first place?

Why would people begin farming in the first place? This is one of archaeology's most enduring questions. As with other topics, single-factor models just don't seem to work to explain the origins of agriculture, probably because different groups had different reasons to take up agriculture in different places at different times. Some interesting (but, ultimately, failed) ideas about the origins of agriculture include:

- ✔ The *unilineal evolution* group of theories suggests that all people were on the track to becoming civilized and that all would eventually take up horticulture and then graduate into agriculture. These theories make no sense for people who live in areas where agriculture simply isn't reasonable, like the hunters or reindeer-herders of the Arctic, who aren't in some time bubble but rather live here in the modern day.

✔ The *vitalist* group of theories suggests that as humanity strove to improve itself, it would naturally take up farming because farming was obviously superior to foraging. These theories fail to actually define in what way farming was so much better. It's farmers who are up at 4 a.m. to milk the cows; foragers actually work a bit less for their daily food. Farmers also actually tend to live in poorer health than foragers.

✔ The *population pressure* group of theories argues that as forager populations increased after the ice ages, population pressure on the landscape forced people to devise new ways of making a living, including farming. These theories ignore the fact that foragers tend to be very careful about letting their populations exceed what their landscapes can support in the first place and already have (nonfarming) ways of coping with population pressures. Foraging groups often spread out if, as one unit, they're stressing the resources of a particular foraging ground. (You can read more about the effects of high populations on human culture in Chapter 10.)

✔ The *climate change* group of theories argues that as climates changed worldwide after the end of the last ice age (around 12,000 years ago), humans invented new ways to survive, including shifting to domestication from foraging. These theories never really explain how this move happened, and just attributing domestication to climate change isn't good enough support.

Although archaeology currently has a decent handle on what farming is, when and where it first appeared, and what effects it had, it still has no theories that comprehensively explain *why* farming first appeared. If the Nobel Prize folks gave an award in archaeology, nailing this agriculture question would be a good way to get your hands on it.

For a long time archaeologists referred to the change to farming as the Agricultural Revolution — it was also known as the Neolithic Revolution to distinguish it from the previous stone age. Although the term *Neolithic* can present some confusion (see the sidebar "Palaeolithic to Neolithic: An adventure in confusing terminology" in this chapter), just remember that it's the period in which farming is first evident.

Having said all that, I'm now going to deal with what archaeologists do know: when, where, and under what general circumstances farming first appeared as a way of life across the Earth. Figure 9-1 will help you keep track of these developments. (***Note:*** Although the figure shows the centers of early domestication, it doesn't number them chronologically, so read carefully.)

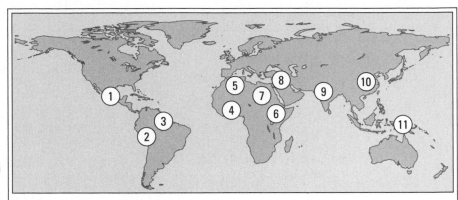

Figure 9-1:
The main
centers
of early
domesti-
cation.

1=Mesoamerica   7=Nile
2=Andes   8=Fertile Crescent/Near East
3=Amazonia   9=Indus
4=West Africa   10=China
5=Sahel   11=New Guinea
6=Ethiopia

The Sumerian farmer's almanac

In 1949, a University of Chicago/University of Pennsylvania expedition to Iraq discovered a series of nine clay tablets in the ruins of the ancient Sumerian city of Nippur. When translated they turned out to be an invaluable look at Sumerian agriculture, with the following good advice for the farmer:

"Keep an eye on the man who puts in the barley seed that he make the seed fall 2 fingers uniformly . . . Where you have plowed straight furrows, plow (now) diagonal furrows; where you have plowed diagonal furrows, plow (now) straight furrows . . . When you are about to cultivate your field, take care to open the irrigation works (so that) their water does not rise too high in it (the field). When you have emptied it of water, watch the field's wet ground that it stays even; let no wandering ox trample it. Chase the prowlers and have it treated as settled land. Clear it with ten narrow axes (weighing no more than) ⅔ of a pound each. Its stubble (?) should be torn up by hand and tied in bundles; its narrow holes shall be gone over with a drag; and the four sides of the field shall be fenced about. While the field is burning (in the summer sun) let it be divided up into equal parts. Let your tools hum with activity (?). The yoke-bar should be made fast, your new whip should be fastened with nails, and the handle to which your old whip was fastened should be mended by the workers' children."

In the Near East

The world's first domestication seems to have taken place in a region called the *Fertile Crescent* of the Near East, from Israel up to Southern Turkey, across to Northern Iraq, and then down the west side of Iraq's Zagros Mountains.

Archaeologists begin to see traces of experimentation with domestication of both plants and animals in this region at about 12,000 years ago. Specifically:

- ✔ **The domestication of wild grasses:** Domesticated wheat (emmer and einkorn varieties) and barley appear around this time.

- ✔ **The domestication of goats and sheep:** This domestication may have occurred before that of the plants, though this question remains unresolved.

- ✔ **The appearance of small, sedentary communities:** The Natufian villages in modern-day Lebanon and Israel are sedentary and include burials of generations of people under houses, indicating a deep connection with certain places on the landscape that contrasts to the mobility philosophy of foraging peoples.

- ✔ **The slow transition from hunted foods to domesticated foods**: Food refuse from some villages shows a transition from mostly antelope and deer remains to the remains of sheep, goats, and the main forms of wheat.

Eventually, the list of domesticated Near Eastern plants includes wheat, barley, peas, chickpeas, and lentils; fava beans, carrots, beets, safflower, and olives; and figs, dates, and *fenugreek* (a legume-like herb).

In Africa

Archaeological evidence accumulated over the past two decades has shown that domestication of plants, and perhaps some animals, occurred in Africa around 7,000–10,000 years ago; certainly by 5,000 years ago, people on the Nile, organized as the Egyptian civilization, were full-fledged farmers, using tools such as the *shaduf* (shown in Figure 9-2) for irrigation. Some main evidence:

- ✔ One kind of domesticated wild grass — emmer wheat — was present in highland Ethiopia as early as 7,000 years ago; not long after, the main domesticates of the Near East appear on the fertile banks of the Nile.

- ✔ As early as 10,000 years ago, people may have domesticated wild aurochs into cattle; in the long run these cattle were popular among both African pastoralists (cattle herders) and agriculturalists.

- ✔ Small, sedentary communities appear; villages of mud brick spaced along the Nile were apparently economically and politically independent until unification by early rulers around 5,200 BP.

Eventually, the list of domesticated African and Nile plants includes sorghum, millet, tef (a millet-like crop), cow pea, oil palms, watermelon, and okra.

Figure 9-2:
Egyptian
shaduf
irrigation
tool in
modern
times.

© Erich Lessing / Art Resource, NY

In East Asia

People of Eastern Asia were cultivating wild rice by 9,000 years ago, and soon they were domesticating and farming it as well. Today, rice supplies about 20 percent of the world's calories.

Domesticates cultivated independently in Eastern Asia include the aforementioned rice plus pigs, chickens, cattle, dogs, and ducks. Small, sedentary communities such as the Lungshan villages appeared around 5,500 years ago; these sites have many remains of cattle and pigs and storage pits for millet and other crops. Eventually, the list of domesticated East Asian plants includes apricot, peach, cucumber, sesame, radish, turnip, canola, tea, apricot, and water chestnut. As in other areas, food waste indicates a shift in diet from hunted foods to domesticated items.

Herodotus and Egypt, "gift of the Nile"

Around 500 BC, the Greek geographer Herodotus traveled to Egypt, and, impressed by the richness of its Nile-watered farms, called the whole civilization "the gift of the Nile." He also described a certain aspect of ancient Egyptian agriculture, and although he perhaps overstated how easy it was, it remains a good description nonetheless:

"It is certain however that now they gather in fruit from the earth with less labor than any other men ... for they have no labor in breaking up furrows with a plough nor in the hoeing nor in any other of those labors which other men have about a crop; but when the river has come up of itself and watered their fields and after watering has left them again, then each man sows his own field and ... when he has trodden the seed into the ground by means of ... swine ... he waits for the harvest, and when he has threshed the [harvest] by means of the swine, then he gathered it in"

In the Western Pacific

By 10,000 years ago, peoples in highland New Guinea were exploiting and cultivating several plants, including taro and banana; by 6,500 years ago, they were clearing land and building horticultural plots for such plants; and by 4,500 years ago, they were digging simple earthen waterways.

By 3,000 years ago, some of the folk of the Western Pacific were exploring east into the open ocean, carrying on their sailing vessels domesticated animals and plants, as well as seed stocks to use when they eventually found land.

The major Western Pacific domesticates included the versatile breadfruit, yam, coconut, and banana, plus dogs, pigs, and chickens. Eventually, the list of domesticated Western Pacific plants includes grapefruit, mango, lemon, cloves, and arrowroot.

In the Americas

In recent years, the origin of domestication in the Americas has been pushed back by new archaeological discoveries. For decades, archaeologists thought cultivation took place in North America very late, but today evidence indicates the cultivation (horticulturally) of sunflowers in the region close to 10,000 years ago. The general consensus was that agriculture in Central Mexico was only 5,000 to 7,000 years old, but now both corn and squash have been dated to around 10,000 years ago as well.

The agricultural wonders of Tenochtitlan

In 1520, the conquistador Hernan Cortez wrote about the Aztec capital of Tenochtitlan (today's Mexico City). In this letter, he described some domesticates of the Aztec world, giving anthropologists a good look into the vibrant agricultural engine of an ancient civilization.

"There are all kinds of green vegetables, especially onions, leeks, garlic, watercresses, nasturtium, borage, sorrel, artichokes, and golden thistle; fruits also of numerous descriptions, amongst which are cherries and plums, similar to those in Spain; honey and wax from bees, and from the stalks of maize, which are as sweet as the sugar-cane; honey is also extracted from the plant called maguey, which is superior to sweet or new wine; from the same plant they extract sugar and wine, which they also sell . . . [I have also seen] maize or Indian corn, in the grain and in the form of bread, preferred in the grain for its flavor to that of the other islands and terra-firma; patés of birds and fish; great quantities of fish — fresh, salt, cooked and uncooked; the eggs of hens, geese, and of all the other birds I have mentioned, in great abundance, and cakes made of eggs; finally, everything that can be found throughout the whole country is sold in the markets, comprising articles so numerous that to avoid prolixity, and because their names are not retained in my memory, or are unknown to me, I shall not attempt to enumerate them."

Important characteristics of New World domestication include

- **The domestication of wild grass:** Several kinds of wild grass, including the corn-like *teosinte,* were slowly but surely domesticated into corn.
- **The domestication of llamas and turkeys:** Interestingly, no animal to be widely ridden was domesticated in the Americas.
- **The cultivation of beans and squash:** Beans were a staple; squash was popular as food but also for its gourd, which made a good container for all kinds of substances.
- **The cultivation of condiments:** These crops included peppers, mint, and chiles.
- **The cultivation of the potato:** The potato first appeared in South America, and, like many other New World crops, was taken back to the Old World after conquistadores "discovered" it in the 16th century.

Eventually, the New World domesticates, which include those of the Andes and Amazonia (both in South America) included quinoa, corn, sunflower, common bean, manioc, squash, papaya, sweet potato, peanut, peppers, avocado, cashew, and pineapple.

Chapter 10

The Development of Civilization

- -

In This Chapter

▶ Searching for the origins of modern civilization

▶ Distinguishing various methods of human subsistence and organization

▶ Connecting the characteristics of civilizations

▶ Tracking the rise and fall of two ancient civilizations: Egypt and the Incan empire

- -

Civilization, it's often said, is the pinnacle of human evolution, the point that evolution has been building to in the first place. Is that true? What does anthropology have to say about it? Like many lessons of anthropology, we're in for a lesson in humility. Humanity hasn't been striving for civilization, abandoning every other way to live in a quest for SUVs and transparent tape; our species has invented many ways to live, and many humans continue to live happily without cities or the many products of civilization.

So what is civilization, if not the inevitable result of human evolution? This chapter tells you exactly what civilization is, when and where it first came up, and a bit about what it was like to live in some of the ancient civilizations.

Human Subsistence and Social Organization

The first thing to remember about *civilization* — the most complex form of human social organization — is that it appeared only in the last 6,000 years or so. The species *Homo sapiens sapiens* has been around for 100,000 years, so (calculators ready?) civilization has been around for less than 10 percent of that time; it really is a very recent development.

In all time before civilization, humans gathered or grew their daily foods in some distinctive ways, each of which had important effects on the shape of human societies. Knowing about these ancient ways of life is important to understanding civilization itself. In this section, I discuss the connections between *human subsistence* (the way people get their food) and social organization before delving more deeply into civilization itself in later sections.

Human subsistence

All animals, humans included, have worked out a way to survive. All animals must meet the following basic requirements for survival:

- ✔ **They must obtain food.** Humans require about 1,000 calories per day just to stay alive; active people in civilizations may require 2,000 to 3,000 calories, and active foragers like polar hunters as much as 4,000.

- ✔ **They must obtain water.** Humans need about 2.5 liters (about half a gallon) of clean water per day to remain healthy and may need a lot more depending on the amount of work they do.

- ✔ **They must be able to regulate temperature.** Temperature regulation keeps animals warm or cool; most humans are comfortable in a small temperature spectrum, feeling cold below 50 degrees Fahrenheit (10 degrees Celsius) and hot above 70 degrees Fahrenheit (21 degrees Celsius). This temperature range is only about 20 degrees Fahrenheit (or 6 degrees Celsius) above or below the Earth's average temperature of about 60 degrees Fahrenheit (15 degrees Celsius); staying warm or cool is very important.

- ✔ **They must ingest the proper nutrients.** *Nutrients* are vitamins and minerals required to keep healthy; the recommended varieties and amounts vary wildly from species to species. Some vitamins important to human health include vitamin A, vitamin B, and vitamin C; many societies acquire these nutrients by trade if they're not available in native foods.

To fulfill these requirements, every human society has devised a kind of subsistence. Obviously, the distribution of resources such as food and water on a landscape has a strong effect on how humans make their living; the kind of subsistence practiced also affects things like social structure, *mobility* (how far people move around each day), and even religion and ethics. The main subsistence modes humans have invented are described in the following sections, with notes on how these modes of subsistence affect other variables such as social ranking and concepts of property ownership.

The idea that a society's mode of subsistence directly explains its religion and ethics is called *environmental determinism.* Like many *-isms,* the idea has some value — social factors are certainly affected by subsistence factors. That said, you can't attribute everything in a culture to how its people subsist; human culture is just too complex for that.

Foraging

Foraging (also known as *hunting and gathering*) is the subsistence mode in which humans move across a landscape on a near-continual basis, collecting their food and water every day. Humans and early hominids have been practicing foraging since at least 2.5 million years ago, and although most humans today subsist on *agriculture* (which I discuss later), many foragers continue to hunt and gather on a daily basis. Some important features of the foraging subsistence mode include

- ✔ **High residential mobility,** meaning that housing normally isn't permanent

- ✔ **Limited food storage,** meaning that environments or foods are unsuited to being stored (for example, they rot)

- ✔ **Lack of emphasis on material culture,** meaning that although some artifacts are important (like tools for food gathering), the society's cultural symbols are rooted in its *oral traditions* (cultural information, including histories and myths passed down through storytelling)

- ✔ **Lack of emphasis on social ranking,** meaning that people in the foraging culture have equal access to all resources (an arrangement known as *egalitarianism*)

- ✔ **Lack of emphasis on possession,** meaning that most (although not necessarily all) items are communally owned, and symbolic units of value (like money) are absent

Foraging was the original way of life for the human species. Early *Homo* emerging from Africa, the Aborigines of Australia, the Baka of Central Africa, the native people of Arctic Alaska and Canada, the Chinook people encountered on the Lower Columbia River by Lewis and Clark, the cave-painting peoples of ice-age Europe — they were or are all foragers. Their lifestyles, though very different from our own today, sustained them for thousands or even tens of thousands of years. Today, as *sustainability* (maintaining core resources such that you can continue a practice indefinitely) shapes many of our decisions (and rightly so), we'd be smart to take as many lessons as possible from these folks.

Foragers are often portrayed as poor because they don't own many of the objects we in civilization cherish. But foragers' wealth isn't reliant on objects; their cultural richness resides in their oral traditions and their histories. Foragers don't see themselves as poor, and neither should you.

Pastoralism

Pastoralism is the practice of herding animals to provide subsistence, moving them — and the social group that herds them — across a landscape of grazing land and water sources according to a complex seasonal cycle. Pastoralists include the Samburu people of northern Kenya, who herd cattle, and the

Saami of Arctic Scandinavia and Russia, who herd reindeer. Pastoralists eat some meat, but rely more on their herds to provide secondary products such as milk, butter, cheese, and hides. Pastoralists domesticate their animals, making them tame (or very nearly tame). The following list describes some common characteristics of pastoralists:

- **Moderate food storage,** including *meat on the hoof* (the idea that living domesticated animals are themselves a kind of stored food).

- **Moderate emphasis on symbolic material culture,** meaning they put some emphasis on elaborating the symbolism in the people's artifacts in the form of decoration or symbols; this is often because animals can be used to carry those artifacts (whereas in foraging societies, people essentially must carry everything).

- **Moderate emphasis on social ranking,** meaning some people have greater access to resources than others. These folks are often leaders of families that own certain herds of animals; higher livestock counts normally mean higher social rank for the owning family.

- **Moderate emphasis on possession,** meaning that, as compared to foragers, pastoralists value their goods — including their livestock, which they exert a great deal of energy to protect — to a greater degree.

Pastoralists move around landscapes, but not quite as much or continuously as foragers; they may stay in one place for weeks or months as the quality of a grazing patch dictates. Interesting pastoral subsistence adaptations include the Maasai (East Africa) custom of mixing live cattle blood with milk to provide a high-calorie, nutrient-rich broth as delicious to Maasai kids as milkshakes are to kids in the U.S. Cultural anthropology has revealed that dietary choices depend on the resources — they're not universal.

Horticulture

Horticulture involves low-intensity farming, in which people grow crops without the massive investment of irrigation and fertilization and emphasis on storage seen in *agriculture* (see the next section). Horticulturalists include the Maori people of New Zealand and the Fore (for-*ay*) people of highland New Guinea, each of whom grow yams and raise pigs. These folk practice a form of subsistence not seen in foragers and seen only sparingly in pastoral societies: *domestication,* which is the raising of plant and animal species entirely for human purposes. (Check out Chapter 9 for a more extensive discussion of domestication.) Because horticulturalists farm the land, they're tethered to that land, staying in one place on the landscape longer than foragers or pastoralists. Among the characteristics of horticulturalist societies are

- **Moderate to high reliance on food storage,** including extensive processing and drying of foods so that they're edible for months to years after harvest

- ✔ **Strong emphasis on symbolic material culture,** meaning that a great deal of effort is put into embellishing artifacts — from houses to costumes — largely because horticulturalists don't move as often as foragers or even pastoralists

- ✔ **Strong emphasis on social ranking,** meaning that some people have greater access to resources than others; these citizens are often leaders of families that own lots of livestock and extensive and unusually productive patches of farmland

- ✔ **Strong emphasis on possession,** meaning that (as compared to foragers and pastoralists) horticulturalists place a great deal of value on their goods and personal property (farmland, food-processing and storage facilities, corrals, and so on) because they invest so much time in that property

Horticulture is often practiced as *swidden* or *slash-and burn* farming, in which croplands are farmed for a few years before the social group moves on to another cropland, which is cleared (slashed and burned), renewing the soil to be farmed for a few years before moving on to another slash-and-burn site. This practice prevents overtaxing the soil and allows it to replenish its nutrients, and in many societies the farmlands are returned to repeatedly in a multiyear cycle.

Agriculture

Agriculture is intensive farming facilitated by the use of massive water-control facilities (such as irrigation ditches and dykes); intensive food-processing practices (such as *winnowing*, or separating grain from chaff); and massive reliance on stored foods, which may last for years after harvest. Agriculturalists eat some of the crops they reap, but they also rely on these crops' secondary products, such as oil from olives, and cheese from domesticated animals. Every ancient and modern civilization rests on an agricultural foundation to supply basic sustenance. Important characteristics of agricultural societies include

- ✔ **Almost total reliance on food storage,** including extensive processing and drying of foods so that they're edible for years after harvest. (Exotic import foods are normally delicacies rather than staples.)

- ✔ **Very strong emphasis on symbolic material culture,** meaning that a great deal of effort is put into embellishing artifacts largely because of not having to move as often as foragers or even pastoralists.

- ✔ **Strong emphasis on social ranking,** meaning that some people have greater access to resources than others; these people are and were often leaders of families that own lots of livestock and extensive and unusually productive patches of farmland.

> ✔ **Strong emphasis on possession,** meaning that (as compared to foragers, pastoralists, and horticulturalists) agriculturalists place the most value on their goods and personal property (farmland, food-processing and storage facilities, corrals, and so on) because they invest so much time in that property.

Agriculture has only been around for at least 10,000 years, but even when cultures did take up full-time farming, it didn't immediately lead to modern civilization. People have floated dozens of theories to explain why humanity first took up farming full-time, but none has convinced all anthropologists. For example, some have proposed that farming began when populations of foragers grew so high that the land could no longer support daily foraging, and required a new method of subsistence: agriculture. But that theory ignores the fact that foragers normally prevent their populations from growing beyond what the landscape can support in the first place (for example, by *infanticide*, the killing of infants, or *social fission*, splitting a foraging group up when the food supply on a landscape can't support everyone). Today the question surrounding the origins of agriculture is one of anthropology's greatest mysteries.

Earlier in this chapter, I mention that subsistence modes clearly have important effects on the nature of human society; in the following sections, I cover the main kinds of human social organization. Not surprisingly, they basically reflect the four main modes of human subsistence.

Human social organization

The different modes of subsistence had important effects on the kind of social organization people have practiced through the ages. This section describes the four main kinds of human societies and provides a handy table summarizing how subsistence and social organization are interrelated. I discuss these modes of social organization in further detail in Chapter 16 as well as the sidebar "Social organization and subsistence among humanity past and present" later in this chapter.

Keep in mind that the terminology anthropologists use varies. One of the most frustrating things I learned throughout four years of undergraduate work and thirteen years of graduate school worldwide was that every rule seemed to have an exception. No matter how I tried to pin down humanity (in the present or the ancient worlds), just when I thought I had a good line drawn around a subsistence mode or a social type, for example, I'd find out that things just weren't so simple. Still, the types of subsistence and social organizations mentioned in this book are generally applicable to the study of humanity at large; just remember their edges are blurry, not sharp.

Bands

Bands are normally relatively small groups of foragers who travel long distances across their foraging landscapes. They're essentially egalitarian, giving a little respect to the best hunters and gatherers in the group but making sure to socially shout down anyone who tries to *self-aggrandize* (gain social status by boasting or giving extravagantly).

Tribes

Tribes can be somewhat larger than bands and may travel less; they include pastoralists with their herd animals but may be specialized hunters like the Arapaho Native Americans (who focused on buffalo hunting). Tribes have chiefs, but they have more influence than actual power, and they can be kicked out of position by the population. Tribes have slightly more members than most bands.

Chiefdoms

Chiefdoms, which often rely on some kind of horticulture for subsistence, include the Maori of New Zealand. They're led by hereditary elites, people of a royal bloodline born into positions of power. These chiefs have more power than the leaders of tribes and can't be so easily ejected; still, their power is mainly that of coercion and influence, except over their slaves, whom they could trade, injure, or kill at will (in the past, anyway — most or all of today's chiefdoms don't own slaves).

States/civilizations

States or *civilizations* (like most archaeologists, I use these terms interchangeably) are characterized by massive and strict division of the population into elite, commoner, and lower-class/slave classes (at least in the ancient civilizations). They're largely sedentary, relying on intensive agriculture and stored foods, and their very size and population make the number of connections and interactions between the members enormously complex compared to those in chiefdoms, tribes, or bands.

Today, not all people are fully engaged in what typically qualifies as civilization. This discrepancy doesn't mean they're not fully modern humans, just that they carry on lifestyles like foraging, pastoralism, or horticulture that were invented long before civilization. These groups often have some contact with civilizations, such as the foraging Inuit, who buy snowmobiles from civilization but use them to hunt in their foraging lifestyle. Because civilizations have spread so widely, many of these indigenous folks have been pushed far from their original territories and/or placed on reservations, and this relocation — combined with their trade and cultural contacts with civilization — makes it appear that they're trapped in some kind of time bubble. But they're not. They're modern people just like you; they just happen to have very different modes of subsistence than the agriculturalists of the world's civilizations.

Social organization and subsistence among humanity past and present

In the following table I summarize some of the main characteristics of bands, tribes, chiefdoms, and civilizations. These are general notes — they're generally accurate, and chiefdoms are definitely different from states, for example — but remember, each type of social organization is more of a shade on a spectrum than a rigid category.

	Band	*Tribe*	*Chiefdom*	*State/ Civilization*
Subsistence	Foraging	Foraging/ pastoralism	Horticulture or (rarely) foraging	Agriculture
Mobility	High	Medium/cyclic	Low	Lowest
Food storage	Little: days to months	Little: weeks to months, or meat on the hoof (among pastoralists)	Medium: seasons to a handful of years (some stored food crops)	High: with reliance on stored foods
Attitudes toward property	Low but present	Medium: Among pastoralists, herded animals are property of individuals	High: elites own special material goods that are not owned by commoners	High: commoners and slaves are prevented from owning certain material items, such as clothing restricted to wearing by elites only
Attitudes toward social ranking	Low: generally equal access to resources for all members	Medium: Among pastoralists, families with more animals have higher rank	Strong: hereditary elite class exists but has more power to coerce than command	Very strong: High rank can be achieved or ascribed, and access to resources depends on social rank

	Band	*Tribe*	*Chiefdom*	*State/Civilization*
Population	10–150	Fewer than 200	Low hundreds to 1,500	Tens of thousands to millions or billions
Example	BaAka of Central Africa, Paiute of North American Great Basin, Inuit of Arctic Canada	Maasai of East Africa (cattle herders), Saami of Arctic Scandinavia (reindeer herders), Cheyenne of North American plains	Maori of New Zealand, Vikings of medieval Scandinavia	Ancient Egypt and Greece, Shang China, Maya (Mexico and Guatemala), United States

The Characteristics of Civilization

The preceding section shows you how civilization differs from other kinds of human social organization; now take a look at some of the main characteristics of civilization. This section details 14 characteristics that most archaeologists agree are indicators of civilization. But remember, since the beginning of professional archaeology over 150 years ago, prehistorians have argued about the characteristics that define ancient civilizations, generating one list after another. In this book, I'm using a list of characteristics culled from a number of eminent prehistorians, but you should remember that each ancient civilization was a little different. At the very least, any society with these characteristics was so different from any known band, tribe, or chiefdom that it may as well be considered a civilization.

Remember two things: The following list comes in no particular order, and every characteristic connects with other characteristics; although I discuss them separately, they don't exist independently. Finally, if one characteristic underpins all the rest of the characteristics of civilization, it's an agricultural subsistence mode. Most of these characteristics were supported from the beginning by a surplus of food. Craft specialists who focused on making goods could only increase their special skills if they weren't out gathering food half the time.

A false impression: From Savagery to Barbarism to Civilization

For a long time, anthropologists believed that all human societies would progress through a known series of stages of evolution; this was the concept of *unilineal* (one-way) social evolution. The stages were Savagery (marked by simple, low-population societies with low-grade technologies), Barbarism (marked by slightly more complex, medium-population societies with medium-grade technologies), and Civilization (marked by massive populations and high technologies). But anthropology and archaeology have shown that this hierarchy just isn't true. Modern traditional Arctic people continue to forage for their daily subsistence and keep their populations low, and not every horticultural society has evolved into a full-blown civilization. The unilineal evolution concept, devised by European anthropologists in the Victorian era, was built primarily to contrast European society — considered civilized — with non-Europeans by sticking the outsiders with the loaded term *uncivilized*. But every human society evolves on its own path, and comparisons just don't work. Because some societies actually did go from foraging to farming, you may be inclined to think that every society should. The truth is that not all societies progress the same way, and that doesn't make them any less human than us. It simply means that those societies evolved a little differently. Civilization is only one way to survive as a human in the modern world.

Urbanization

Urbanization is the concentration of a human population into an area that can't support the population ecologically; the populations must import foods and other goods. Essentially, urbanization is the growth of cities, where you find high populations of *non-food production specialists*, people like potters and blacksmiths who work at trades other than farming or food-processing. Urban centers are basically cities, and even in the ancient world they had apartments, markets, administrative centers, temples, and other religious facilities. In the ancient world, massive fortifications like the heavy stone walls of Troy (in modern-day Turkey) often defended these cities. In some civilizations, like the Maya of Central America and the Egyptians, a few main cities existed, but more people actually lived on farmland. In others, like Rome and Sumer, many people were packed into dense cities very similar to today's metropolises.

Long-distance trade

Ancient civilizations used extensive trade networks to import and export a variety of goods. Normally, these goods weren't staples but *exotics*, items made valuable simply because they came from distant lands. Semiprecious stones were imported to ancient Egypt from the mines of Afghanistan hundreds of miles away. In Incan civilization, elites were buried with a sprinkling of the dust of the thorny oyster shell, only available from coastal communities hundreds of miles to the north. Ancient civilizations rarely imported staples such as food; the Romans conquered and annexed Egypt as a giant farm (the so-called breadbasket of Rome) to feed its troops on their massive expeditions to conquer mainland Europe. Normally, imports and exports like the semiprecious stones and thorny oyster shell were goods for elite consumption. Importantly, long-distance trade employed many non-food production specialists who worked at occupations other than farming, such as the Aztec *pochteca* or the Inca *mindala,* guilds of long-distance traders. Remember that these folk and their activities were important parts of the economies of all ancient civilizations.

Some civilizations outsourced or contracted some of their long-distance trade to other peoples; the Egyptians — not wanting take on the cost of a trade navy — hired Phoenician and Minoan peoples of the eastern Mediterranean to do their sea trading for them.

Social stratification

Unlike most foraging societies, ancient civilizations didn't necessarily guarantee equal access to resources for all their members. Civilizations ranked individuals according to a strict hierarchy, the practice of *social stratification.* In every case, a ruling elite managed the affairs of the populace (common people), and in most cases the kings and queens were at the top of the top because they were considered to be living gods, or at least people closer to the gods than the populace. These elites were members of royal families, each of which formed a *dynasty* that ruled the civilization until the bloodline was broken, often by assassination or other intrigue. Among the elites (either within the royal family or close to it) were the highest priests, the military officials, and the regional governors. Below them were commoners, including merchants, artisans, scribes, and lower priests, and below these — forming the bulk of the population — were the low commoners: the farmers and herders that most people today can claim as ancestors (unless you're descended from the royal family!) The middle commoners and the farming population were the largest part of the tax base, financing all kinds of state projects including the building of monumental architecture and military adventures.

Durable record-keeping/writing

As populations increased and the complexity of the whole system of civilizations became more complex, each ancient civilization devised means of keeping track of that complexity. These systems usually involved some kind of *durable record-keeping*, using hieroglyphs, letters, or other symbols to set down permanent records. When the taxman came around in ancient Sumer, he inscribed a farmer's payment on a clay tablet, which was later archived in the state record halls; Sumerians even wrote on clay nails used in ceremonies commemorating the building of important structures, like temples (as shown in Figure 10-1). In Inca civilization, sets of strings called *quipu* were complexly knotted into codes indicating how many troops should be moved from one province to another, where to send 5,000 laborers to clear a stretch of landslide-covered stone road, and so on. Because most people of the ancient civilizations were illiterate, scribes, who normally had somewhat privileged positions in society, made and read the durable records.

Figure 10-1: Sumerian clay tablet, an example of durable record-keeping.

Standing armies and extended warfare

Each ancient civilization was engaged in warfare — some to expand the civilization's territory to ensure buffer regions, and some to actively conquer their neighbors. Whatever the case, standing armies carried out various goals in warfare very different from the kind of hostility you see in chiefdoms or other types of human social organization. In those societies, warfare is normally carried out for short-term goals, like revenge for some injustice; however, because storage is somewhat limited even among horticulturalists, everyone eventually has to get back home to tend to the farm, preventing massive armies or protracted engagements. In civilization, however, massive silos of state-controlled grain could be used to support massive *standing armies*, military forces that didn't assemble only when needed but rather were always training and deploying. These armies were used for *extended warfare*, a new kind of conflict in which military forces went beyond the civilization's boundaries and for long periods of time, often laying siege to urban centers. Some of the earliest archaeological evidence of extended warfare in the Mediterranean includes the citadel of Troy, where over 3,000 years ago the Mycenaean built massive fortifications against expected siege, complete with built-in escape passages as well as tunnels to fresh-water sources.

Money

Like durable record-keeping, the complexity of life, interactions, and transactions in ancient civilizations drove the evolution of a new form of exchange, one in which arbitrary but agreed-upon units of value were attributed to objects such as coins; you know this system as *money*. The old system involved *bartering,* or trading one item for another item of intrinsically similar value — for example, trading a cloth that took a week to weave for a pair of shoes that took a week to cobble together. The difference between money and bartering is that money is basically a state-sponsored unit of some socially accepted value that's independent of the items being traded and the work that went into them. Early civilizations manifested money in very different ways: Early Sumerian money included shell rings, whereas Aztec civilization traded cacao beans. Coins are first known from the Eastern Mediterranean, around 2,600 years ago. The Inca produced wafer-thin bronze plates that were bundled in stacks, just like dollar bills, and traded across vast distances.

Slavery

An unfortunate reality is that some of civilization's characteristics aren't necessarily good for everyone; in fact, I often ask myself, "Who is civilization really good for, anyway?" For the millions of slaves in Rome, Egypt, and Aztec and Incan empires (and really every civilization), it hasn't been much good. *Slaves* are human beings who have been objectified as property; they have no say in their welfare and are typically punished (ranging from injury to death) for attempts to escape. Slaves carried out enormous labor in ancient civilizations, working on agricultural projects and constructing massive buildings. Slaves were often captives of military expeditions, the citizens of enemy states brought home in chains after a military victory.

Perhaps a kind of slavery is still underway in our civilization. Although the modern conception of slavery — people bought and sold in chains — has been largely abolished, some argue that a slave class still exists: the people of the lowest income bracket. Carrying out jobs no one else can afford to do and being for all practical purposes immobilized (except for a few, always well-publicized, exceptions) in the lowest economic ranks, these folks are the working poor. Classifying these people as slaves is an uncomfortable thought in societies that proudly talk about the lack of social class, but it's a reasonable argument that I find hard to refute.

Territorial sovereignty

Each civilization maintained its *territorial sovereignty* (its independence) by maintaining boundaries with some kind of armed force and often building frontier walls, fortresses, barracks, and other military outposts on their borders. Egypt built massive fortresses in its south, to defend from the super-chiefdom of Nubia, and Rome built the Antonine and Hadrian's Walls to mark its northernmost boundaries (just south of modern Scotland). These outposts had to be maintained by standing armies, and each solider and officer was a non food-production specialist who had to be fed, watered, armed, trained, and paid.

Vassal tribute

Every ancient civilization expanded its territory, and most routinely swallowed up any neighboring semi-civilization or chiefdom that couldn't resist the civilization's armies. Aztec civilizations worked on a kind of protection racket principle: They would amass on a neighbor's territorial boundary and send out an emissary offering Aztec citizenship and protection from assault for the price of total surrender. Anyone rejecting the offer was overrun and annexed anyway. In this way, ancient civilizations increased their tax base by increasing their population; the new citizens became vassals. *Vassal tribute* was the practice of generating wealth by demanding certain items or services *(tribute)* from the conquered peoples. One Aztec tribute list indicates the tribute — the number of bales of cotton, polished tortoise shells, rare jaguar skins and quetzal feathers, and other goods — expected to be paid annually by a conquered chiefdom. The Aztecs were so demanding in their tribute lists, though, that when the conquistadores arrived in 1519, they quickly enlisted the help of disgruntled conquered chiefdoms to overthrow their Aztec lords. (It worked, but it later backfired when the conquistadores enslaved their momentary allies.)

Non-food production specialists

Non-food production specialists (also known as *occupational specialists*) were people engaged in activities other than food production. These multitudes included cobblers, jewelers, priests, tax collectors, military personnel (from officers to soldiers), sea captains and their crews, tailors, smiths, masons, woodworkers, and on and on. Because they engaged full-time in their non-food production work, they had to be compensated, housed, and fed, and this demand in turn kept farmers and yet more specialists (such as scribes to keep track of everything with written records) employed. Each of these citizens was engaged in a complex non-food production economy.

Astronomy and/or mathematics

The religious systems of ancient civilizations were all acutely aware that no matter what spells they cast or gods they tried to influence, one kind of phenomenon was completely beyond their control: the actions of the heavenly bodies. The appearance, disappearance, movement, and so on of the lights in the sky — stars, comets, planets, and so on — simply couldn't be influenced. For this reason (and others, I'm sure), these lights were ascribed to the realm of the supernatural, and ancient astronomers kept careful track of the happenings in the sky, making observations and keeping records in attempts to understand that realm. Observations often took place from specially constructed observatories, such as the Inca's stone towers and the top of Sumerian *ziggurats* (pyramids), and the piling up of records about the lights in the sky drove the evolution of *mathematics,* the manipulation of numbers to carry out operations and identify patterns. The durable record-keeping of priests and scribes helped manage all this activity; each of these record-keepers qualified as a non-food production specialist.

Monumental architecture

Each ancient civilization impressed its citizens (and its rivals and enemies) with massive architectural works meant to display the civilization's might. Some works had other, more utilitarian functions, like the Great Wall of China (to keep out invaders, but — some argue — just as importantly to remind Shang citizens that they were Shang citizens) or the 12,000 miles of stone-paved roads in the Incan empire (used to efficiently transport troops and supplies across the mountainous terrain). In the end, monumental architecture was an important part of ancient civilized economies because it required massive effort to build and maintain. One archaeologist has estimated that the Incan fortress of Sacsahuman, on a hill above the capital of Cuzco, took a workforce of 20,000 people 20 years to build. The champion monumental works, of course, are the three massive pyramids of Egypt's Gizeh plateau. Built around 4,500 years ago, these monuments to the greatness of Egypt still draw visitors today (including archaeologists; though I haven't been there, I simply have to see them before I go into the ground!) Figure 10-2 shows the Sphinx of Egypt, with a pyramid in the background, when European archaeologists first carefully examined them in the early 1800s AD. Today the Sphinx has been excavated so that its entire body is visible, not just the head.

Figure 10-2:
The Sphinx
and
pyramids
of Egypt
in an
early 19th
century
engraving.

© François Guenet/Art Resource, NY

State religion

Civilizations have state-sanctioned religions that provide an interface between the material and spiritual realms for the citizenry. In ancient civilizations, these religions were normally *polytheistic*, having many gods that were considered responsible for many aspects of daily life. For example, in Mayan civilization, the rain god Chac determined the future of the harvests; in Egypt, the goddess Isis reigned over matters of the family, health, and motherhood. In ancient civilizations, citizens rarely had the freedom of choice you enjoy today; in Aztec civilization, police ensured that all citizens attended religious rituals carried out at the massive pyramids.

State religions had a couple of important characteristics. First, they required a priestly class, whose main occupations were administering the religion through *divination* (making predictions based on the reading of omens), the maintenance of temples, and the scheduling and proper execution of ceremonies. Monumental architecture was also a key element in these religions; large, publically visible structures (often pyramids) were part of many ceremonies to remind citizens of their engagement in the state religion. See Chapter 16 for more on religion.

Taxes

Every ancient civilization collected taxes from the citizens in exchange for protection from real or perceived threats and/or to provide public services such as municipal waterworks or access to state food supplies and other goods in times of hardship. Ancient Sumerians gave roughly a quarter of their harvest to the tax wagons that came by like clockwork, and Incan citizens toiled at looms to make cloth, which was among the most valued of Inca material goods. Sometimes taxes were paid in labor, as in ancient Egypt, where entire families could be relocated to a builders' village to work on the latest monument, temple complex, or pharaoh's tomb. Inscription was also a common form of taxation, with male citizens being forcibly invited into military service (as in Sparta and the Aztec civilization) for a number of years. Whatever the details, the citizenry provided the ruling elites with a massive wheel of economy through labor, material goods, and/or harvested foods.

Charting the Rise and Fall of the First Civilizations

Although each ancient civilization manifested the characteristics of civilization (described in the preceding section) in different ways, they all mark a kind of human social organization that differs significantly from all others.

So when does all of this manifesting happen? When and where do the first civilizations occur? Figure 10-3 indicates a basic timeline of the ancient civilizations, and Figure 10-4 shows where they arose.

To get an idea of how civilization pans out in two completely isolated cases, the following sections look at Egypt and the Inca, civilizations that flourished in North Africa and in South America's Andes Mountains, respectively. Although every ancient civilization was a little different, archaeologists may have a good point when they see so many similarities that they offhandedly comment, "After you've seen one ancient civilization, you've seen 'em all."

Egypt

I don't think I've ever met an archaeologist who wasn't fascinated by Egypt. Whatever archeologists may study, from animal bones to chips of stone, they seem to love Egypt for its majestic architecture, the romantic notions of its early exploration by eccentric Europeans, and the splendors of the tombs of the pharaohs. I simply couldn't write this book without sketching out a few of its characteristics.

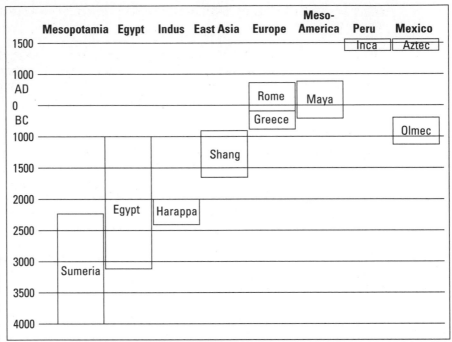

Figure 10-3: Timeline of the ancient civilizations.

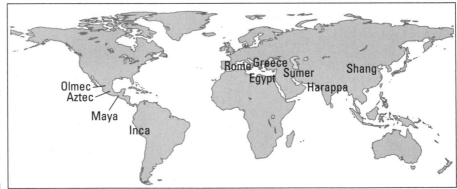

Figure 10-4: World map of the ancient civilizations.

Chronology and origins

The origins of Egypt reach back to around 3,000 BC (5,000 BP), when King Narmer (also known as Menes) united the farming communities of Upper and Lower Egypt. Narmer — shown on one ancient tablet smiting a rival chief — was the first pharaoh of Egypt. The concepts of civilization in Egypt may have been provided by Sumer, where the world's first civilization was already well underway (refer to Figure 10-3), but Egypt was clearly its own creation and not a product of Sumer.

The origins of Egyptian civilization, then, seem to be in conquest; the might of Narmer was too great for anyone to resist. Narmer and the other pharaohs were depicted wearing crowns displaying both the cobra (the symbol of Lower Egypt) and the vulture (the symbol of Upper Egypt).

Flourishing

Egypt flourished as an active, energetic civilization for about 3,000 years, from 3,000 BC (5,000 BP) to 300 BC (2,300 BP). During this time — despite two dark ages marked by chaos and the breakdown of the state institutions of religion and taxation — Egypt was a distinctive entity with a pantheon of hundreds of gods and goddesses believed to rule the supernatural world that was the ultimate destination of every person. Thousands of priests and other religious officials were in charge of keeping track of the deities' actions, and appeasing them to maintain a harmonious world and civilization; in Egypt, modern ideas of "religion" didn't even have names because they were interwoven into every aspect of life.

Both the ruling elites and the commoners spent considerable time and energy in their preparation for the afterlife, which ultimately resulted in mummification (for those who could afford it) and burial in a tomb. Modest, apartment-sized tombs could be within the means of a well-to-do family.

Common people worked in many occupations; males often went into the armed forces (voluntarily or otherwise), and some were lucky enough to go to school as scribes. Women found employment as musicians, priestesses, or treasurers. Most of the citizens of ancient Egypt, of course, were farmers or people associated with the great agricultural engine that carried the civilization. I think my fantasy job in Egypt would have been as a long-distance trader sailing down the Nile and then out into the Mediterranean to meet Phoenician or Minoan trading partners in their ships.

Decline and how it ended

Some civilizations were overthrown from outside, and others decayed from within. Some of each occurred in Egypt; it suffered heavy blows when invading Persians defeated it in the 500s BC (2,500 BP), but it also weakened with civil war and breakdowns of religious institutions. Just as today, people in the ancient world were ready to die fighting for their religions, and when invaders destroyed temples (or the state could no longer finance them), the fabric of civilization often frayed.

Egypt faced many attacks throughout history; everyone wanted to get their hands on the fertile banks of the Nile River, one of the great farmlands on Earth. In the 600s BC, attacks came from the Assyrians, members of a fearsome warrior civilization based in what is today's Northern Iraq. A century later, the Persians showed up, and in 330 BC Alexander of Macedon (Alexander the Great; Macedon is Greece) invaded Egypt and made himself pharaoh. One of the greatest, longest-lived civilizations of the world had effectively come to an end.

Inca

In contrast to Egypt, Incan civilization lasted only a few centuries; it was also a New World civilization, emerging and flourishing in what are today Peru and Ecuador.

Chronology and origins

The Incan empire begins long after Dynastic Egypt was dust, and at the same time as medieval Europe in the 1400s AD. Around this time, a number of competing chiefdoms of the Cuzco region of highland Peru — each very powerful and populous, and bordering on being a civilization in its own right — unified as a single entity after being conquered, one after another. As in Egypt, then, the origins of the Incan empire are rooted in conquest.

Be careful with the idea that only one factor (in this case, military rule) can account for the origins of all civilizations; for instance, Harappa, on modern Pakistan's Indus River, shows no sign of such military origins to its civilization. Time and again, I've found that -isms and single-factor models just don't work in explaining humanity. That doesn't mean you can't know anything about humanity, only that attributing major trends to single factors normally just doesn't pan out.

Although the Incan mythology names some important early ruling families engaged in the conquest of their neighbors, archaeologists have found evidence suggesting that many successive leaders took several centuries to conquer and bring their neighbors into submission. But the Incan elites preferred a simple ideological story of lightning victory, so it seems they invented a narrative; propaganda is found throughout the ancient civilizations.

Flourishing

The Incan empire — which flourished from about 1400 AD to 1532 AD, when it was conquered by the conquistador Pizarro — spread rapidly from Cuzco, building a massive, 12,000-mile road network to move their troops from place to place for military conquests and to put down revolts. They conquered peoples of Ecuador to the north and peoples of Chile to the south; the only directions they didn't expand were west (because there lay the Pacific Ocean) or east (because there lay the vast Amazon basin). One after another, anyone who couldn't resist Incan domination was quickly subjugated; to preserve a little of the conquered peoples self-respect and prevent uprisings, the leaders of the conquered became regional governors — honorary pseudo-Incas, if you will. Many of the Incan affairs were military in nature. Whereas Egypt fought largely defensive battles, or offensive ones to establish buffer states, for the Inca, civilization was about expansion and conquest.

As in other civilizations, the Inca conquered only some — not all — of their neighbors. They were better off to let the coastal Ecuadoreans (the Manteno people) alone; because these people were expert long-distance traders who imported ritually important goods that the Inca needed in their religious ceremonies, the Inca allowed them their independence. Such peripheral societies on the margins of civilization can have strong influences on civilizations.

As in Egypt, the Incan ruling elites (all blood members of a single royal family) ruled the millions of citizens for decades. Commoners enjoyed protection from invasion, but they paid a heavy price for it. Few objects actually belonged to individuals, and most everything was state property. Individual freedom was limited: Professions were assigned, and taxation on labor and produced goods was so high that individuals could do little to change their economic positions in life. Males were often drafted into various military adventures, and women engaged in tremendous amounts of spinning and weaving cotton and other textiles, which were more precious to the Inca than gold.

Decline and how it ended

Incan civilization came to a quick and violent end, rather than the protracted weakening that brought down Egypt. The conquistadores arrived in 1526, and by 1532, they defeated the civilization, which was weakened by European disease (as well as wracked by civil war even before the conquistadores arrived). Like the Aztecs of Mexico (defeated by Cortez), the Incan collapse was swift.

Civilization Today: Will It Fall, Too?

What's the meaning of the word *civilization* today? What's the difference between Western and Eastern civilization? To be honest, that's hard to say. The sheer volume of communication and interaction in the modern world seems to create more commonalities and connections than clear lines demarking people and ideas. Today, civilization may best be considered an economic phenomenon that binds many diverse people and perhaps the world population.

All things considered, I think it's possible to spot characteristics of a distinctively Western civilization today. It's the civilization that has spread globally. It's the reason millions in India wear suits and ties rather than the indigenous clothes they wore a century ago. It's the civilization best typified by Europeans and North Americans.

Western civilization has its roots in Greece about 500 BC (2,500 BP), and Rome, which rose as Greece declined. Mainland Europe didn't have civilization until it was directly imposed on them by the Romans, who came up from Italy in the southeast; in the 50s BC, Julius Caesar brought the concepts of cities, occupational specialization, money, and so on to mainland Europe, which at the time was a vast province of competing farming chiefdoms. And by 476 AD, Rome itself was dead, conquered by its enemies after being overextended too far on too many battlefields. For the next thousand years, the fragmentation and disunity in dark-age or medieval Europe is hard to really call a civilization, if you compare it with the splendors of Egypt or the Aztecs at their height.

So should you start planning for the fall of Western civilization? You often hear that the civilization is waning, and it may be; however, it's a massive and powerful juggernaut, an engine of immense power and complexity. It takes some imagining to consider a loss of all unity such that the peoples of North America and Europe would suddenly be living as semi-independent farming villages, perhaps ruled by chieftains of some kind.

The force of the disruption needed to bring this end about seems hard to imagine, but of course the forces of nature are far more powerful than humans are, and agriculture is clearly fragile. A few years of crop failures, and the whole structure could fall apart. And, of course, every country and its brother seem to have or want nuclear weapons; though the Cold War is over, it could restart. As a teenager, I often wondered when coming home from a camping trip whether the cities could have been wiped out while I was in the mountains.

Finally, remember that the citizens of the Classical civilizations of Egypt, Greece, Rome, or the Incan empire couldn't have imagined their own ends. Each thought of their world as entirely modern, the pinnacle of human existence, the best way to live, and the one way that would never fall apart. And today they're all dust.

Part III
Cultural Anthropology and Linguistics

The 5th Wave   By Rich Tennant

"I've lived among them my entire life, and I can tell you, 'fetch,' 'roll over,' 'sit,' 'stay,' and 'bad dog,' is the extent of their vocabulary."

In this part . . .

Humans talk (a lot), and what they talk about depends on the culture they grew up in, be it Armenian or American. So why do humans talk so much? And what's culture, anyway? This part answers these questions by introducing cultural and linguistic anthropology and discussing culture, language, and the related issues of race and ethnicity, religion, politics, and gender.

Chapter 11

The Spice of Life: Human Culture

- -

- -

*O*ne basic question about humanity is "Why aren't all cultures the same?" That is, if all humans are basically biologically the same, why don't we all have the same behaviors? At the root of the answer is the fact that human behavior isn't guided largely by instinct; it's guided by culture, by the information that you learn in the course of life.

Surviving by relying on cultural information is one of humanity's most distinctive characteristics, so this whole chapter is devoted to what culture is (and isn't) and how it changes through time.

Demystifying the Definition of Culture

A lot of fuzziness surrounds the definition of culture. Culture isn't an easily defined entity. Where do you draw the line between, say, English culture and American culture? They're more similar to one another than either is to polar Inuit culture, but they're clearly not the same. At the very least, they drive on opposite sides of the road.

Never fear. I'm here to clear the air by listing some characteristics of culture that not only explain it better but also show you why culture is so difficult to define:

> ✓ **Culture exists in the abstract only.** Culture is often talked about as though it is a thing, a concrete entity, a noun. But actually culture is a whole nebulous set of ideas, and it's hard to draw a line around. Even though you, the reader, and I, the writer, may both say we belong to

"American" culture (and some extraterrestrial anthropologist observing our behavior patterns would probably agree), we probably have many differences; not *all* of our ideas are the same.

✔ **Cultures contain subcultures.** To further blur the picture, remember that cultures can contain all manner of subdivisions, such as *subcultures* (for example, the "Elvis impersonator" subculture in the U.S. or Japan's "1950's Pop Americana" subculture) or *ethnic groups* (people who share specific geographical, historical, and cultural roots, such as Sicilian Americans). These divisions are defined in many ways; for the moment, just keep in mind that they're subdivisions within a larger culture. You can learn more about such subdivisions, like ethnic groups, in Chapters 14 and 17.

✔ **Culture constantly changes.** Keep in mind that culture isn't a concrete thing or entity; it's a cloud of ideas, a set that changes and varies from mind to mind. Because the characteristics are always changing, no culture is an easily defined block.

✔ **Culture adapts, but not perfectly.** Just because cultures can adapt to various environments worldwide doesn't mean that every culture is perfectly adapted to its environment. A culture can develop *maladaptations*, behaviors that aren't good for the population. For example, overconsumption of resources may be adaptive in the short run but doesn't work in the long run because resources are depleted to collapse.

✔ **Cultures contain conflicts.** Cultures aren't all sweetness and light with regard to the interactions of their members; conflicts inevitably rise within cultures. In every culture, forces work to promote innovation, and other forces oppose them to promote conservatism. I don't know of any culture that goes for long without some kind of social friction.

What Culture Is and What Culture Isn't

Culture has been defined hundreds of times. Because cultural anthropologists disagree on exactly what culture is, most anthropology texts define it in slightly different ways. Still, most anthropologists agree on some basic properties, the most important being that information is handed down from one generation to the next (mainly through language) rather than inherited genetically. The real significance of culture is that it directs human behavior much more than simple instinct or reflex does.

For better or worse, humans are guided by what they learn, not just by instinct. Every myth, symbol, point of etiquette, prayer, war-whoop, greeting, insulting phrase, ideological stance, food preference, all of it — all of that is culture. For this reason, I think of *culture* as a set of ideas about what the universe is like and how to behave in it (or, a little more flippantly, what I'm supposed to do about it).

Culture versus cultured

Culture is the whole set of ideas and beliefs shared by a group of people about their world and how they should act in that world. Your cultural ideas tell you how to greet your neighbors, what foods are suitable for certain occasions, who your friends and enemies are, and generally how you should act in the world. Cultural ideas don't ride on the genes: You don't get them by instinct. You get them from your parents, at first, and later from your peers, books, the Internet, television, and any other kind of media. Now, you may choose not to believe what you read in the paper or see on TV, and that's fine; the point is that culture comes to humanity in all kinds of media, from conversations with friends and family to what you read on the Web, hear over the radio, and so on. Culture is the spice of human life; it's what makes people different around the world.

And although this all seems obvious, it has profound implications. Every other animal life form operates by instinct, and, in some species, a little of what they learn during their lifetime. But humans learn not just what their parents know, but what their parents' parents knew, and what their neighbors and friends know, and what those parents' and neighbors' parents and neighbors knew, and so on. In this way human culture is distinctly cumulative over time. It's an ever-expanding archive. It ensures that — unless your ideas are really out of vogue — your ideas will survive you. Although other animals leave behind only skeletons, humans leave behind ideas as well.

Keep in mind that other animals — notably other primates — do survive by learning a lot from their parents. But only humans are absolutely dependent on culture to survive. You'll learn just why throughout this chapter.

Culture, then, isn't just high art, the opera, or the product of an elite education; it's simply information. A given cultural information set would *contain* the opera (by containing the definition of opera and how it's to be staged, sung, scripted, and attended), and people with elite educations may acquire more cultural information through learning (which they'll be sure to let you know), but culture itself is just information without any connotation of high-status lifestyles.

Why human behavior differs

Why isn't every human culture the same? For example, why do some cultures believe in monogamy (males having one wife,) and some in polygamy (men having several wives)? Cultures and behaviors differ for a number of reasons:

 ✔ **Ecological determinism:** Cultures directly reflect their physical environment. So cultures are tailored to the environment in which the people live. Clearly, desert peoples' culture will differ from the culture of folks who live in rain forests

Of course, no -*ism* is ever perfect. For example, many in the 19th century thought hot climates promoted sloth, which is why civilization was centered in cooler Europe. This theory conveniently ignored the fact that many of the great ancient civilizations (think Egypt, Sumer, Aztec) arose in hot regions.

✔ **Encounters with other cultures:** Another reason for cultural diversity is that groups of people move from place to place and exchange ideas when they encounter other cultures in those movements. As a result of these encounters, each culture is slightly altered.

✔ **Internal change:** Cultures can also change internally by themselves so that over time they differ from other cultures. How this change happens is the study of cultural innovation, a fascinating topic I discuss later in this chapter.

In fact, each culture is shaped by each of these factors, creating nearly endless diversity and complexity. In cultural evolution, nothing is simple.

Cultural Universals

Although the specific characteristics of any given culture are unlikely to be the same as those of another, there are some *cultural universals,* things that each culture has specific instructions for how to do appropriately (although what's considered appropriate differs per culture.) These concepts include

✔ **Communication:** Each culture has a distinctive way of speaking and a set of gestures — including body language — used to describe the world and to move all the cultural information from one generation to the next (as well as to move cultural information around among the members of a current generation).

Languages change over time, and several cultures may in fact share the same language or dialects of the same language.

✔ **Ethical/justice system:** Every culture has rules about truth-telling, killing, and stealing (even if the concept of personal property isn't as strongly developed as in other cultures) and specific ways of administering justice when ethical codes get broken.

✔ **Right and responsibility assignments by age and gender group:** All cultures have concepts of what are appropriate behaviors for people of different age ranges or *life stages* (for example, infant or adult) and different genders; generally speaking, much of this has to do with the division of labor in the culture.

Ejengi: the living forest

Among the BaAka Pygmy hunter-gatherers of the Central African rainforests is a custom known as the Ejengi dance. *Ejengi* is the BaAka name for the spirit of the rainforest. As hunter–gatherers, the BaAka depend on the rainforest during much of the year for their livelihood. Their shelter and food all comes from the forest, and more importantly, their knowledge of the forest. To survive in the rainforest, the BaAka have to know exactly where to hunt at what times of day and which times of the year. They have to know which plants are edible (and which are good medicine) and where to find them in the forest, and they need to know where the water sources are. They also must learn how to avoid dangers, such as elephants and gorillas — which are both extremely territorial and can attack intruders — and how to avoid snakes and other poisonous animals.

Because they rely so heavily on the forest for their survival, it's not surprising that they view the forest as a living entity, with the rewards of food, water, and shelter to those who know and understand the forest and the punishment of hunger, disease, and possible death for those who don't. The BaAka talk of being able to "see" Ejengi; the younger children learn how to "see" the forest spirit from their parents and older siblings by living with them in the rainforest for long periods of time. During the times of year when they're not living in the rainforest but rather in clearings near small farming villages, the BaAka and their children often have an Ejengi dance.

These dances usually take place at dusk or in the evening, are often unplanned, and occur something like this: As older boys and men begin to drum and the women lead the younger children in song and teach them to dance to the rhythm, one of the village elders slips away from the group and dons a costume made from *raffia* fibers (the bark of a vine common in Central Africa). The costume is relatively simple; the fibers from the vine have been made into many strings attached to a wide-brimmed straw hat. The fibers hang down from the brim of the hat to the feet. The costumed elder slowly dances from the edge of the forest and over to the children who squeal with delight as he twirls around and the strings fly out. The women encourage the children to get close to Ejengi as he dances around, but not to let him get close enough to grab them. The children each run up and try to touch the swirling strings, but if Ejengi starts to dance over to one of them, they run from him, laughing, and try to circle to another side of him (a relatively difficult task considering the fiber strings completely cover the face and body of the wearer, and the children can't tell his front from his back!) and touch his swirling strings again.

As part of their study of other cultures, anthropologists try to understand and explain human behavior. Is this behavior of the BaAka "just something they do?" Or is there a deeper meaning to it, something that the BaAka adults may not even be aware of? A *functionalist* anthropologist (read more on functionalism in Chapter 12) would probably say yes. In essence, functionalism holds that there is an adaptive purpose behind the behaviors and ceremonies of a culture, and somehow behavior or laws or customs help the society in question better survive in its environment. In the case of the BaAka, a functionalist interpretation of the Ejengi dance would go something like this:

The belief that the rainforest isn't so much a place or a thing but a spirit; Ejengi, that can be known like one person can get to know another, makes it easier for the BaAka children to understand that they can and need to "see Ejengi," or learn about the forest. The fact that the children are encouraged by the women to run up and get close enough to touch Ejengi, but also to run from him if he starts to chase them reinforces to the BaAka children not only the importance of their traditional forest environment but also the need to be wary of the dangers it contains.

✔ **Mythos/ideology:** Cultures have distinctive concepts of the supernatural — often ritualized in religion — as well as ideological, political, and economic positions; these distinctions are often the source of cultural friction between those who prefer innovation and those who prefer conservatism.

✔ **Bodily decoration and/or clothing:** Cultures have distinctive ways of expressing themselves by adorning the body directly (think Maori tattoos and East Indians' hennaed hands) and/or by wearing distinctive clothing (such as the robe-like clothing of the Berbers of Tunisia); "style," as people normally think of it, is usually about identity, although globalization has dampened the wearing of distinctive ethnic clothing in some areas, such as in China, where Western clothing predominates.

✔ **Family structure:** Although family structure varies widely, every culture has guidelines for what it considers a *family*, a social unit typically composed of married people, their offspring, and possibly other relatives. (You can read more about families in Chapter 15.)

✔ **Sexual regulations:** Cultures have *incest taboos* — rules against procreating with close kin — that prevent the ill effects of a small genetic pool.

✔ **Food preferences:** Cultures have distinctive concepts of what tastes good or bad and what foods are appropriate at different social functions.

Having an Out-of-Body Experience

Although identifying exactly what culture is presents problems, I can safely say that, generally speaking, cultural behavior is humanity's most important way of adapting and surviving. Humans don't rely on their bodies so much as on their behavior and tools to adapt. In this way, some have defined culture as humanity's "extrasomatic means of adaptation." This technical term basically just highlights the fact that human adaptations are mostly nonbodily, which is important to understanding humanity (and makes a great conversation starter at parties).

It's easy to think of the extrasomatic means of adaptation as just the objects made by people to survive; these objects (like a fur coat in the Arctic) are normally called *material culture*. But much more is involved. Again, culture is the *whole set* of group-specific information people acquire throughout their lives, including instructions for behavior, the definition and justification of values, and the instructions for making material objects. In the sections that follow, I explain each aspect of this group-specific information, along with the implications of adapting to this information.

Adaptation and its implications

One of the unique characteristics of humanity is that we survive and adapt to our environments culturally as well as biologically. For example, our essentially subtropical body form isn't well suited to life in the Arctic because we don't have the fur of polar bears or the thick, insulating blubber of sea mammals. But we can make fur clothing, shelters to contain warmth, and weapons with which to hunt and defend ourselves. These items are cultural adaptations and nice examples of "extrasomatic adaptation."

The extrasomatic definition of culture emphasizes evolution by highlighting how culture is used to survive the natural world; keep in mind, though, that people must also survive the cultural world they inhabit, and that's just as important. For example, if you don't greet your neighbors the right way, you may cause bad feelings; in the same way, your grandfather may not appreciate your elaborate, back-slapping handshake the same way your buddy does. So although culture does help you survive the natural world, it also tells you how to survive the cultural world of social interactions.

A focus on culture as extrasomatic adaptation has some important implications First, because culture isn't carried on the genes, it has to be passed on to the next generation socially; in societies without writing, that means myths, fables, and other aids to memory known as *oral tradition*. Also, aspects of culture that directly relate to physical survival (such as when to migrate to a certain area to pick berries or hunt a particular animal) are relatively slow to change because they're so important to survival. However, despite conservatism in some aspects, cultures can promote innovation and experimentation, and behaviors or inventions that are useful in promoting survival are often quickly adopted.

Behaviors

Think of *behavioral elements* of culture as the things you're supposed to do or not do in a given situation. For example, in many Native American societies, people just moving through adolescence go on a *spirit quest* or *vision quest* to find a spirit animal that will guide them for life. The quest involves specific instructions for where the person is to go (often into the mountains, alone) and what he's to do there (often, go without food or water, or deprive himself in some other physical way until he sees the spirit or vision).

Much of culture is about what behavior is and isn't appropriate in any given circumstance. Learning it all is a constant process. Early in life, children normally get leeway for breaking the boundaries of appropriate behavior, but among adults breaking social customs can lead to everything from souring

100 percent American

In 1936, cultural anthropologist Ralph Linton published an essay in his book *The Study of Man: An Introduction* revealing a number of aspects of all-American life that actually originated in different countries. This humorous essay pointed out how much of American identity is actually rooted in the customs of other countries.

For example, Linton pointed out, on a typical American morning "our solid American citizen" sleeps in a bed built to a Middle-Eastern pattern that was modified in Europe before being exported to America, wears sleeping clothes invented in India, and washes with a kind of soap invented in ancient France. He then eats an orange — a fruit of the eastern Mediterranean — for breakfast with maybe a slice of cantaloupe (from Persia — today called Iran), a cup of coffee (first domesticated in the Arabian peninsula), eggs from an animal first domesticated in Southeast Asia, and "thin strips of the flesh" of a pig, first domesticated in the Near East and cured by a process invented in Northern Europe.

"[H]e reads the news of the day, imprinted in characters invented by the Semites upon a material invented in China by a process invented in Germany. As he absorbs the account of foreign troubles he will, if he is a good conservative citizen, thank a Hebrew deity in an Indo-European language that he is 100 percent American."

business transactions to war. Breaking normal behavioral limits is also a common form of comedy; you can laugh when *Seinfeld* character George Costanza double-dips his chips at a party after biting from them, but you're not likely to try this practice yourself because it breaks some pretty serious social conventions about hygiene. Even if you do brush your teeth.

Values

Values are judgments of what's good, bad, and in between in a given culture linked to the culture's ethical/judicial system of ideas. In other words, they're about what is and isn't worthwhile, what is and isn't desired.

Values are often broadly divided into judgments in the moral or aesthetic fields. *Moral* judgments typically deal with justice and personal interactions. They're so basic to a culture's sense of itself that they're not the opinions of individuals but rather givens that (according to the members of a culture) don't require justification; they're often used to evaluate outsiders, which can lead to friction. Breaking moral conventions normally involves a victim and a perpetrator, and the conflict's resolution involves the cultural system of the administration of justice.

Values may be taught formally or informally, but many receive so much repetition every day, in every utterance and action of cultural members, that the values become common sense to members of the culture. However, they may not make so much sense to people from another culture, and when cultures bearing deeply held but fundamentally differing value systems come into contact, situations can get difficult.

Aesthetic judgments, such as preferences in artistic expression, are also cultural. Aesthetic judgments are endlessly varied and each has a complex history; imagine the artistic styles of Western civilization, from Greek to Postmodern visual art, for example. Social, economic, religious, and moral concerns are all involved in shaping the aesthetic ideals of a given culture at any given time.

Objects

Items made or used by humans are called *material culture*. Material culture isn't just limited to tools for physical survival. Every object, from a distinctive wedding costume to an ancient Greek clay container for transporting wine to your car or bicycle, is a cultural object.

Even seemingly mundane objects carry cultural information in their design and/or decoration. Credit cards, for example, often bear images of what cardholders value, like mountains, a cityscape, or a piece of art; these designs are cultural information that they've selected from a pool of options to say something about themselves. Even if you don't buy into this business of having fancy images on your credit card, that decision also says something about you; you may even be proud of your plain, nonconformist card (which, of course, is a statement in itself). Figure 11-1 shows a woman from Myanmar showing her cultural identity with traditional dress and ornamentation such as earplugs and necklaces.

Figure 11-1:
A Myanmar woman wearing traditional clothing and body ornamentation.

© Erol Gurian/CORBIS

Language: Passing the baton of culture

Language moves information; therefore, language is important to culture because culture is cumulative. Cultural information has grown through time, such that today humans fill libraries and archives with information they want to remember. This accumulative nature of culture has allowed for the adaptation of behavior to the environment. Every new fact allows a potentially better understanding of the world. This applies not just to current Western civilization but to all cultures worldwide across time. Of course, just because things are better understood, doesn't mean that cultures necessarily act on that understanding.

In this case, the environment means *both* the physical environment, such as the desert ecosystem inhabited by the Paiute Indians of the American Southwest, as well as the social environment, such as the interactions among ancient Polynesian chiefs and their subjects.

Over time, human culture has grown to today's massive, unmanageable size. How did cultures organize and communicate everything they needed to communicate without libraries or other means of storing information outside the body? In many societies, the answer has been "through language," often in the form of myths that represent or symbolize a culture's basic ideas and values. Traditional myths aren't just stories to be told around the hearth; they normally pass on lots of traditional knowledge. The human mind best remembers stories with a beginning, middle, and end, and the narrative structure of myths is an important aid to memory.

Storing cultural information outside the body is called *external data storage;* its invention by around 75,000 years ago (probably in Africa — you can read more about this in Chapter 7) was a major event in the history of human mind evolution. It allowed for storage of an effectively infinite amount of cultural information that would otherwise be subject to the limits of human memory.

Opening Your Human Behavior Owner's Manual

The fact that you can reduce culture (in an analytical sense) to a set of instructions for behavior has some important effects, including the ability to conceptualize and study human culture as information that's transferred from one mind to another by language. That ability is significant because, as scientists have learned more about how language, memory, and the mind work, they've gained a better understanding of how culture actually is stored in the mind, recalled by memory, and processed by language.

Culture = software, brain = hardware

Although many anthropologists don't like the following analogy for the brain and culture, I think it's effective and useful so long as you don't take it too far. I trust you not to do that. The analogy I'm talking about is that of the mind as a computer. This analogy has gotten a bad rap due to its oversimplification of both culture and the brain, but it works if you remember that it's just an analogy.

In this analogy, the brain is the hardware, roughly equivalent to your PC with a basic operating system onboard (like your hard-wired capacity for language). (You can read more about the nature of language in Chapter 12.) Culture is the software you add into your computer/brain, for example, by loading games, music, or a word processor (all legally obtained, of course).

This parallel allows the understanding of culture as a set of information in the mind of an individual. Other individuals may share much of that information, but no two are identical (just as two people may buy the same computer model but load it with different programs). This example allows you to understand the individuality of each human and avoid the stereotypical conception of a culture.

The brain is a physical object, composed of *neurons* (specialized brain cells); memory is stored as the connections between certain neurons in certain parts of the brain, and the *mind* is what the brain does, such as retrieve or archive memories and process information.

Problems with the software/ hardware analogy

The hardware/software analogy has its problems, though, so the following are a few caveats to keep in mind:

- **The brain is far more complex than any computer.** Yes, the brain is a memory storage-and-retrieval device, but the way it stores and associates memories is fantastically more complex than anyone ever suspected when people began experiments in artificial intelligence programming.

- **The mind is far more complex than any computer program.** Although some computer programs can beat humans in games, nobody has succeeded in getting a computer to really understand or compose a poem with intent or become self-aware and capable of intelligent thought.

✔ **Culture is far more complex than any computer program.** Not only that, but it's ever-changing, and although computers can simulate the movement of ideas in a culture, such simulations are crude because they can't simulate the complexities of each individual mind through which the information is filtered, interpreted, and then passed on to the next mind.

So always remember that although the analogy has some uses, you shouldn't take it too far.

Getting Your Cultural Education

Enculturation is a lifelong process during which humans are continuously loaded with cultural information. During childhood, humans pay a lot more attention to *discrete* enculturation, in which parents basically teach their children how to be functional members of the culture. The children aren't just learning how to react to situations, though: Through the very words, symbols, and myths they learn to describe their world, children also learn how to perceive and understand their world.

Some enculturation occurs formally — in Western society, people send children to school. It also happens informally as children learn what's appropriate (and what's inappropriate) behavior in a home setting. Later, as people move away and/or build their own families as adults, enculturation continues (often largely without formalities) as people continue to learn about their place in their culture. In the following sections I explain the stages of life and how people learn in each of those stages.

Life stages

Every culture has ideas of what are appropriate activities, rights, and responsibilities for each gender and age group, and all this information spreads through enculturation. Many cultures recognize at least the following stages even though the ages they represent vary from culture to culture; for example, in Iceland in the early 1900s, old age would have been in the 30s for both men and women, who died very early compared to Americans today.

✔ **Infancy:** Someone (parents, siblings, other relatives, and so on) cares for the individual.

✔ **Childhood:** The individual begins to form a distinctive personality, takes steps towards certain possible futures, and takes on more responsibilities.

- ✔ **Sexual maturity (sometimes known as "puberty"):** The individual has the potential to become a parent and learns all the attendant rules of sexual behavior.

- ✔ **Adulthood:** The individual achieves economic security, marries, and raises children (at least ideally for most cultures.)

- ✔ **Old age:** The individual may be relieved of some responsibilities (such as some physical labor) and assigned others (such as making decisions about inheritance.)

Because every member of a culture is affected by the various rights, roles, and responsibilities of their position in the stages of life, anthropologists spend a lot of time identifying just how these life stages play out.

Stages of human learning

Although each culture has its own way of bringing up children, French biologist Jean Piaget identified some cross-cultural universal stages of learning that are important for understanding enculturation.

- ✔ **The Sensory-Motor stage (birth–18 months):** The child learns motor control (which influences cultural gestures and postures later in life) as well as identifies herself as an individual.

- ✔ **The Preoperational stage (18 months–7 years):** The child acquires the functional language that describes her universe by about 3 years old. Fully developed language comes in a later stage; therefore, the child doesn't fully appreciate deep symbols such as complex metaphors at this time.

- ✔ **The Concrete operational stage (7 years–11 years):** The child acquires logical understanding of physical properties, such as numbers and weights, and the ability to step out of the self and begin to think from the perspectives of other people. Her understanding of metaphor also increases.

- ✔ **The Formal operational stage (from 11 years on):** The child acquires adult reasoning, allowing her to use and generate deeply symbolic metaphors.

Although these stages exist in all human cultures, the length of each stage varies. Still, most agree that Piaget identified the basic stages of learning in humans.

From Mop-Tops to Mötley Crüe: What Is Cultural Change?

One conclusion all anthropologists can agree on is that culture is dynamic, not static or unchanging; how else do you account for the difference in popular music between the Beatles in the 1960s and the so-called hair bands of the 1980s? Does change like this just happen? No. Few cultures live, or have lived, in total isolation, and connections of marriage or trade have long fostered the movement of ideas from one culture to another. Culture changes in several ways; most cultural anthropology textbooks discuss innovation and diffusion (which I cover in the following sections), but I also want to look at how culture evolves through time.

Diffusion versus assimilation

In anthropology, *diffusion* is the movement of cultural information from one population to another. It can happen in many ways, but migration and border diffusion are particularly important.

One way for culture to change is for migrating donors to move ideas to recipient cultures. Physical *migration* is the movement of people from one region to another. Because humans carry their culture in their brains (as sets of ideas) and sometimes in books or other external media, culture comes along for the ride when humans move. When cultures meet, ideas from one culture (the *donor*) almost invariably get transferred to the other (the *recipient*). What this really means is that people of the recipient culture begin to perceive and remember new ideas from people of the donor culture. Whether those ideas spread or are shunned (or some combination) depends on the circumstances. Of course, these cultural transactions rarely run one way; aspects of a recipient culture can rub off on a donor culture, reversing the roles and making the interaction that much more complex.

Another type of diffusion, *border diffusion,* happens when one culture borders on another and frequent interactions between the cultures promote the exchange of ideas, words, phrases, and even entire languages. This interaction and exchange process is called *acculturation*.

Assimilation, on the other hand, is the inclusion or absorption of one culture into another, more dominant, culture. However, cultural information from the minority can have important effects on the dominant culture. For example, American rock-and-roll music (which is today widespread) originated at least in part from the early 1950s subculture of traditional African American folk music.

Innovation

Innovation is the new association of ideas; it's what happens when two ideas that have never before been combined are combined to make a new idea. If social conditions are suitable and the idea is something communicable like an art or musical style, the innovation can spread and change the culture.

The key here is *social conditions.* People have to experience the innovation if they're going to imitate and spread it, and many cultures use social mechanisms such as censorship to prevent the spread of what they consider inappropriate or profane ideas. Today, an innovation is available worldwide the moment it reaches the Internet. Of course, millions (perhaps billions) of people do not have access to the Internet, and while information moves very rapidly today, it doesn't affect or reach every human population in the same way.

Cultural Evolution

So does cultural change follow any particular pattern? Does culture evolve in steps or stages, from a simple to an advanced stage? Can you apply principles of biological evolution to cultural change?

The answer is yes, but carefully. Early attempts to apply evolutionary concepts to the processes of culture change made a big mistake. At the time (the late 19th century), people thought evolution was trying to improve life forms — using some kind of intent or inner drive to strive toward the pinnacle of evolution (which was, predictably, the Victorian male Londoner). If this was the case, people reasoned, culture would do the same: Worldwide, every culture must be somewhere on a path from the simplest form (Savagery) to the most complex (Civilization). Later, anthropologists found that this wasn't the case but that each culture was on its own path, and anthropology ditched the unilineal concept of cultural evolution.

Anthropology was wise to ditch the unilineal concept of culture change, but unfortunately anthropologists also began to dismiss any concepts of cultural evolution. Culture does, indeed evolve, as I describe in the following sections.

How culture evolves

Cultural information is moved from one mind to the next like genetic information is moved from parent to offspring generations (although culture is passed on socially, not biologically). Not all the information is perfectly reproduced (or moved from mind to mind), just as genes aren't perfectly reproduced; as in genetics, mutations are introduced to the population. Cultural variations are new ideas, or innovations. Along these lines, culture has the properties of an evolving system: Information is *replicated,* but not always perfectly, so it *varies* from individual to individual. Over time, variations spread or disappear due to *selection* for certain variations and against others.

Cultural variations aren't necessarily selected for because they make sense or are beneficial to everybody; many societies are hierarchically structured so that certain people, such as royal families, do much of the selection in cultural evolution. This bias leads directly to the consideration of power relationships: Who, in a given culture, has the power to select *for* certain ideas (by promoting them in the media, for example), and who has the power to select *against* ideas (by practices like censorship)? These questions apply to Western civilization as well as ancient Egypt, the Polynesian chiefdoms of the Pacific, and everyone in between.

For many reasons, archaeologists (in particular) and some cultural anthropologists feel that these similarities between genetic and cultural information aren't just trivial but rather very real and important to study.

What cultural evolution doesn't mean

When you start thinking about the evolution of culture, keep in mind that

- Although natural selection (in the wild) has no intent and doesn't *try* to shape change through time, humans do have intent and do try to shape culture over time — typically by promoting or resisting change.

- Although biological evolution really does improve the species over time (because only useful characteristics tend to be preserved), cultural evolution doesn't necessarily phase out aspects that aren't good for everyone (think racism).

- Although biological evolution is relatively slow, only moving information (genes) in one direction (from parent to offspring), members of a culture can share cultural information (ideas) among themselves *within* a given generation, such that cultural evolution is very fast.

Chapter 12

From Kalahari to Minneapolis: How Cultural Anthropologists Work

Cultural anthropology is the study of living humans and their societies, and all societies exist in some sort of physical space. The field is the space that an anthropologist visits in order to study and interact with the culture she's studying, whether that space is in the Amazon, the Gobi desert, or downtown Chicago. In fact, one of the main ways that cultural anthropologists examine human cultures is by going into the field to experience ways of life different from those of Western civilization. (Anthropologists do study Western cultures, but this is more often the job of sociologists.)

The anthropologist does this fieldwork systematically by observing and recording every aspect of life very carefully — from calories consumed per day to drugs used to shamanic initiation rites performed. Such close observation leads to a better understanding of human life in all its variety, from the nomadic peoples of Mongolia to the foragers of the Amazon.

But cultural anthropologists don't just barge into a village and start asking questions — not if they want to be welcomed by the local people and learn anything other than native curses. (Imagine what you would say if an Australian Aborigine appeared at your doorstep one day and asked to live with you and study you to fulfill his curiosity!) Anthropologists have devised many methods that enable them to do successful fieldwork and report their findings accurately.

In this chapter, you first get a brief history of the development of anthropology. Then, you get to see how cultural anthropologists do their job and how valuable this kind of anthropology is for helping them gain a better understanding of humans everywhere.

Watching Cultural Anthropology Grow Up

Cultural anthropology has its roots in the 16th century during the Age of Discovery, a time when Europeans were discovering other continents and encountering the peoples who lived there. But the study of cultures has transformed dramatically since then, as I show you in this section.

Battling ethnocentrism

In the 16th century, Europeans referred to the people they encountered during their explorations as "Others." The Europeans knew nothing of these native people — they weren't, for example, accounted for in the Bible. Explorers often wrote detailed, vivid (and occasionally completely fictional) accounts describing how these people lived. These accounts were the only information people back in Europe had about newly discovered lands and people.

Most of the European explorers' accounts were heavily *ethnocentric,* meaning they were written from the perspective of the explorer's own society, such as explorers judging Native Americans from the Christian European perspective. Consider Figure 12-1, which shows a woodcut of Native Americans created by an artist in Europe who had never visited the Americas. It depicts the native people of what is today Paraguay. By European standards, their nakedness was shocking and taken as an indication of their supposed savagery. (For the native people, of course, the European habit of walking around heavily clothed in a hot environment was just as strange.)

SCHERVES.   Cap. 36

Figure 12-1: Image of Native Americans by 17th-century European artist Theodore de Bry.

Consider a present-day example. Say you're an American tourist visiting Bali, Indonesia, and you observe a kite festival. From your perspective — which is that kites are flown for recreation — you may conclude that the Balinese are just playing, and that it's funny to see adults doing so out in the fields. But actually the Balinese attach deep religious significance to the annual kite festival, in which the kites represent Hindu deities. The tradition holds that agricultural success depends on how well teams from each village fly their kites. Because you don't know this — and can only understand what the Balinese are doing based on what kite flying means in your own culture — your view that the kites are just toys is an ethnocentric interpretation.

Getting scientific

The flaws of ethnocentric accounts became more apparent as people started to travel more often and to interact more frequently with people from other cultures. At the same time, the value of studying other cultures became more apparent as well. As a result, in the early 20th century, anthropologists started taking some serious steps to improve the credibility of their work.

Many of the changes in the early 20th century came from a recognition that cultural anthropologists should attempt to understand other human cultures rather than judge them. This approach, called *cultural relativism,* promotes the idea that each culture should be understood in its own terms, rather than judged by outsiders. Cultural relativism is one of the cornerstones of cultural anthropology.

Another key factor in the changes that occurred in the early 20th century was the recognition that if anthropologists wanted to improve the credibility of their research results — so anthropology would be taken seriously as a discipline — their methods would have to be more scientific. That meant accomplishing several things:

✔ Defining their terms more clearly

✔ Building a comprehensive theoretical framework

✔ Developing ways of observing humanity more objectively than subjectively (that is, without making value judgments)

Defining their terms

Anthropologists began to more clearly define exactly what they meant by terms such as *marriage* or even *dance*. Because different cultures expressed these things differently, defining them in ways that all anthropologists could agree on was important in order to understand them across cultures.

But this defining process has been harder than you may expect. For example, some anthropologists are content to say that human social groups can be classified in some major types, such as *band*, or *tribe*. But others say these are more artificial constructions, things that anthropologists expect to see (because of their theoretical perspective), rather than what's actually there.

Still, a working vocabulary has been developed for cultural anthropology, allowing most cultural anthropologists to communicate. One online resource you may be interested in is oregonstate.edu/instruct/anth370/gloss.html, Oregon State University's "Definitions of Anthropological Terms" Web site.

Building a theoretical framework

By the early 20th century, many scientists used the *scientific method* to guide their research. Essentially, the scientific method says that you ask a question, do some background research, create a hypothesis based on what you believe your research into that question may show, conduct the research, and then analyze the results.

As anthropologists worked to improve the credibility of their studies, they started to adopt (and adapt) the scientific method. The result was that they didn't just haphazardly collect information about a culture by writing down observations about whatever happened to look most interesting. Instead, they would start with a topic of interest — for example, how Maori (native New Zealander) dance was used to remind Maoris of their ancestry and cultural traditions — and then make observations specifically about that topic of interest.

Some cultural anthropologists began to make *cross-cultural* studies in which a theory was tested by seeing whether or not it accounted for cultural behavior around the world. For example, many anthropologists knew that an *incest taboo* (a prohibition against sexual relationships among close blood relatives) seemed to be present in all human societies. To be sure, anthropologist George Murdock first defined incest and then looked at anthropological literature on 250 societies worldwide to see whether it really was universal. It was, provided that incest was defined as sexual relationships between people within a *nuclear family*, a married couple cohabiting with children. In this way, Murdock was asking a question (in other words, defining a research problem), making his terminology clear, and then doing a large-scale study to answer the basic question — is the incest taboo universal in human culture?

Using a *theoretical framework* (a specific set of definitions and ideas that guide thinking about a particular question) to guide their research has certainly helped anthropologists up their game. But keep two key issues in mind:

- ✔ An anthropologist must be honest and forthright about his theoretical stance before going into the field. This ensures that the reader of the anthropologist's work can see where the anthropologist is coming from — for example, if he or she sees the world through a particularly feminist lens — and be on the lookout for potential bias caused by that stance.

- ✔ Carrying too much theory into the field can lead to distortions, such that the anthropologist's findings conveniently confirm his favorite theory; so although anthropologists tend to have ideas about what human culture is like in the first place, they try to keep their minds open to new possibilities and interpretations.

Promoting objectivity: Etic research

In the attempt to steer clear of ethnocentrism, anthropologists began to use a certain approach to field studies: the *etic* approach. It basically entails an anthropologist observing another society without really interacting with the people, focusing instead on how the anthropologist sees the culture he's studying in a kind of detached way. Some say this is a good idea, but others argue that it ignores the reality of the culture itself and that an etic approach is simply invalid. The jury is still out on this issue.

The Golden Bough: Armchair anthropology

Perhaps the best known "armchair scholar" of early cultural anthropology was Englishman Sir James Frazer, who in 1890 published *The Golden Bough,* a work that encompassed much of what was known at the time about different cultures across the world, discussing various religions in terms of cultural (as opposed to theological) roots. Frazer hoped that he could uncover universal truths about human psychology through studies of human societies across the globe. He never undertook any of his own field research but relied on written reports and the stories and descriptions of others who had spent time overseas with different peoples.

Embodying the etic modernist approach: Bronislaw Malinowski

The changes that occurred in the early 20th century led to what anthropologists now call *modernist* cultural anthropology — characterized by a scientific, systematic approach to the understanding of human diversity. This type of anthropology is perhaps best exemplified by Bronislaw Malinowski, who did fieldwork from about 1914 to 1918 among the Trobriand Islanders of Melanesia, an island northeast of Australia.

Raising the bar for ethnographies

An Austro-Hungarian citizen living in Australia at the start of World War I, Malinowski was exiled to the Trobriand Islands for the duration of the war because of fears that he harbored sympathies for the Germans. Sustained by a regular food drop, Malinowski spent some time pouting and counting the days.

But he also authored what many regard as the first modernist *ethnography* — or written description of a culture — *Argonauts of the Western Pacific*. This widely acclaimed work established a standard both for the performance of anthropological fieldwork and the writing of ethnographies. In this book and his subsequent teachings, Malinowski stressed that the anthropologist must be objective and scientific — in other words, somewhat etic.

Setting the standards of study

To achieve objectivity, Malinowski called for anthropologists to make direct and systematic observations of the people they studied. For example, rather than just recording what you happened to observe, you would go from one house to the next asking each person the same question and documenting the various responses.

Malinowski also recommended what he called a "natural period of time" for the observations, usually at least a calendar year so that the society's activities during all seasons could be observed.

Focusing on how cultures function

Malinowski became associated with *functionalism*. Functionalism also holds that just about every aspect of a culture—from its ceremonies to its myths and religion— has an adaptive purpose and that somehow a society's general behavior, laws, and customs help the culture to better survive in its environment. For an example of a functionalist interpretation of a dance in African society, see Chapter 11.

Setting the stage for structuralism

Following on the heels of Malinowski was Claude Levi-Strauss, a French anthropologist born in 1908 who was also significant in developing modern cultural anthropology (and no, he's not the Levi Strauss of blue jeans fame). Levi-Strauss founded the school of thought called *structuralism*, which basically holds that human societies are structured by basic concepts that are expressed in every symbol, myth, ritual, and so on. These structures often amount to oppositions of general cultural concepts like raw-versus-cooked, hot-versus-cold, and male-versus-female. Furthermore, Levi-Strauss proposed that some "Universal Structures of the Mind" exist cross-culturally. (The jury is still out on that one.)

Unlike Malinowski, Levi-Strauss was far more theoretical than grounded in field observation, basing most of his theories on a year that he spent in the Brazilian Amazon.

Wading through jargon

Every scientific discipline uses its own terminology to communicate complex and esoteric ideas within the discipline. To an outsider, a conversation between experts can be incomprehensible; even the subject of the conversation may be a complete mystery.

An unfortunate byproduct of early anthropology's desire to be regarded as an objective science was that it began to use unnecessarily complicated jargon and expressions. As anthropologist Edmond Leach wrote about Claude Levi-Strauss's works, "The outstanding characteristic of his writing, whether in French or English, is that it is difficult to understand; his sociological theories combine baffling complexity with overwhelming erudition. Some readers even suspect that they are being treated to a confidence trick."

Obviously, any conversation or writing between anthropologists will use terms and concepts specific to anthropology, but many anthropologists feel that they're doing a greater service for society if their works are more accessible to the average reader.

A More Personal Approach: Emic Research

Although injecting a healthy dose of objectivity into their work helped anthropologists join the ranks of respected scientists, not everyone was satisfied with the hands-off, *etic* approach to researching another culture (see the earlier section "Promoting objectivity: Etic research"). Many researchers in the field felt that the etic approach was too cold and distant and, therefore, couldn't produce an intimate understanding of human cultures. The best way to understand a culture, some anthropologists suggested (if not insisted), was to walk a mile in the shoes of the people being studied (the *subjects*). From this idea came the concept of the *participant–observer*, who would use what anthropologists call the *emic* approach to research.

The participant–observer studies a particular people by living among them, working with them, and interacting with them in most aspects of their daily lives. By participating in the daily activities of the subject people this way, anthropologists learn a lot about the lives and social structures of human cultures around the world firsthand.

But, of course, the question of objectivity arises again with this type of research. The anthropologist's presence can alter the behaviors of the subjects, and the researcher may simply have a tougher time recording information without bias in this situation. I discuss the challenges of the emic approach to research in the following sections.

Recognizing how a researcher's choices influence the results

Recently, anthropologists have generally accepted that any *ethnography* (written description of a culture) is really as much about the person writing it as it is about the culture being studied. For example, if you and a friend spent a week in France doing the same things at the same time with the same people, your account of your trip would differ from that of your friend. Sure, the descriptions of the places and people would be generally similar, but the two of you would each have perceived a person or place differently or concentrated on different facets of a particular experience.

Of course, in an ethnography you really have to get down to details; the descriptions of people, places, and events need to be much more in-depth than in a travel journal. So any anthropologist worth his salt will gather information from multiple sources and not rely simply on a single observation.

But who the anthropologist chooses to observe and get information from impacts the outcome when he's studying a complex society. No matter how objective he tries to be, he has to make choices about which *informants* (people within the culture who share information about it with the anthropologist) to use, and those choices determine the outcome of the research.

Consider the example of a traffic court in the United States. Many people fill the courtroom: defendants, lawyers, bailiffs, police officers, witnesses, and the jury. Each has a different view of the case. The defendant is probably nervous, the bailiffs and police may be bored, the lawyers have a great stake in the outcome of the proceedings, and members of the jury (although all in the courtroom for the same reason) each have different impressions of the proceedings.

An outsider unfamiliar with how a U.S. court works — say, a New Guinea highlander studying American culture — may choose the defendant as the informant and get the defendant's perspective, which may be very different than that of one of the jurors. And if the New Guinea highlander enters the courtroom to study the proceedings in full ceremonial dress, you can imagine that the behavior of the whole courtroom will change; people may become more cordial than normal, for example, so as to give a good impression.

The same idea applies to picking informants in cultural anthropology. Just one person, carelessly chosen, won't do. Anthropologists need to learn from lots of people from across the spectrum of the culture — and understand that their choices will determine how the research unfolds.

Realizing that the act of observing affects the results

We also have to consider what effect the act of observing has on the people being observed. Some observations in science are *passive*, meaning that they have no impact on the subject being observed; photographing the planet Mars, for example, doesn't affect its geology or its atmosphere. But in anthropology, the participant–observer lives among the people she's studying, and her mere presence changes the behavior of the members of the culture in question, at least initially.

Individuals and even groups change their behavior when being observed by an outsider, even if they're unaware of it. For example, subjects may become self-conscious and avoid the anthropologist or hide ceremonies or rituals they don't want the anthropologist to see. They may also change their normal clothing, work, recreation, and dietary habits in an attempt to show the anthropologist what they think she wants to see.

Cultural critique, Margaret Mead, and the importance of good writing

Many modern anthropologists believe that the real promise of cultural anthropology is to serve as a critique of current society and suggest ways people can improve their own lives. To do this, an anthropologist departs Western society and lives among a non-Western society for some extended period of time. On returning to the West, the anthropologist is accustomed to seeing the world in the way of the people he has just been living with, and is in a position to look at his own society from a new perspective. The anthropologist can point out aspects of his society that others living in it take for granted.

In the mid-1900s, it became somewhat popular for cultural anthropologists to write two different reports or *paired works* about the culture they had studied: a traditional academic study, and a more free-flowing, descriptive text written almost like a novel. The rationale was that although the academic text was necessary, only a deeply personal account of the time spent among the host society could completely convey the fullness of the experience.

Some good examples of paired works are David Mayberry-Lewis's *Akwe-Shavante Society* and *Savage and the Innocent,* Paul Rabinow's *Symbolic Domination* and *Reflections of Fieldwork in Morocco,* and Napoleon Chagnon's *Studying the Yanomamo* and *Yanomamo: The Fierce People.*

In the early 20th century, American anthropologist Margaret Mead picked up on this tradition of writing for the general public by drawing parallels and contrasts between the societies she studied and her own. In one of her better-known works, *Coming of Age in Samoa,* Meade offered a detailed explanation of how boys and girls in traditional Samoan society transition from childhood into adulthood and ultimately choose their spouses. She also compared and contrasted how children make this transition in Samoan and American societies. By doing this, she helped make anthropology more relevant to the average American.

Mead wrote *Coming of Age in Samoa* in simple and engaging terms for a wide audience. This doesn't mean that she wasn't as serious about anthropology as other scholars; a generation of anthropologists emulated her methods of both careful observation and notetaking. But by relating her understanding of a different culture to the American public at large (and not simply other academics), Mead captured the interest of many Americans and other Westerners who otherwise wouldn't have known or cared anything about Samoan society (or anthropology in general).

The only real cures for the disruptive presence of the anthropologist are the passage of time and establishing a rapport. To observe the most natural behaviors of a culture, you have to wait until they become comfortable with your presence. This adjustment period is one reason why short field programs just don't work; settling into a routine can take months. The anthropologist has to become part of the background as the subjects settle into their *normal* routine, which is what anthropologists want to observe.

Considering Recent Developments

Although many of the research methods still used by cultural anthropologists emerged in the early 20th century, the science certainly hasn't stood still since then. In the following sections, I discuss how postmodern theory and increased cultural interaction have influenced anthropology.

Chewing on postmodernism

In the late 1980s, anthropology's postmodern movement sought to find a better way of conducting fieldwork and writing up the results. This movement almost completely rejected the etic approach and essentially said that because all knowledge is socially constructed — because all people are a product of their own, ethnocentric culture — nothing is really "real." For the postmodernists, everything anthropology had ever learned was just a reflection of the times, a social construction. For example, early anthropologists "discovered" several main races of humanity *because they were looking* for those race designations to justify 19th-century political activities such as colonialism. Colonial domination sure sounds a lot nobler if you frame it in the context of civilizing the supposedly savage native races.

Postmodernism was founded on the writings of several 20th century French philosophers, notably social critic Michel Foucault and deconstructionist Jacques Derrida. Although some anthropologists continue to explore these philosophies in hopes of establishing a new framework for anthropology, most continue to conduct traditional, modernist fieldwork. Basically, postmodernism has turned out to be just too wide a swing of the pendulum away from the etic approach; it's hyper-emic — it's too much. Clearly, anthropological questions *could* be strongly conditioned by the times — and anthropologists do have to be careful about that — but anthropologists can recognize and adjust for that tendency and still actually learn something about the world.

Keeping pace with cultural change

The world is rapidly changing and growing smaller as communications and ease of transport bring more people closer together every day. As this interaction happens, cultures change one another; in fact, today many cultures studied by early anthropologists have vanished, diluted by the globalization of Western civilization. (You can read more about cultural change in Chapter 11.) The days of *first contact,* when a Western anthropologist encountered a society that had never even heard of Western society, are most likely over.

Today, wary of grand, sweeping explanations of human behavior that haven't worked out so well in the past, many anthropologists focus their investigations on specific facets of culture, such as dance, food preparation, mythology, and so on. Ethnography today uses both etic and emic approaches, often to test a particular theory or hypothesis through collection of observable data. At the same time, many have recognized that being completely objective is impossible, so many years of schooling prepare the fieldworker not to be overly ethnocentric.

Striving for Accuracy

With all the challenges involved in observing natural behaviors and getting an accurate idea of a people's culture, how can cultural anthropologists be sure they're getting any accurate information at all?

Well, they start by asking good questions. Then they learn as much as humanly possible about the culture in question, including the native language, before going into the field. Being aware of the problems that may come up — perhaps learned from prior anthropologists — is a good start. And being a great observer is one of the cultural anthropologist's greatest assets.

Although I can't give you an A to Z education on how to become a cultural anthropologist, I can at least introduce you to some common issues these scientists face and ways to address them. That's what the following sections are all about.

Recognizing potential research pitfalls

No matter how well trained anthropologists may be in observation or how long they've spent with a particular people, certain variables can impede or complicate the relationships between anthropologists and the people they're studying. Some of the major variables that every anthropologist must contend with are discussed in the following sections.

Individual versus group dynamics

Answers to sensitive questions can change depending on whether the anthropologist is talking to an individual or a group. Personal or political dynamics between members of the same society when they're speaking with a stranger (the anthropologist) can affect their answers, especially if the questions are sensitive. For example, a young Samoan male may claim to have had more sexual relationships than he has in order to impress peers. In Arabic culture, exaggerations and distortions of the truth are common when speaking privately and less likely in public, so group size can make a big difference when it comes to the accuracy of answers. In general, people in groups may tend to seek a consensus from the others instead of answering truthfully.

Truth versus lies

Anthropologists can be lied to just as easily as anyone else. The subjects aren't necessarily being malicious — informants may simply enjoy the anthropologist's company and attention or the special status they receive in dealing with the foreigner. For these and other reasons, informants may just tell the anthropologist what they think she wants to hear in hopes of staying in her favor. That's why crosschecking information through other informants and with direct observation is important.

Time and space

Variables of time and space may be the hardest to reconcile. Cultures may have distinct variation in group behavior over geographical space. For example, an anthropologist studying the culture of Oregon would have to consider the major political and economic differences between residents of urban, wealthy, mostly liberal Portland, and residents of rural, less wealthy, mostly conservative Pendleton — and that's no small task. So it's very important for the anthropologist to document exactly where he conducted a particular study.

The same goes for time; every culture on Earth changes with the passage of time. (Check out Chapter 11 for more on cultural change.) The Trobriand Islands today aren't what they were in Malinowski's time, and undoubtedly many elements of that society have changed a lot. In the same way, many American restaurants are now found almost worldwide. Some of the most significant changes in non-Western societies occur as their contact with and *assimilation* (cultural absorption) into Western societies increases. With the spread of rapid communication and transport, contact with the West is becoming almost unavoidable. Unfortunately, some parts of the world have seen the disappearance of entire non-Western cultures. (You can read more about the problem of disappearing traditional languages in Chapter 18.)

Motivations (self and informant)

Lastly, the motivations of the anthropologist and his informants have to be considered. The anthropologist is presumably confident of his objectivity and research design, but it's easy to fall victim to *confirmation bias*, the phenomenon by which everything observed conveniently confirms what you already believe. Cultural anthropologists have to be very aware of themselves and what they're thinking because they're as subject to the influence of preconceived notions as anyone else.

The motivations of cultural informants also have to be considered. Traditionally, informants were paid for answering questions, but of course this doesn't ensure correct or honest answers and turns the anthropologist-informant relationship in a businesslike rather than friendly direction. A more emic approach helps the anthropologist get closer to the informant by participating in the events and activities of the subject people's daily lives, and perhaps paying for information in ways other than simple cash exchange. Malinowski paid his informants in tobacco, but he noted that they only seemed to be interested in answering his questions when they wanted a fresh tobacco supply.

Watching cultural anthropology in action

Anthropologists do fascinating work that helps them better understand humanity despite all the difficulties I outline in this chapter. Of course, nobody's perfect, and mistakes happen, but anthropologists do their best to understand humanity in spite of these setbacks.

Today, anthropologists often do their best to work in the interest of the cultural groups they're studying because so many traditional cultures are on the verge of complete assimilation into Western civilization. This work occurs in a variety of contexts worldwide. The following sections show two examples of cultural anthropology success stories.

The Kalahari

One well-known anthropologist who has worked among a society very distinct from Western civilization is Richard Lee, who is famous for his work among the !Kung of the Kalahari desert. (Once known as "Bushmen," the !Kung, today, are also known as the Nyae Nyae or the Jo-hoansi, pronounced *zhu-wahnsi*.) The *!* symbol in the !Kung language is a click sound made with the tongue.

Having spent many seasons with these foragers of South Africa, Lee has written extensively on every aspect of !Kung life: geography, subsistence, kinship, politics, conflict resolution, mythology, material culture, and on and on. These outward observations have led him to an intimate understanding of their religion, worldview, and perceptions of social change.

One of Lee's surprising findings was that, contrary to common belief, the !Kung had to work hard to prevent anyone from trying to get too much power in the small band. For a long time, anthropologists thought that the human species was inherently *egalitarian*, meaning that all people would have equal status and access to resources. But when Lee tried, one evening in the late 1960s, to give the !Kung a fat cow as a present, they shunned the gift and asked him to get the flea-bitten bag of bones out of their camp. After much pleading, Lee finally persuaded the !Kung to accept the gift. Lee had discovered that although the !Kung were basically egalitarian, they had to work at it; they had social mechanisms, in this case ridicule, to prevent anyone in the group from trying to become, essentially, a big shot. This was a fascinating discovery for anthropology.

Minneapolis

Cultural anthropology isn't limited to non-Western culture. Anthropologists have found that American culture can serve as a mirror for humankind. Take, for example, James Spradley and Brenda Mann's study of the subculture of cocktail waitressing in the mid-1970s.

Using the same methods of observation as they would have if they'd been studying a non-Western society, Mann and Spradley selected a subject area (a bar). Mann adopted an emic, participant–observer approach and actually began to work as a cocktail waitress, while Spradley observed etically. Among their observations were how this subculture classified its members:

- **Employees:** Lowly ranked in relation to the highly ranked bartenders
- **Customers:** Classified either as *regulars* (the highest rank), *people off the street,* or *female* (the lowest rank)
- **Managers:** Bar owners, who were often also bartenders

Mann and Spradley recorded their observations and published the results as an ethnography covering traditional ethnographic topics such as social structure, division of labor, and concepts of territory among the cocktail bar scene. The book, though unconventional at the time, provided a good illustration of the social dynamics between the sexes in a common American institution (the cocktail bar) and shed some light on gender relations in contemporary American society.

Going into the Field: Getting Prepared for Less-Than-Ideal Conditions

The far-flung and exotic corners of the world are no longer the only acceptable places to conduct anthropological studies. Especially since the dawn of the postmodern era (see the "Chewing on postmodernism" section earlier in this chapter), anthropologists have showed up just about everywhere. What identifies them as anthropologists is that regardless of their subject and any theory they may be testing, they're going into the field (whether it's the

Kalahari or Minneapolis) to make observations about people in that field, and they draw conclusions about some facet of the human experience based on those observations.

Still, many anthropologists do voyage to places far off the beaten path, and they have to be ready for a variety of circumstances before going out to do their fieldwork. This isn't just travel advice — many cultural anthropological projects have gone wrong because researchers have arrived in the study area completely unprepared for the conditions.

In the heyday of modernist cultural anthropology, nobody aspiring to a career as an anthropologist dared to think that they could get away without doing fieldwork in some extremely inhospitable part of the world. Fieldwork was considered an important rite of passage in the field of anthropology, and if the professors had suffered months of tribulations in steaming jungles, arid highlands, or other difficult conditions, so would the graduate students.

Even today — much as in the time of Malinowski — many areas in the developing world are still hard to reach and have very limited facilities of the kind that Westerners often take for granted. In many cases, luxuries such as telephones, toilets, and showers — and even necessities such as drinking water — can range from hard-to-find to nonexistent. Anthropologists who choose to work in these conditions have to be prepared for long periods spent away from the comforts of home.

Ready access to medical treatment is often limited if it's available at all, and disease can be common, so some provision must be made for medical evacuation. (Global communications systems such as satellite telephones make this escape much more likely than even five years ago.) Specialists in infectious diseases should be contacted before setting out because in the world of tropical diseases an ounce of prevention really is worth a pound of cure.

Communications must also be considered. How will the anthropologist stay in touch with the folks back home? Mail service may be unreliable, and although Internet access is increasingly available in more places around the world, it's still not a given.

Chapter 13

Can We Talk? Communication, Symbols, and Language

● ●

In This Chapter

▶ Looking at ways human and non-human animal communication differ

▶ Understanding the difference between shallow and deep symbols

▶ Reviewing the main characteristics of human language and its acquisition

▶ Considering theories on how language first evolved

● ●

*A*ll animals communicate using a variety of methods to exchange information. Strictly speaking, anything that one entity does that conveys
a message to some other entity is communication. Bees signal the location
of resources by dancing in their hives, gorillas stick out their tongues, grunt,
and beat their chests to intimidate intruders, whales call to one another
across vast distances, and humans talk . . . and talk, and talk. All around the
world, information moves from one living thing to another every second of
every day.

Of all these communication methods, human communication — typified
by speaking — is unique in many ways. Human language is especially fast,
accurate, and subtle, and can address many listeners at a time (billions with
global communications). Infants acquire language piece by piece in basically
the same way worldwide, regardless of the culture they're born into. In the
human linguistic system of communication, a single word can be used to
mean many things or to increase the power of a statement.

Of all the kinds of animal communication, human language has the greatest
potential for creating innovations. Human sounds assembled into words,
phrases, and sentences don't have one stand-alone meaning; they can be
combined with other words to build unique new messages. Our language is
ever evolving and has essentially infinite potential for creating and communicating new meaning.

Because human language is a unique characteristic of our species, here's a full chapter about it. In it I discuss what language is, how it differs so much from the communication methods of other non-human animals, how it's used and learned, and how anthropology approaches this fascinating facet of being human.

Exploring the Complexity of Human Language

Human language, strictly speaking, is a system of communication using defined units combined in a systematic way. That is, any culture's spoken language is a set of sounds assembled according to a set of rules so that all who understand the rules and can hear the assemblages of sounds can understand what's being said.

Messages are created in the mind of one person, converted to sounds assembled in a comprehensible order, spoken, heard, and then interpreted by other people. Each stage involves the potential for miscommunication and misinterpretation; in some ways, the fact that human language works at all is amazing! Here I'm largely talking about human speech, but keep in mind that this topic includes body language, symbolic postures, tone and volume of voice, and other facets of human language.

Speech refers to the use of certain anatomy to make the sounds used in human vocal communication, whereas *language* can refer to that speech as well as to body language (gesture) and writing. In this chapter I'm mainly using "language" to refer to human vocal communication. The important thing to remember is that "speech" is about anatomy whereas "language" is about cognitive rules.

In this section, I provide some context that sheds light on the phenomenally complex and subtle form of animal communication that is human language. I begin by explaining how non-human animals communicate and the importance of symbolism before showing the main characteristics of our amazing language and how it helps to shape the human mind.

Screeching and howling: Non-human animal communications

To get a true picture of what makes human communication unique, you need to understand how other animals communicate.

Humans *are* animals. It's easy to fall into the old human habit of drawing a line between our species and all others, but to be accurate we need to refer not just to "animals" but "non-human animals."

Chemical

Pheromones are chemicals emitted by an animal to communicate with others, and they're the most important communications in the non-human animal world. They include chemical *trails*, which are used by ants, for example, to indicate the direction to a food source and can also be blocked by other pheremones to indicate a dead-end trail. *Sex pheremones* indicate readiness for mating. The systematic study of pheremones is only a few decades old and still holds plenty of mysteries to be solved; for example, why is it that female Asian elephants emit the same sex pheromone as more than 100 species of moth? Finally, many animals also use scent to mark their territories.

Visual

Visual communication occurs among animals with eyes or other light-sensing organs. It involves many variables, including the nature of the light source, the background against which the body of the signaler is set (for example, an off-white polar bear against a white, snowy background), the signaler's intent, and the receiver's interpretation of the signal.

Visual communications relay messages about aggression, sexual receptivity, or territoriality. They can be combined with audio signals, although generally speaking, visual signals are used across shorter distances than audio signals and some chemical signals. They're particularly important among the primates, in which facial expressions, gestures, and bodily postures are very important. (See Chapter 4 for more on primate behavior.)

Gesture

Gesture, or visible physical action used in communications (also known as *body language*), is an important part of human language. Many researchers have suggested that bodily "speech" using mimes and bodily postures was the precursor to vocal speech. Recently, psychologist Merlin Donald has gone so far as to say that mimes and gestures certainly evolved first, and that speech, though important, evolved simply as a subset of gesture — a more efficient way to communicate but nothing more than an elaboration on gesture.

Whatever the case, humans still use gesture in their communication today. Gestures can increase the specificity of a description, "hold" a concept in mind as you search for just the right words to describe it, and increase the accuracy of instructions you're giving. Of course, you can also use them to add emphasis or to spice up communication with comedy, insult, irony — the possibilities are limitless.

Audio

Audible communications include a wide array of sounds — mostly *vocalizations,* in which the lungs move air through the mouth or beak to produce sound (as in dogs and birds, respectively). Audible communications also include the rattlesnake's rattle, whale-song, insect sounds made by rubbing the wings and legs, and many others. Audio communications are effective over longer distances than visual signals — African elephants can identify other individual elephants up to more than a mile away based on vocalizations — and are common in environments that impair clear fields of vision, such as heavy jungle foliage.

Among audio communications, of course, is humanity's spoken language. It can also be combined with visual cues such as body language. But aside from falling under the same broad category as barking and insect sounds, our language has fairly little in common with non-human animal communications. The following section begins to explain why.

Contrasting non-human and human symbolism

Understanding just how different human and non-human symbols are is critical to understanding humanity. A *symbol* is something that represents something else. Many non-human animals have some kind of symboling system, but most are very simple compared to human symbols.

A red stop sign, for instance, displays the word *STOP*, but even without the word, you'd slow down if you saw the red octagon. You know that in this context the color red and the octagonal shape means you have to stop. Now, the octagonal shape and the color red have nothing to do with stopping or going. Red may indicate danger, but the octagonal shape is completely random. And yet you know immediately the message the sign is conveying because culturally, that sign represents the idea that you must stop your vehicle.

Symbols, then, are (or can be) entirely arbitrary. They refer the mind to something other than what they are. Other examples just use words: The letters *C-A-T* convey "cat" to English-speakers, but they don't have any cat-like qualities; they're also completely arbitrary, and in fact its constituents, the letters *c, a,* and *t,* can be rearranged to have a completely different meaning, for example, as *A-C-T.* Again, neither "cat" nor "act" has anything to do with the things it represents or symbolizes.

So, what's the significance that symbols are arbitrary? Well, that depends on just how arbitrary they are. In the case of shallow symbols, it's important to the life of the animal, but not as important as when the symbol is deep. The following sections describe these kinds of symbolism in more detail.

Shallow (non-human) symbolism

Many animals use audio signals to indicate danger, for example, or safety from danger, or to call their fellows (scientifically called *conspecifics*) over to a food source.

Compared to human symbols, which I describe in the next section, these symbols are relatively shallow; a monkey's aerial predator alarm screech, for example, is *only* used to mean aerial predator. It doesn't indicate, for example, "aerial-predator-like" qualities in some other monkey. I call it a *shallow* symbol because it lacks depth or even potential depth. The concept is closed rather than open. The fact that these symbols are shallow has several important ramifications:

- ✔ Messages are typically short in duration.
- ✔ Messages are relatively simple.
- ✔ Messages are essentially literal, with no multiple meanings.
- ✔ Messages are rigid and offer little symbolic innovation.

The shallow symbols used by many animals are very effective for them; they work well for the kind of lives that those animals lead. But human symbols are fundamentally different, and it's important to see how.

Deep (human) symbolism

Deep symbols can mean many different things (rather than the single meaning attached to shallow symbols). What do you think of when you read the words "to be, or not to be" or even the single word "revolution"? These words can mean different things to different people, so depending on what you've read, how you reacted to it, your own personal history and knowledge, and so on, your reaction to the phrase will probably differ from that of many other people. This makes metaphor and deep symbolism a key part of one of humanity's most important characteristics: *individuality*, or the fact that humans aren't interchangeable automatons but rather individual beings with unique identities. You can read more about this fascinating characteristic of our species in Chapter 15.

The power of deep symbols lies in their ability to trigger so many other ideas. The human capacity for limitless metaphor allows for infinite variation of ideas in the human mind. Humans often rely on figures of speech rather than more literal explanations to get their points across. You may say "That's the way the cookie crumbles," resigning yourself to some fate you can't control, and your friends know just what you mean without thinking you're talking about an actual cookie.

The origins of ritual and religion?

The use of metaphor and deep symbols does so much to promote individuality that the late anthropologist Roy Rappaport believed that ritual and religion were essentially invented in order to reduce the potential for disorder (that is, nonuniformity) that human language presents.

Rappaport wrote that ritual and religion establish rigidity, not fluidity, of thought. They use sharp definitions of things, rather than blurry, to channel thought in a particular direction, and those definitions (because of their sacredness) aren't allowed to be questioned, further dampening individual thought. They use ceremonies, where people are expected to be quiet, to remind people of their unity and shared concepts (called Ultimate Sacred Postulates) rather than promoting the individual, "messy" thinking that's almost inevitable when people converse freely.

Keep in mind that Rappaport wasn't trying to bash religion. He was presenting an anthropological explanation for its roots, connected, in his way of thinking, to the evolution of language.

Don't get your figures of speech mixed up. A *simile* uses the words *like* or *as* to compare things: "Writing this book is like herding cats." A *metaphor* is a comparison in which you claim one thing is another ("all the world's a stage") or has characteristics of another ("the walls have ears").

The characteristics of the objects compared in a metaphor can be pretty vaguely similar, and if they're not similar enough, the metaphor can fail. But most humans are very good at using metaphors to more accurately convey a message. The title of Ursula K. Le Guin's 1998 book on writing, *Steering the Craft*, nicely conveys what she means to teach you: how to guide the art (craft) of writing as though you were steering a water vessel (craft).

I can't overemphasize the significance of metaphor as a communication tool. One of the most fascinating aspects of metaphors is that they're not made more effective by *restricting* what they mean; you don't reduce them down but rather open them up. You blur the edges of a concept until it becomes a metaphor. For example, I could say "I'm on thin ice" if I'm in a dangerous situation, but I don't really have to be on ice; I could be facing a difficult exam (well, not anymore, thankfully) or something else ominous. The meaning of "thin ice" has blurred such that it can convey the *essence* of something else; ice is no longer just an insubstantial layer of frozen water. The symbol system is open.

Identifying characteristics of human spoken language

This chapter is largely about spoken language because speech undoubtedly evolved before written language and because even today many people don't write or read but do speak and comprehend spoken language. Writing, which you can read about in Chapter 10, is typically associated with the social organization called civilization, and first appears around 6,000 years ago.

The following are the characteristics that make human spoken language distinct:

✔ **Only our anatomy will do.** Spoken human language requires the coordination of many anatomical structures to succeed: The lungs force air through the larynx and then through the mouth and nose, the tongue presses on the roof of the mouth, the vocal cords vibrate, and the lips shape carefully depending on the desired sound. Figure 13-1 shows some of this anatomy.

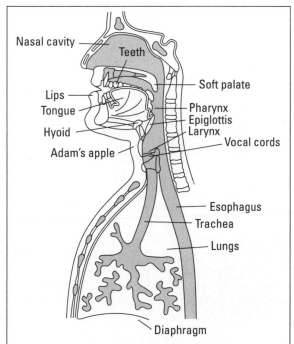

Figure 13-1:
Diagram
of human
language
anatomy.

Nasal cavity
Teeth
Lips
Tongue
Hyoid
Adam's apple
Soft palate
Pharynx
Epiglottis
Larynx
Vocal cords
Esophagus
Trachea
Lungs
Diaphragm

Although chimpanzees and gorillas possess some anatomical similarities to humans that allow them to make some human-like sounds, they don't make all our sounds.

- **It follows complex rules (otherwise known as *grammar*).** Even more important to human language than making complex sounds is the cognitive ability to use complex rules — grammar — to assemble and decode messages. (After all, people who can't talk or hear spoken language can convey complex thoughts with sign language.) This capacity is far beyond that of even the brightest non-human primates who have been taught various forms of sign language in laboratory settings. The same goes for parrots; they mimic human sounds and may use some very simple rules, but they don't use complex syntax or grammar to assemble unique new phrases.

- **It's learned, not genetic.** The capacity to learn language seems to be hard-wired, or instinctual, in humans; any infant placed in a cultural setting quickly observes people using language and begins to learn it. (You can read more about language acquisition later in this chapter.) But the actual information the infant has about language is all learned, not transmitted genetically as instinct.

You can think of the physical brain as hardware and language as software, but don't take the brain-hardware/language-software analogy too far. The mind and language are far more complex than any machines or computer programs ever devised.

- **It's voluntary, not automatic.** Although you may yelp (or curse) if startled, you're often able to stifle such impulses — many other animals can't. And you can choose to begin assembling complex statements at any time (even though you may self-censor, for whatever reason); this voluntary self-activation is pretty uniquely human.

- **Abstraction is allowed.** Because of its symbolic nature, human language allows you to speak about things that aren't necessarily present at the moment. For example, you can talk about past, future, and even hypothetical events without any time constraints. This practice is called *displacement*, and it's important because it allows a degree of abstract thought (that is, *may be* versus *actually is*).

- **It allows for invention.** As I explain in the earlier section "Non-human and human symbolism," other animal communication systems are largely closed in that one signal (for example, a squawk) can only mean one thing. But one signal in human language (such as the word *pool*) can mean many things. In this way, human language is an open system that allows the invention of new words, new meanings, and new combinations of words.

Mark Twain on "The Awful German Language"

Understanding what someone is saying can be humorous, but so can *not* understanding it. In 1880, American writer Mark Twain published his travel classic *A Tramp Abroad* and in Appendix D wrote the following about his frustration with German grammar:

"Surely there is not another language that is so slipshod and systemless, and so slippery and elusive to the grasp. One is washed about in it, hither and thither, in the most helpless way; and when at last he thinks he has captured a rule which offers firm ground to take a rest on amid the general rage and turmoil of the ten parts of speech, he turns over the page and reads, 'Let the pupil make careful note of the following exceptions.' He runs his eye down and finds that there are more exceptions to the rule than instances of it. . . . German books are easy enough to read when you hold them before the looking-glass or stand on your head — so as to reverse the construction — but I think that to learn to read and understand a German newspaper is a thing which must always remain an impossibility to a foreigner."

Linking language to the mind: Tapping its true power

The real power of human language isn't just that you can make new meanings by rearranging words and sounds; the power and potential lie in what happens with those meanings in the mind and in the ability to think in the abstract.

Nobody knows just why, but human memory allows for one idea to trigger another rather easily; that is, when you hear the word *major* you may immediately think of a military officer or an academic focus during college. This is deep symbolism.

Even the most well-trained chimpanzees and gorillas, on the other hand, largely use their shallow symbolism to communicate about the present, or the very near future or past; their lives are a series of things that happen to them, whereas human experience and language promote complexity of thought and contemplation. This is the real power of language, the key to how it makes our minds different from any others.

Exactly what constitutes the mind is hard to say. For the moment, think of the *mind* as the activity of the brain (which, in this context, is strictly an anatomical structure).

Stuff you've long forgotten: Syntax and grammar

We all learned them, and we all use them, but few of us have thought much about them since high school. I'm talking about syntax and grammar, and I'm here to remind you what these two words mean.

Syntax is the rule system pertaining to the word order of a sentence. For example, in most human languages, sentences are composed of a subject, verb, and object (and in many cases, in that order). In English, the syntactical rule is that the subject is first in the sentence, the verb next, and the object last, such that the sentence "The dog bit the man" has a very different meaning than "The man bit the dog." The words are the same in both sentences, but you must follow the specific word order rules of English to communicate the information accurately.

Grammar is a language's rulebook; it's a system of ideas that tell how a language is and isn't to be expressed. Each language has a grammar, but not all grammars are the same. For example, French has rules about the genders of nouns.

In French, you would say *le mur* ("the wall") rather than just *mur*, "le" indicates the gender of "mur," and the sentence would be incorrect with another gender article or none at all.

Although grammars differ, all grammars inform the proper use of the following language elements:

- ✔ The use of *nouns* (people, places, things, or ideas)

- ✔ The use of *verbs* (descriptions of action or states of being)

- ✔ The *case* of nouns (either as subject or object of a sentence)

- ✔ The use of *modifiers* (like the *-s* suffix in English to indicate plural)

- ✔ The use of *gender* (using masculine, neuter, or feminine nouns)

- ✔ The use of *tense* (past, present, and future)

Humans use language in some unique ways. We comprehend it very quickly — up to 15 sounds per second (whereas other sounds of that frequency tend to blur into an indistinguishable hum). We speak entirely on the fly, making up new phrases and sentences from one moment to the next rather than using a detailed script; in fact, we continually make new idea-associations as information comes to us. Finally, we rarely make major, repeated structural errors, such as saying "I am getting in my banana and leaving!" rather than "I am getting in my car and leaving!" Even under great stress, such errors are very rare in healthy individuals.

Ready to Swear: How the Human Mind Is Hard-Wired for Language

Anthropological studies have shown that infants aren't born with an "on-board" vocabulary but with the *capacity* to learn any language; in other words, any healthy infant can acquire any language. This shows that human language isn't transmitted genetically — you don't inherit it from your parents — although the ability to learn human language is. This tendency is informally referred to as being *hard-wired* for language. Humans are, and it's very important.

One reason (the use of) language is so important for people is that humans rely on their culture to survive. *Culture* refers to the whole set of instructions about how the world works and how to function and survive in it. Now, all those instructions — from how to greet a rival chief to how to make a fire in the rain to where to fish when the river has been high for a week — aren't genetically transmitted; they don't ride on the genes any more than language does. So one generation has to transmit them to the next, and the mechanism of that transmission is language. Humans use language to move critical survival information from one generation to the next, so getting that information right is important. In this way, human biological survival was promoted by a cultural phenomenon: This *biocultural* interaction is a good example of how human evolution has been particularly complex and fascinating.

What's most surprising about human language acquisition is that we don't really learn it through discrete teaching; parents rarely actually describe the intricate rules of their language to their offspring. In fact, most people don't even know all of the specific rules of their language; they just know what "sounds right."

So if humans don't pick up language through enlightening discussions about grammar and syntax, how is it that people are talking at all? The learning process starts almost immediately — infants accumulate language in a discrete series of stages that don't vary culturally. These stages are universal (which also argues strongly for the concept of humans being hard-wired for language acquisition at birth). Generally speaking, kids first learn phonemes (sounds), then basic morphemes (words), syntax (word order in a phrase or sentence), grammar (complex rules of language construction), and finally they expand their vocabulary of words. Fully adult speech isn't really achieved until ten or so years of age. Before then, all children acquire language through some universal stages, which I describe in the following section.

First four months

In the first four months of life, children work out the basic sounds of a language: the phonemes.

A *phoneme* is the smallest unit of sound that differentiates meaning in a word; for example, the sound denoted by the letter *v* as opposed to the sound denoted by the letter *t*. Phonemes aren't normally words in themselves (like "I" or "a"), but you combine them to make words.

Technically speaking, phonemes aren't necessarily syllables, but in terms of speech comprehension, most people hear them as syllables. You can pretty safely think of them as syllables, but know that this isn't a hard-and-fast rule.

Worldwide, the first phonemes learned seem to be the sounds *p, m,* and *a*. These basic sounds require little motor skill to make (as opposed, for example, to *ing* as in "ending"). After four months or so, the number of phonemes that kids learn drops radically. Although children can learn many languages after this time, learning correct pronunciation in each of those languages will be more difficult than if they learned multiple phonemes early on.

Six to twelve months

In this period of babbling, kids attach phonemes to make simple words like "dada" or "mama." The child learns subconsciously that combining insignificant single sounds can create meaning, at this stage perhaps only apparent to the child as a reaction to the word by the parent. Experiments have shown that after a few minutes of exposure to a new two-phoneme word, many children learn that word and file it away in their memories.

12 to 18 months

By one year of age, children can assemble basic speech, having learned the basic phonemes and how to produce them anatomically. They're also able to build basic, two-word phrases from the words they've learned, such as "get cat" or "more milk." One set of words, called *pivots*, are used repeatedly as actions on which other words, called *open words* are hinged. For example, "get" is a pivot, and "cat" is open. "Get" can be used as action for any number of open words. Building these basic sentences requires a basic understanding of syntax ("get cat" is different from "cat get"). Children use short sentences for a number of reasons:

- To locate and/or name something: "see mama"
- To demand or indicate desire: "want candy"
- To negate: "no stairs"
- To describe or qualify: "big bird"
- To indicate possession: "daddy car"
- To question: "where ball"

18 to 24 months

Before 24 months, most children have learned to use the words "what," "who," and "where" to form questions. These words begin to expand meaning out of the near or recent, into more abstract concepts of distance in time and space.

36 months and later

By three years, most children are speaking complex sentences that incorporate phonemes and rules indicating tenses such as present, past, plural, and possessive. After about three years or so, an accent develops, vocabulary increases greatly, and the dreaded word "why" makes its debut. Life suddenly gets very complicated.

Watching Human Language Evolve

How did all this happen? How did humans come to possess the ability to learn such a complex system of communication? Certainly, the explanation has roots in evolution because evolutionary forces have shaped humanity. But just saying "language evolved as some form of communication" doesn't tell anthropologists everything they want to know. For example:

- How did humans get from shallow to deep symbols?
- When did fully modern speech effectively replace bodily gestures?
- If all humans are in the same species, *Homo sapiens sapiens*, why don't we all speak the same language?

Admitting our uncertainty

What do anthropologists really know about language evolution? Not much. Even the origin of language is up in the air; theories on when human language first appeared vary wildly:

- **Just over 2 million years ago:** Some say language must have been present to allow the large-brained, relatively fragile new genus *Homo* to survive on the open savannah.

✔ **About 1.8 million years ago:** Some match the use of symbolic language with the appearance of the symmetrical stone tools used by early *Homo erectus* because, according to proponents, the symmetry of hand axes was itself a symbol.

✔ **About 200,000 years ago:** Some say that language would have appeared with the first representatives of *Homo sapiens,* the very-large-brained species that goes on to become modern humans, dated to more than 170,000 years ago.

✔ **About 100,000 years ago:** Some say that only when anthropology sees plenty of evidence of deep symbols can it be sure that relatively modern human language emerged, as indicated by symbolic artifacts dated to this period.

Researchers have based their theories on the evolution of language on various types of evidence, but each line of evidence has a flaw. For example:

✔ **The size of the hypoglosseal canal:** Some say the larger this nerve-bundle conduit located at the base of the skull is, the more the mind is engaged in language. This is because the canal is used to control fine movements of the mouth, but research has showed it's just as large, relatively speaking, in the minds of nonspeaking, non-human primates as in humans, so it's of little use.

✔ **The hyoid bone:** Some say a modern-appearing hyoid bone — which is part of the speech anatomy situated at the base of the tongue — would indicate language, but the hyoid is very delicate and rarely fossilizes; the analysis of the few that have been found has been so contentious that I don't put much stake in it. Some say it indicates that Neanderthals could make the full range of modern phonemes, others that they couldn't — nobody knows for sure.

✔ **Symbolic artifacts:** Some say that language is an example of symbolic thinking, and that it must have been used by the bearers of the first symbolic artifacts; these are close to 100,000 years old. Others argue that symbolic thinking and language could have occurred for thousands of years before they showed up in artifacts, and so the earliest use of language might be archaeologically invisible.

Explaining language diversity

It appears that as modern humans emerged from Africa around 100,000 years ago and colonized the rest of the world (you can read more about this migration in Chapters 7 and 8), foraging groups developed their own dialects and then languages, perhaps driven by a need to describe the new plants, animals, and environments they encountered.

Language was very important as a means of survival because humans aren't born with much useful instinctual knowledge; we certainly don't instinctually know how to grind a sliver of bone into a needle, thread it with seal gut, and then use that to sew together clothing to live in the Arctic. All the knowledge of how to negotiate your place in a society, all of the knowledge of your family history and myths and dreams — all that culture — had to be transmitted from one generation to the next, and language provided that link. The better the language reflected the environment, the closer the fit of the people to the environment. A culture's vocabulary and capacity to model, in their minds, the environments they encountered were measures of that culture's likelihood of survival.

Over time, many languages evolved; today, anthropologists know of about 6,000 human languages, though many are spoken by only a few people. Most humans speak one of nine main languages: Mandarin Chinese, Spanish, English, Bengali, Hindi, Portuguese, Russian, Japanese, and German. (You can read more about the alarming loss of traditional languages worldwide in Chapter 18.)

To understand the evolution of human languages, anthropologists have used methods such as *glottochronology*, which estimates the rate at which languages change. Combining archaeological and linguistic anthropological data, anthropologists have identified the main language groups, called *phyla*. You can find maps showing their distribution at webspace.ship. edu/cgboer/languagefamilies.html.

Not all linguistic anthropologists agree on what languages go in which groups in the language phyla. Some would move certain specific languages from one group to another. Still, most of these groups are widely accepted.

In the same way, Figure 13-2 shows the relationships between some of the main language groups; most linguistic anthropologists would consider this diagram a reasonable approximation of what's known about human languages today.

Figure 13-2:
Diagram
of modern
languages
and their
relations.

Making room for new theories

Thousands of researchers, from every discipline, have contemplated the origins of language. By 1865, the Linguistic Society of Paris — fed up with wild speculation — refused to publish in its scholarly journal any further papers on the origins of language; until more was known, they said, all was guesswork. Within a few years the Philological Society of London said essentially the same thing.

As anthropology was growing as a discipline in the early 20th century, the need for a scientific understanding of language to understand humanity became clear. Years of research have shown that humanity evolves, like all other life forms, with a long and complex evolutionary past. If anything separated humanity from the rest of the animal kingdom, it was spoken language, and that meant language had to be understood. The range of explanations has been enormous.

In my view the most compelling recent theories of the evolution of language have been proposed by physical anthropologist Robin Dunbar and psychologist Merlin Donald. (You can read more about each of their models of language evolution in Chapter 7.)

Social grooming

In short, Dunbar's *social grooming hypothesis* states that language evolved as a way of making social relationships in primate groups easier. In non-human primates, Dunbar observes, social order and cohesion are maintained by long periods of physical grooming, where individuals clean each other's hair by picking out parasites; this practice promotes close bonds and intimacy and dampens social conflict.

Dunbar argues that because most human talk is small talk about others in one's immediate social sphere, language evolved as social grooming a more effective way to communicate that includes complex vocalizations as well as physical action. Speech, Dunbar points out, can be used to address or "groom" more than one member of society at a time.

Representing ideas

Psychologist Merlin Donald believes that whatever language was used for among our ancient ancestors, it was most importantly a new and more efficient way to represent ideas. The word "represent" is important here, because for Donald, the fact that humans continually and voluntarily recall (that is, re-present) old ideas and memories of past events is of major significance; it breaks the mind out of the here and now, allowing for abstraction and deep symbolism, two hallmarks of the human mind.

Personally, I think these theories are both great ideas. To show you just how little anthropologists know for certain, though, have a look at this list of questions posed in a recent research article on the origins of language; these are questions that linguists and linguistic anthropologists themselves are asking (taken from M.H. Christiansen and S. Kirby's 2003 article "Language evolution: Consensus and Controversies"):

- Can an evolutionary approach help us discover innately determined features of language?
- What role does evolution by natural selection have to play in explaining language origins?
- Can genetic and archaeological evidence converge on a timetable for the origins of language in hominids?

For the moment, I think it's safe to say that anthropology just doesn't know when speech or language first appeared. But I do think we're closing in on the answer. The work of Robin Dunbar and Merlin Donald, to me, are the most interesting at the moment. I think it's safe to say that human language evolved as an efficient way of making social commentary. Until anthropology knows more, that's all I'm going to hang my hat on.

Chapter 14

Types of Types: Race and Ethnicity

*W*hat kind of person are you anyway? We all have an answer: black, white, Hispanic — no, Latino! Every society classifies humans into ethnic groups and races, often blurring the two or simply making them up for convenience.

In this chapter I describe how anthropologists think of race, and just what ethnic groups really are. Although the concept of race is dead as a doornail in the world of anthropology, many people outside anthropology still believe in it, which can have terrible consequences such as racial discrimination. Differences between ethnic groups can also cause terrible conflict. To better understand the human species, you have to know what anthropology has discovered about these "types" of the one "human type" of the primate order.

The Kinds of Humanity: Human Physical Variation

People come in many colors and shapes; people of the Mediterranean, for example, are obviously darker-skinned than those of Scandinavia, and natives of the Arctic are shorter and stockier than the tall, lean Samburu of East Africa. Why is this? How did these variations come about, and what do they mean for humanity as a species?

The answer comes from the study of human biology by physical anthropologists. In this section you see how human populations have adapted to their varying environments by the same evolutionary process that shapes all living things.

The race card: Racial types and physical anthropology

Like all living things with sensory input, humans have to classify their perceptions into some kind of order: These things go with these others but don't belong in this group. Some people have darker skin, so they're in the "darker skin" category. And so on. Obviously, not all human beings look the same, so humans have spent some time putting people of different colors, body shapes, and so on into different categories sometimes called races. Unfortunately, this tendency has had some very bad consequences for millions of human beings over the centuries.

Biologically speaking, a *race* is a group of organisms of the same species that share similar physical (and genetic) attributes and specific geographic regions. In short, they're subdivisions of a single species — meaning they can mate and have offspring that are healthy enough to have their own offspring — exhibiting some characteristics reflecting their geographical origins.

This definition is pretty slippery, though, because finding good examples of distinctly different races is difficult. The most visible non-human animal races are those of dogs. From Chihuahua to Great Dane, all dogs are in the same species — *Canis familiaris* — but they have obvious physical differences. Strictly speaking, they're of different races — and even this isn't so strict, because these differences come from humans selectively breeding these animals for certain characteristics, not from their originally inhabiting very different environments. Once, all dogs (most likely first domesticated about 20,000 years ago) were wolf-like, and their modern diversity is more a result of human selective breeding than geographical adaptation.

Just like any other living thing, human beings adapt to their environments through an evolutionary process. Throughout this book I emphasize that our species adapts mainly through cultural means; that is, we survive our environments not because we've adapted to them biologically, but with artifacts and complex behavior. (For more on cultural adaptation, see Chapter 11.) Having said that, human bodies *have* adapted to certain conditions over time.

Adaptation is a process — behavioral or biological — that increases the likelihood of survival for an organism. An adaptation can be a mutation that confers an advantage. For example, a frog that has better-camouflaged skin than its siblings has a lower chance of being snapped up by a fish, and therefore a stronger chance to survive and have offspring that will carry the gene for better-adapted camouflage. In humans, adaptations include complex behavior, such as making tools. These behaviors aren't passed on genetically but rather culturally.

Some of these bodily adaptations are pretty easily visible, and some are only visible when you look very closely at the genes. Skin color — one of the most visible human characteristics — is a good example of adaptation to a particular environment. The darkest skin appears in populations originating in tropical zones, such as Africa and Asia. The lightest skin is traditionally found in northern Europe because over time, natural selection favored darker skins in areas that received extensive and more intensive sunlight, because individuals with lighter skin in these areas were more prone to skin cancers. Darker skin, then, is an adaptation to the geographical conditions of Africa.

What's the adaptive value of lighter skin? It has to do with vitamin D, of all things. Vitamin D is a nutrient that helps human bones form properly. Without enough vitamin D, deformities like the disease *rickets*, which normally includes bowed legs and a misshapen pelvis, will occur. In females, rickets result in a deformed birth canal, which makes normal childbirth hazardous if not lethal.

Humans naturally produce Vitamin D through the skin when they're exposed to sunlight, but cloudier parts of the world — like northern Europe — are exposed to much less sunlight than regions in the tropics, where the species began. As early human populations were expanding into northern Europe around 40,000 years ago, those individuals with darker skin were less able to manufacture Vitamin D and probably experienced a much lower birthrate than those populations with lighter skin. (You can read more about this expansion in Chapters 7 and 8.) Lighter skin, then, is an adaptation to the geographical conditions of Europe because over time, the prehistoric colonists of Europe who happened to be born with lighter skin (simply by chance) had more offspring, who themselves carried the genes for lighter skin.

Biological adaptations aren't instantaneous. They take place over the span of generations, so an African moving to Europe won't evolve lighter skin, nor will a European travelling to Africa evolve darker skin (except for some tanning). A suntan is a lighter-skinned body's defense mechanism — the release of dark-pigmented melanin — against too much ultraviolet light. See Figure 14-1 for a skin color map of the world. Note it shows shades in a spectrum from very dark to very light, and the cutoff point for various shades of skin color are essentially arbitrary. The map could change a bit as the cutoff points shift.

Also, note that these are shades of native peoples' skin, and mixing native and non-native populations has the tendency to change skin shade.

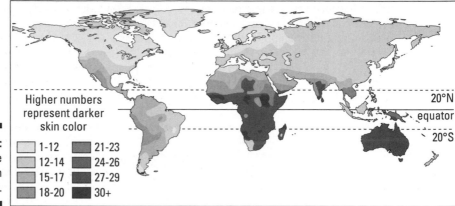

Figure 14-1:
Worldwide
human skin
color map.

Another example of biological adaptation in human beings is the difference of stature between arctic (such as Inuit) and East African (such as Maasai) folk. In biology, *Bergmann's rule* indicates that in colder regions, warm-blooded animals will have stockier bodies than their counterparts from warmer regions, because stockier bodies are more efficient at retaining body heat. In the cold polar regions, the Inuit have a short and stocky build; the Maasai of East Africa have taller and more slender bodies that don't have to retain so much heat — they actually have to dump excess heat in their hot environment, which is facilitated by their body shape. Body stature in these cases is an adaptation to the geographical conditions of hot African and the cold Arctic.

The rapid physiological changes that occur in one's lifetime — like a mountaineer's adjustment to lower oxygen levels at high altitude — are referred to as *habituation* or *acclimatization*. These *aren't* passed on genetically to the next generation (because changes acquired during life can't be encoded in the genes,) and they're reversible (as when the mountaineer returns to lower elevations.)

The lowdown: What anthropologists can say for sure about human races

So do human races exist? Very strictly speaking, yes. *Homo sapiens sapiens* does feature geographically based differences within the species. However, you must consider two very important points.

First, these genetic differences don't mean a lot, biologically. Because all healthy humans can mate and have healthy offspring, we're all in *Homo sapiens sapiens,* biologically speaking. Don't let anyone tell you different. Not only is it inaccurate to say "the female species" when talking about significant sex differences between males and females, but it's also inaccurate to say "the African race" or the "European race" when speaking of deep differences in these peoples. A look at the genes shows no significant species-level differences — only very minor visible ones such as skin color, shape of nose, or hair texture. Biologically speaking, though, these differences aren't important. For most physical anthropologists (who've spent the most time closely examining human biology), race is nearly meaningless when applied to humanity.

Rather than talk about races, physical anthropologists more commonly talk today of ancestry, a more general term that recognizes the reality of some geographically specific human adaptations but doesn't turn them into loaded, black-and-white races (pun intended.) Ancestry may be important, for example, when considering someone's genetic health because different human populations have developed slightly different genetic characteristics over time.

Second — and most important — is that cultural behavior isn't genetically linked to those geographical differences. This disconnect is one of anthropology's most important discoveries and lessons for humanity. People from Scandinavia aren't reserved — or whatever other behavioral trait you may apply to them — because it's in their genes to be so. It's not. Most of human behavior isn't biologically determined or filtered in through the natural environment — most of it is culturally learned. An infant from Japan can be raised in the Kalahari of Southern Africa and won't automatically remove his shoes when going into a home unless his culture specifically teaches him to do so. Like any human can acquire any language, any infant can acquire any culture; it's culture that really drives behavior, not the genes. The ancient belief that human races have innate behavioral traits — industrious Asians or hot-blooded Mediterraneans — is simply wrong.

One of the main reasons the race concept really doesn't apply to humans is that defining human races is almost impossible: To what race do you assign a person born from a Native American and a native African marriage? Do you create a new race in this case? Although some of these designations do exist, to come up with a race for every possible combination of ancestries would be an infinite job. Plus, it would just be another exercise in drawing lines where they don't really exist. And what's "black" or "white"? Is a Greek person black or white? Of course, they're in between. Assigning people to a race based on skin color becomes an exercise in holding up paint chips to the skin.

Figure 14-2 shows genetic relationship among human populations. Note that although most anthropologists agree that these relationships are essentially accurate, there is always some debate in science. Note also that genetic mixing from one population to another causes a lot of ambiguity. Also remember that political boundaries such as country names aren't genetic boundaries, so here I have tried to avoid naming countries and focus instead on regions.

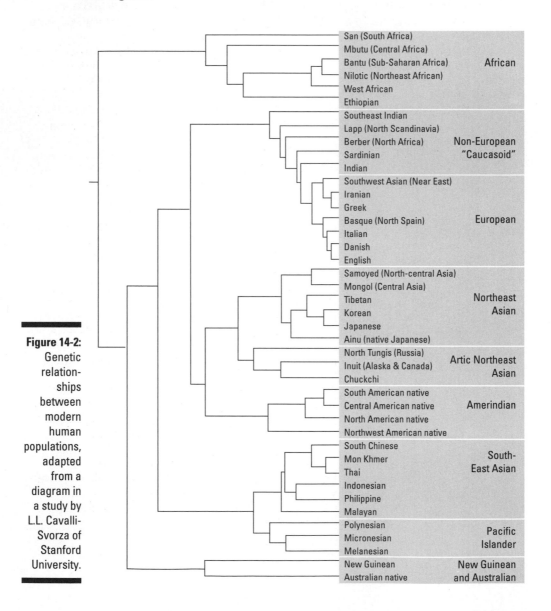

Figure 14-2: Genetic relationships between modern human populations, adapted from a diagram in a study by L.L. Cavalli-Svorza of Stanford University.

The history of racial typing

If race is such a nonissue for humanity, why has anthropology been so concerned with it for so long? And why is it such a big issue today? Answering these questions requires looking at how long humans have been talking about race and seeing what the concept of race has meant for anthropology.

Like all animals, humans have undoubtedly been classifying their neighbors in various ways for a very long time. So far, I'm unaware that any archaeologist has spotted depictions of different races in early cave art, and unfortunately — though modern human behavior seems to begin around 100,000 years ago — most cave art ranges from roughly 35,000 to 11,000 years ago. Some of the first records of humans classifying others as certain "types" come from ancient Egypt, where by 1350 BC you can see records of them classifying humans by skin color: Egyptians were red-skinned, people south of Egypt were black-skinned, those living north of the Mediterranean Sea were white-skinned, and people to the east were yellow-skinned.

By the the16th century, during the Age of Discovery, Europeans voyaging around the world were encountering many previously unknown peoples and developing racial classifications of their own. Because skin color was so noticeable, many racial classifications were based only on that factor. Additionally, these unknown people weren't Christian and didn't share European culture and values, so the Europeans labeled them Savages. In fact, they thought they could use racial type as an indicator of just how Savage a person was. The less European-looking, of course, the more Savage. Though most have ditched this concept today, many racial supremacists still believe that cultural behavior correlates with skin color, nose shape, hair texture, or what have you.

Some naturalists in the 16th through 19th centuries proposed that savages were even a different *species* than white Europeans, saying that they shouldn't even be considered human. This classification made persecution and enslavement of different peoples purely because of how they looked much easier.

Early attempts by Europeans to categorize people into racial schemes were extremely biased and hierarchical, associating morality and intelligence with skin color and other physical attributes. These schemes always placed Europeans at the top of the scale, and the successively darker-skinned peoples at the bottom.

Biological determinism: Knocked on the chin

Linking physical appearance to cultural attributes went beyond skin color. In the late 19th century, any trait seemed to distinguish the moral character or industriousness of a population group. Any physical trait chosen always seemed to justify the inferiority of the darker skinned peoples. Take this example from a book on human origins published by S. Liang in London in 1892:

"And the form of the chin seems to be wonderfully correlated with the general character and energy of the race. It is hard to say why, but as a matter of fact a weak chin generally denotes a weak, and a strong chin a strong, race or individual. Thus the chimpanzee and the other apes have no chin, the negro and other races have chins weak and receding. The races who, like the Iberians, have been conquered or driven from plains to mountain, have had poor chins; while their successive conquerors, of

Aryan race — Celts, Romans, Teutons and Scandinavians — might almost be classified by the prominence and solidity of this feature of the face."

Liang expected his reading audience to believe that the size or shape of a person's chin could be equated with "character" or "energy." Additionally, Liang ranked human populations according to their skin color, with whites being at the top, darker-skinned southern Europeans below them, and peoples of African origin at the bottom, closer to the non-human primates. Today, anthropologists know all humans are genetically very similar, and all are equally distant from the non-human primates; our genus, *Homo*, split from them many millions of years ago. Many writers, like Liang, were really attempting to find supposedly scientific facts to justify the great social injustices that existed in their societies.

By the mid-1800s, naturalists began using a method of describing the shape of the head called the *cephalic index*, a ratio measurement of the length and width of the head. *Dolichocephalic* peoples had long and narrow heads (like most northern Europeans), and *brachycephalic* peoples tended to have broad heads — like many southern Europeans. Not surprisingly, this classification scheme and others like it led to many arguments about which peoples were superior to the others.

The root problem of all this flailing around at the identification of human types was *biological determinism*, the idea that physical traits were somehow linked to behavior. Many thought traits like intellect, values, and morals were all products of one's race. Today, most people know better, although some people still wear sheets and call for "racial purity," an impossible and destructive idea I discuss later in this chapter.

A similar way that everyone — including early anthropologists — had this idea all wrong was in the application of Darwin's principles of biological evolution to societies. This led to a concept known as *social Darwinism,* the idea that as societies and nations evolved and competed, the morally superior societies would prevail as the less-moral, "savage" societies were weeded out, and that this was all natural and good. Around this time debates about the superiority or inferiority of particular groups continued and some began to fear that civilized (meaning northern European Christian) society was slowly being destroyed by "unfit" peoples who, for one reason or another, were not being weeded out.

With behavioral characteristics "linked" to genetic characteristics in the minds of many (including scientists), some in the 19th and early 20th centuries even advocated for state regulation of marriages, family size, and whether to allow an individual to reproduce. This practice became known as *eugenics*, and the Nazis took it to a terrible extreme during World War II. In Germany, the Nazi party began to systematically kill those members of society that it considered inferior to the northern-European Christian ideal they held. Using eugenics as the basis for its acts, the Nazi party killed millions of Jewish people, Gypsies, homosexuals, and others it considered inferior in an attempt to create a master race.

The problems with the concept of a master race — aside from the obvious moral issues surrounding eugenics — is that biological variation is necessary for the health of a population. Basically, if all members of a population are the same, the population has no buffer against a particularly lethal or catastrophic disease or any other major change in the species' selective environment. If everyone is the same, everyone is susceptible to the same potential disaster. For this reason, many biologists measure the overall health of a species by its very genetic diversity. So even if a master race were possible, and one could (and would want to) manage to prevent any interbreeding, the end result would be a genetically uniform and genetically vulnerable population. The idea of a master race is therefore suicidal.

Even today, the U.S. military still uses its old-school letter identification system on some paperwork to describe a person's ethnic group. This ridiculous system designates *N* for Negro, *C* for Caucasian, *M* for Mongoloid (more properly known today as Asian), and *R* for Native Americans (which I can only guess stands for Redskin). Time for Uncle Sam to get with the times!

The grand illusion: Race, turns out, is arbitrary

Over the years, various anthropologists have attempted to classify the human species into various races, such as Caucasian, Black African, Asian, and so on. The problem is that the physical traits used to identify which group an individual belonged in aren't binary opposites like black or white, period, with no middle ground. They're *continuous* traits, meaning that a whole spectrum exists between, say, "black" and "white" skin designations.

Any attempt to classify human races raises a number of questions. Although Asians look pretty clearly different from Europeans in some respects, what do you do with people who look, well, partly Asian and partly European? And does "European" end in the Middle East, where some African traits are present? Where does Africa even begin, genetically speaking? Who's going to draw up the lines between "black" and "white" (and what qualifies that person for the job, anyway)? One thorough 1972 study by Harvard anthropologist R.C. Lewontin concluded that "Human racial classification is of no social value and is positively destructive of social and human relations. Since such racial classification is now seen to be of virtually no genetic or taxonomic [classifying] significance either, no justification can be offered for its continuance."

Bottom line: For most professional anthropologists today, human "race" is an antiquated concept. For biomedical reasons (and sometimes forensic identification of bodies), the reality of genetic ancestry can be important, but color-coded races, loaded with behavioral traits, are basically arbitrary.

Why Is Everyone Different? Human Cultural Variation

Although all humans are of the same species, they don't all act the same; human behavior varies tremendously worldwide. If race doesn't control a person's characteristics, what does account for human behavioral variation?

In short, the answer is culture. Cultures differ because people live in different conditions, be they ecological, economic, social, or what have you. For example, each culture is ultimately a unique adaptation to the social and environmental conditions in which it evolves. The culture of the Amazonian foragers has certain characteristics, and they value certain things and act certain ways, because they have evolved in a particular ecological environment, one different from highland Scots, whose own culture is an adaptation to their unique environment. This difference is ultimately why human behavior isn't the same worldwide.

Of course, human cultures have been evolving for thousands of years — and in the modern age, with mass communication and mass movement of peoples from one environment and culture to another, culture has changed very quickly. So it may be a stretch today to see the direct ecological reason for any given human behavior; in fact, the winds of history have probably shaped modern cultures as much as, if not more than, the ecological adaptations that they were in the first place.

The American Anthropological Association's position on race

In 1998, the American Anthropological Association released a statement on race that you can find at the following Web link: www.aaanet.org/stmts/racepp.htm. Here are some excerpts:

"In the United States both scholars and the general public have been conditioned to viewing human races as natural and separate divisions within the human species based on visible physical differences. With the vast expansion of scientific knowledge in this century, however, it has become clear that human populations are not unambiguous, clearly demarcated, biologically distinct groups . . . . Throughout history whenever different groups have come into contact, they have interbred. The continued sharing of genetic materials has maintained all of humankind as a single species."

"Historical research has shown that the idea of "race" has always carried more meanings than mere physical differences; indeed, physical variations in the human species have no meaning except the social ones that humans put on them. Today scholars in many fields argue that "race" as it is understood in the United States of America was a social mechanism invented during the 18th century to refer to those populations brought together in colonial America: the English and other European settlers, the conquered Indian peoples, and those peoples of Africa brought in to provide slave labor."

"It is a basic tenet of anthropological knowledge that all normal human beings have the capacity to learn any cultural behavior. The American experience with immigrants from hundreds of different language and cultural backgrounds who have acquired some version of American culture traits and behavior is the clearest evidence of this fact. Moreover, people of all physical variations have learned different cultural behaviors and continue to do so as modern transportation moves millions of immigrants around the world."

The "racial" worldview was invented to assign some groups to perpetual low status, while others were permitted access to privilege, power, and wealth. The tragedy in the United States has been that the policies and practices stemming from this worldview succeeded all too well in constructing unequal populations among Europeans, Native Americans, and peoples of African descent. Given what we know about the capacity of normal humans to achieve and function within any culture, we conclude that present-day inequalities between so-called "racial" groups are not consequences of their biological inheritance but products of historical and contemporary social, economic, educational, and political circumstances."

Distinguishing ethnicity from race

What does all this have to do with ethnicity? A lot. For a long time, many people have used the terms "race" and "ethnic group" interchangeably — and wrongly so. An *ethnic group* is a collection of people who share some cultural characteristics because they share a common history. That history may include marrying people of the same general physical types — such as whites tending to marry whites in 1950s America or Italians tending to marry Italians when they immigrated to the U.S. — and here is where *race* (or physical characteristics) and *ethnicity* (or cultural characteristics) get mixed up.

An ethnic group is a subdivision of a larger culture in which it normally exists. Like culture, ethnic groups are difficult to define. For example, an active, vibrant Sicilian American ethnic group centers on a wonderful little restaurant in Portland, Oregon, but how would I define it? Making a list of its shared beliefs, values, traditions, and so on would be difficult. Still, it's there — and I'm happy for it, because they serve the best food in town.

Ethnic groups tend to be bonded by rituals and traditions that remind their members of their ethnicity and their shared trials and triumphs through time. They also usually identify with a specific geographical area — even if their ancestors migrated away from that area in the distant past — that they often remember sentimentally in their myths and traditions.

A common horror: Ethnic cleansing

Ethnically based conflicts can be very fierce because the shared history and values of the ethnic groups are in conflict. Ethnic groups that are in the minority are often very careful to maintain their identity; it may be all they really have, so they're fiercely protective of their historical claims, such as claims to land, and traditional values, such as those found in their religion.

The power of ethnic identity has often been exploited by tyrannical leaders who often try to divide and conquer by pitting one ethnic group against another. The attempt to eliminate an ethnic group is called *genocide*; former Serbian president Slobodan Milosevic directed one of the worst cases of genocide in recent history. After the collapse of Yugoslavia in the mid-'90s, many areas of the former country splintered along ethnic lines. Milosevic and others felt that ethnic Albanians and Croatians living in Serbia posed a threat to the integrity of Serbia, and so began a process they called *ethnic cleansing,* which is essentially another name for genocide. Milosevic and his subordinates began to rid Serbia of ethnic Albanians and Croats by murdering them by the thousands.

A few years earlier, in the eastern African nation of Rwanda, a similar situation developed. The Hutu, a traditional farming ethnic group, decided that there wasn't enough land for it to coexist with the Tutsi, a pastoralist ethnic group in the same region. Extremists among the Hutu began to murder the Tutsi, and before the violence was quelled, the Hutu had killed an estimated 1 million Tutsi.

A common delight: Ethnic identity

Ethnic identity provides people with a specific identity, which they often manifest in the following aspects of culture:

- Music/artistic preferences
- Food preferences
- Child-naming traditions
- Language or dialect
- Religion or value system

Most people feel most at ease when interacting with members of their own ethnic group because they value the same way of being human. Of course, this isn't to say that because something is comfortable it's the safest or the best thing to do — on the contrary, interacting with members of different ethnic groups can be a truly enriching experience. It's one reason many people travel.

In addition to learning new ways of looking at the world and our place in it, interaction with other ethic groups and societies allows people to discover their common humanity. By sharing the best aspects of their cultures with one another, humans can create a truly functional *multicultural* or *multiethnic* society, one in which various ethnic groups coexist peacefully without some groups dominating others. With the world population increasing as quickly as it is, members of different ethnic groups are increasingly in contact with one another. Maintaining peaceful relationships is important and requires people to respect the ethnic differences between groups and remember that these differences are cultural, not genetic.

Many people live in a multicultural society already. For example, many people enjoy living in cities where they can experience the cultures of different peoples through museum exhibits, traditional ethnic restaurants, and so on. Additionally, you can read the literature of other groups, learn their histories and artistic traditions, and so on. These are just some of the advantages of living in a multicultural society.

Ethnic group interactions

In a 1985 study, anthropologists George Simpson and J. Milton Yinger classified six ways that different ethnic groups have interacted in recent history. Anthropologist Gary Ferraro subsequently reviewed these forms of interaction and offered generally good examples for each. With some reinterpretations of my own, they're in order here from best case to worst case scenario.

Pluralism

Pluralism is essentially the salad bowl concept, in which several intact, identifiable culture groups coexist in a single society. In Switzerland, for example, German-, French-, and Italian-speaking peoples all coexist peacefully. Each of these groups inhabits a different part of Switzerland, where they maintain their individual ethnic identities, foods, languages, and customs while all recognizing that they're Swiss.

Assimiliation

Assimilation is essentially the Melting Pot concept, in which an ethnic minority is absorbed into the greater society. A good example is Hawaiian society, a culture into which various Asian groups have assimilated. Assimilation involves several stages.

Social assimilation is the first stage, in which a minority group joins the dominant culture and is forced to participate in the society and use the social institutions of that dominant group. Use of the social institutions such as schools, markets, and churches is common. Unfortunately, changing the dominant language spoken by the minority group is often a priority for the assimilating society; this practice often involves outlawing native languages, as was common when native peoples are placed on reservations where schools don't teach their native languages but rather the language of the assimilating culture.

Cultural assimilation, in which minority groups begin to adopt cultural features of the dominant group, is the second stage. This process includes adopting the value system and many customs, such as observing holidays not present in the native culture. The final stage, *physical assimilation,* involves physical integration, in which members of the ethnic minority intermarry with the dominant society and begin to have offspring. These offspring often face considerable challenges as they try to find an identity in either the originating or dominating culture.

Legal protection of minorities

Legal protection of minorities is sometimes necessary in societies where ethnic groups coexist but may be hostile to one another. For example, the United States has afforded special rights and status designed to protect traditional Native American populations; for example, Native Americans have jurisdiction on their reservations (which have been legally set aside for them). This protection can extend into the broader aspects of society as well; committing violence against a member of a minority group just because you dislike that particular group can result in prosecution for a hate crime.

Population transfer

Population transfer occurs when minority groups either can't coexist with the dominant population or the dominant society doesn't want to coexist with the minorities. Population transfer was one of the "solutions" offered by the Serbian government to the minority Albanians living in Serbia. The dominant Serb society didn't want them living in Serbia and encouraged (if you will) them to move out to other countries.

Long-term subjugation

Long-term subjugation occurs in some areas of the world where ethnic groups are politically and economically repressed, either legally or through continued social pressures from the dominant group. For example, slavery was legal in the West African country of Mauritania up until 1980. Even today, many black Africans living in Mauritania do so along the fringes of the Arab-dominated society.

Genocide

Genocide is the mass murder or extermination of a people by a different one. It typically occurs when the differences between groups are significant enough to make a dominant group believe that their own way of life is threatened by the mere existence of the other group. That is, when hatred and fear overtake better human nature. Tragically, I can give you too many examples of such events throughout human history: Serbian persecution of Albanians, Hutu persecution of Tutsis, Nazi persecution of multiple groups, and Turkish persecution of Armenians.

Chapter 15

Guess Who's Coming to Dinner? Identity, Family, Kinship, and Gender

● ●

In This Chapter

▶ Reviewing how humanity thinks of and organizes identity

▶ Looking at how humans organize their family units

▶ Understanding how humans keep track of who's related to whom

▶ Seeing how humans organize activities by gender roles

● ●

*A*ll animals recognize differences between "self" and "other." In human societies, these differences take on enormous significance, partly because humans are so individualistic — rather than being clone-like automatons, humans have individual personalities. We validate that individualism by giving infants unique names. Those names also keep track of who's related to whom, sometimes for generations back into the past.

What's the point of this obsession with who we are? Why am I named "Cameron McPherson Smith" rather than "#4423-A," and why do we go further, adding qualifiers such as "Doctor" or "Uncle" to our names?

To understand themselves as a species, humans have to also understand themselves as individuals within networks of other individuals. This chapter explains the significance of individual identity and how cultures worldwide manage different kinds of identities, such as family, sexual, and gender identity.

Am I "Cameron" or "a Smith"? The Scales of Human Identity

If you ask me where I live, my answer will depend on the context: If we're in Berlin, I may say "the United States" or "Oregon." If we're in downtown Portland, I'd probably say "Northwest Portland." In the same way, humans have individual identities that can vary depending on who's asking and in what context. Personally, I'm "Uncle Cameron," "Dr. Smith," "Cam," or "Cameron McPherson Smith," depending on whom you ask. The capacity for such multiple identities is uniquely human, and that's because of human individuality.

The roots of human individuality are found in language. *Language,* our species' main way of communicating, is so subtle and capable of expression that every mind has a slightly different varied take on things (more on why in Chapter 12). Because of this uniqueness, humans give individual names and titles to keep track of everyone. And boy, do they keep track. One study found that up to 70 percent of people's non-work-related conversation is about other people, as in "Can you believe the nerve of that guy?" and "Why on earth would she move to Denver?" All this careful monitoring, this obsession with a person's place in the network of friends, relatives, and coworkers, is possible by keeping track of exactly who everyone is: by keeping track of identity.

Know thyself: Identity

Human societies universally recognize the importance of gender identity. *Gender* is a social category (relating to biological sex) that indicates what are considered appropriate roles, rights, and responsibilities for a particular gender in a particular society. Human societies also recognize at least two other kinds of identity:

- ✔ **Individual:** The self, "I," "me," identified by a personal name
- ✔ **Intimate family:** Marriage mates and other immediate family (*kin*), identified by a family name; even if this practice isn't formalized by use of a "last name," as it is here in the U.S., some way to indicate family identity is always present

Consider how these identities relate to the individual, intimate family, kin, and gender. For thousands of years, much of human interaction was somewhat smaller scale than it is with today's global communications and the ability for people to move around on the Earth very rapidly.

Because social organization is so important to human culture and often relies on the kinds of identities I've just sketched out, anthropologists have made innumerable studies of how individuality, kinship, marriage, and gender are organized. The rest of this chapter outlines their main findings.

What's in a name?

Every human society has the custom of naming offspring, which, according to anthropologist Clifford Geertz, converts "anybodies" into "somebodies." Exactly how names are chosen, though, and for what purposes, varies enormously.

For example, some parents select names to reflect their ideals (such as Harmony) or religion (Gabriel). In medieval Europe, surnames (last names) reflected trades (Wheelwrights made wheels, Smiths worked metal, and so on). In Iceland, females are given a first name followed by a surname that's attached to the name of their father: Thorstein's daughter Artna would be named Artna Thorsteinsdottir. And so on. All across the globe and throughout history, naming keeps track of who you are, who you're born from, and what rights and responsibilities you may have.

A Family Affair

All human societies have ways of organizing their members into *families*. Worldwide, families generally have the following characteristics:

- ✔ **Coresidence:** That is, family members more or less live together; among the Hmong of Thailand, families occupy large houses, several of which form a village.

- ✔ **Economic cooperation:** Members more or less work with the economic interests of their family in mind, assisting (and being assisted) in times of stress; in traditional highland Peru, for example, the economic activities of each family member — like weaving, done largely by women, and plowing, done largely by men — are complexly adjusted as the family structure changes over time with births, deaths, and so on.

- ✔ **Management of reproduction and enculturation:** Members take part in the process of having children, providing for them, and bringing them to adulthood. Among the native Inupiat of Alaska, traditional strategies for child-rearing that used to emphasize the female's role in childcare (because males were often engaged in hunting) are being adjusted to new economies that don't emphasize hunting.

- ✔ **Management of property:** Members orchestrate the movement — within the generation and from one generation to the next — of the family's property; among the Basque culture of northern Spain, the first-born child of a given couple was the first in line to inherit the family's home and land immediately when they were married. (The inheritor's parents would live with the inheriting child from that time on, but would no longer own the land or home.)

American family definitions

The U.S. Census Bureau collects data on American families, and I've listed its definitions of certain terms in the following list. Remember that the definitions of these terms aren't universal — they're specific to the modern U.S. (or a few years ago, when they were written). One of the lessons of anthropology is that such terms may not be universally applicable.

✔ **Family:** A group of two people or more (one of whom is the householder) related by birth, marriage, or adoption and residing together; all such people (including related subfamily members) are considered as members of one family. . . . The number of families is equal to the number of family households, however, the count of family members differs from the count of family household members because family household members include any non-relatives living in the household.

✔ **Household:** A household consists of all the people who occupy a housing unit. A house, an apartment or other group of rooms, or a single room, is regarded as a housing unit when it is occupied or intended for occupancy as separate living quarters; that is, when the occupants do not live and eat with any other persons in the structure and there is direct access from the outside or through a common hall.

✔ **Married couple:** A married couple, as defined for census purposes, is a husband and wife enumerated as members of the same household. The married couple may or may not have children living with them. The expression "husband-wife" or "married-couple" before the term "household," "family," or "subfamily" indicates that the household, family, or subfamily is maintained by a husband and wife. The number of married couples equals the count of married-couple families plus related and unrelated married-couple subfamilies.

What terms do you think may have to be redefined in the future?

Family membership varies worldwide as well, but is based on a combination of two main kinds of relatives. *Consanguines* are those you're related to by blood (biological brothers, mothers, and so on), and *affines* are people you're related to by marriage (wife, father-in-law, and the like).

Although all human societies have concepts of the family, family membership and the rules related to it vary a great deal worldwide. In North America, the monogamous married couple and their offspring (the *nuclear family*) are widely considered the "ideal" family. But this arrangement is an ideal, not necessarily the reality. In the United States, depending on whom you ask (the online U.S. Census Bureau data are years out of date), only about half of people live in this kind of nuclear family; single-parent households are very common.

In some cultures, the immediate nuclear family is less significant than the *extended family*, which includes multitudes of uncles, cousins, and so on. In these cases, the family may be more interested in the most recent two or three generations than in those many years past simply because of the complexity of relations. In either case, all human societies distinguish between two main kinds of relations: the families one is born from, and the family one begins, which I discuss in the next section.

Families can get very complex, so remember that anthropological categories can often be pretty fuzzy. A very large, extended family living together may be better called a "domestic group" than a family, because it may include long-term visitors, for example, or very distant relations being brought back into the social network. Remember, the world is usually more complicated than any anthropological statement. The human species has found many ways to be human.

Families of origin versus families of procreation

Every human society keeps track of the *family of origin* — the family from which a person was born. Cultures use kinship terms such as *mother, father, brother, aunt,* and so on to indicate a person's role(s) in the family of origin. These can get very complicated. In traditional Chinese kinship there are separate terms for one's elder or younger uncles and aunts, whereas in the Western system there is only "uncle." The *family of procreation,* or the family a person begins when he or she marries and begins to have offspring, also uses kinship terms such as *son, cousin,* and *sister-in-law* to keep track of these additional family members. (In most traditional cultures, marriage is a fundamental step in beginning a family.) See the "Kinship" section later in this chapter.

Incest

Both family of origin and family of procreation are important in the regulation of sexual behavior. One of the most important regulations has to do with the *incest taboo,* which is the prohibition of sexual relations with close relatives *(incest).* Again, exactly who is prohibited from relations with whom varies somewhat worldwide (although one study of more than 250 societies showed that in every case, sexual relations between members of the same nuclear family were forbidden), but the taboo universally involves prohibition of sexual relations between parents and their immediate biological offspring. The universality of the incest taboo suggests its great importance for humanity — if humans interbreed too closely, it can have negative genetic effects.

Marriage

Marriage is the socially sanctioned union of two people — usually a male and a female — with a couple of main characteristics. Although divorce is possible, and in some societies common (as in the U.S. today, and among the Tuareg of the Sahara, where women may have several husbands before the age of 30), the social expectation at the ceremony of marriage is that the union will be permanent. In addition, marriage usually comes with a general expectation that the union will be sexually monogamous between the married pair (although customs vary).

Marriage is a complex union that has many functions; it can join romantic partners, but even in these cases it has a lot to do with the management of property, rights, and offspring. A society's marriage customs largely dictate how it arranges and manages families and what terms it uses to keep track of them. As always, these customs vary quite a bit worldwide. *Arranged marriage* matches individuals not for reasons of romantic love but because the marriage brings honor (and sometimes material wealth and prestige) to the families of the married couple. Also (as in India,) many societies that practice arranged marriage believe that young people can't make good decisions about marriage, and that if their elders make them, the marriage is more likely to survive.

Many factors play into the decision to marry; in the United States, one important factor has been age. In 1890, most couples married around 20 or 25 years of age, whereas today many marry closer to 30 years of age. This delay may have to do with the increase in life expectancy, which was around 40 years in the 1800s and is closer to 70 years today.

Marriage is normally between a male and a female because for many thousands of years the institution has been deeply concerned with the rearing of offspring, and matching up pairs of males and females takes advantage of each parent's qualities to protect the children. But the times, they are a-changin': Particularly in Western civilization, the marriage of same-sex couples is becoming more common. In non-Westernized cultures, same-sex marriage can occur, but it's pretty rare.

Another cultural variation deals with the number of people a person can be married to. One common variation is *polygyny,* or the marriage of a male to more than one female. This practice is very common worldwide: About 70 percent of human cultures approve of the arrangement (at least in principle), but because getting the union sanctioned by multiple family members and providing for several wives at once are both difficult tasks, many more males worldwide aspire to polygyny than actually practice it.

Another similar practice is *polyandry,* the marriage of a female to more than one male. Polyandry is very rare worldwide, practiced only in sub-Himalayan

Asia (Nepal, Tibet, and India); it likely originated with the cultural practice of female infanticide (carried out for complex reasons), which reduced the number of marriageable females in society.

Another dimension of variability in marriages is the question of whether one marries in or marries out. *Endogamy* is the tradition marrying within a specified and well-known social, economic, and/or racial group; for example, royal families are very careful to marry among their own social level (that is, other royals), though even royals buck this trend occasionally, as in the case of the British royal Prince Charles and Lady Diana Spencer (who became Princess Diana). Although Diana wasn't royalty, she was from the aristocratic Spencer family, so Charles hadn't strayed too far from the norm. The opposite of endogamy is *exogamy,* or consciously marrying well outside the boundaries of your closer relations. People often do this to escape certain economic restrictions (such as marrying up to a higher social/economic level) or, more practically (in small-scale societies), to prevent the genetic problems that come from incest, such as birth defects. Some cultures prohibit marrying outside ones' subculture; for example, in the Indian caste system, people are supposed to marry within their own specific social rank.

Kinship

Although marriage deals specifically with whom a person marries, *kinship* deals with all relations, those by blood and those by marriage. It's so complex, in fact, that anthropologists have come up with a glossary of kinship terms and a way of graphically diagramming kin relations that produces diagrams much like a family tree; a very simple example is shown in Figure 15-1. Rather than cover the whole world of kinship terminology comprehensively, the following sections introduce you to some of the kinship basics.

Kinship deals with more than just close relatives; it also deals with many individuals, such as those in *lineages* (bloodlines) or *descent groups*, which are groups of individuals related by ancestry (for example, clans or tribes). Although functions vary, and not all of the following are true of all descent groups, common functions of descent groups (which overlap some functions of the family) include

- **Justice administration:** Entire descent groups may be insulted if one member is insulted, and justice is therefore often managed not between individuals of different descent groups, but between the entire groups.

- **Management of property:** In families, the communally owned property, including material items, spiritual resources (like access to certain ritual sites), and/or political resources are all managed by the descent group rather than by individuals or individual families.

✔ **Identity:** In some cultures, the descent group (not the family or even the individual) is the main unit of identity.

✔ **Endorsement of marriage:** In descent groups, the whole group must endorse marriages, not just the marrying couple themselves.

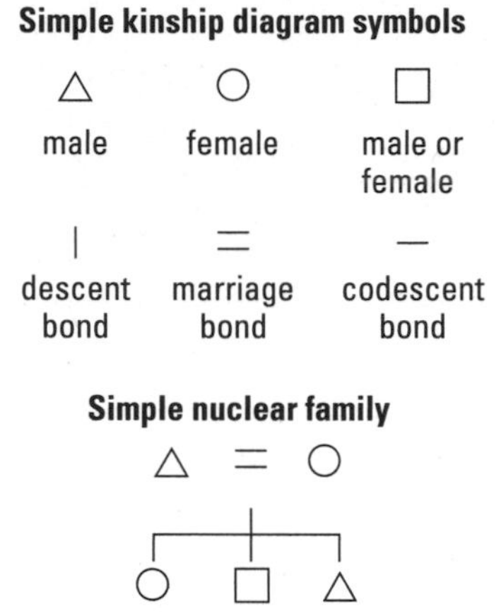

Figure 15-1:
Kinship
diagram for
a simple
nuclear
family.

Simple kinship diagram symbols

△   ○   □

male   female   male or
                       female

| =   —

descent   marriage   codescent
bond   bond   bond

Simple nuclear family

△ = ○

○ □ △

The "male or female" (square) is called "ego" or the person of reference in the diagram. In this case, "ego" has a married mother and father as well as one brother and one sister.

One way to keep track of what ancestry a person has is to consider whether descent groups trace their heritage through one or both of the parents. If a person's descent is *unilineal,* he tracks his relations through either his mother's or father's side (but not both). This practice is or was traditional in just over half of the world's cultures, and was common in ancient Rome as well as the great 18th-century Ashanti kingdom of West Africa.

Cognatic descent is more flexible than unilineal descent because it allows people to track their relationships to the families of *each* parent. Slightly less than half the world's peoples traditionally use or have used this system; although people in the U.S. typically use the last name of the male parent in naming (which seems to imply unilineal descent), they're actually interested in (and make social and economic use of) the relations of both parents' families, so U.S. residents actually practice cognatic descent.

Squirming yet? Ethnocentrism and relativism

Reading about different types of marriage, sexual relations, and so on can be very uncomfortable because cultures are normally quite conservative; individuals tend to hold tightly to their core cultural values and normally consider those values to be the most reasonable option. This ethnocentrism isn't just a Western issue — all cultures seem to believe that they have sorted out the world's best and most appropriate ways to be human. Avoiding ethnocentrism doesn't mean you should never judge anyone for anything. Nobody said that every human adaptation is good for everyone in the culture; cultures have made marvelous things like art and myth that are universally loved, but they've also created terrible institutions such as slavery that today are largely (if not universally) despised. Remember, ethnocentrism is common and leads to friction, but at the same time, a knee-jerk reaction of extreme cultural relativism in which you accept all cultural traits may well be amoral considering today's global connections; for example, by allowing us to ignore clear violations of human rights, such as slavery.

In addition to keeping track of one, or both, sides of the parent generation, globally human cultures specify whether they will track identity through the male or female parental lines. *Patrilineal* ancestry focuses on the relatives of the male parent; this is the most common system worldwide, practiced by about 60 percent of human cultures. *Matrilineal* ancestry focuses on the relatives of the female parent; this is less common than the patrilineal system and is practiced by only about 15 percent of the world's cultures. Either of these tracking systems is an option for unilineal descent trackers; for cognatic trackers, the answer is *ambilineal* ancestry, which allows a person to track descent by either parent's family.

Although matrilineality sounds as though it's a situation in which females have more power than males, male domination of economic and social opportunities and actions within the family is pretty widespread even though possessions, rights, and so on are transmitted through the female line.

In the U.S. today, most people track descent cognatically and ambilineally, and in this way Americans have a lot in common with many cultures worldwide — their families are important to them. But due to a variety of social and economic factors, one topic Americans don't spend too much time on is deciding which family to live with after marriage, which is a big issue in many nonindustrial societies. *Patrilocal* residence keeps the married couple close to the husband's father's physical residence; *matrilocal* residence keeps them closer to the bride's mother's residence. *Neolocal* residence (practiced widely in the U.S. today) allows post-marriage residence away from both the brides' and groom's parental residences.

Sex and Gender

Sex is a biological term referring to whether a person donates sperm or egg in the act of biological reproduction. Human males and females exhibit several main outward differences:

- Males are on average about 10 percent larger (in height or weight) than females.
- Females can breastfeed.
- Females have slightly wider hips and carry more fat on the body.

The possibility or likelihood of differences in male and female perception, ways of communicating, and skills (however defined) is so hot a topic that I'm not even going to touch it. Personally, I think anthropologists have good evolutionary reason to imagine that such differences could exist, but I'm not convinced that anyone has yet documented them in detail.

The differences between sex and gender

Although sex is a relatively straightforward matter of biology, gender can be very complicated. Before looking more carefully at what constitutes certain genders, keep in mind how important gender issues are in society. Worldwide, gender is assigned to individuals for several reasons:

- As part of a person's core identity (informing expectations of self)
- To delineate social expectations
- To delineate economic and political expectations

Masculinity and femininity are important; every culture has some concept of *gender ideology,* or what's appropriate male or female behavior, woven throughout its values and often its religious system. However, these ideologies differ from culture to culture. In some cultures (for example, Arabic culture), males are permitted and even expected to hold hands with their friends, whereas this action would be considered effeminate and suspicious in other cultures. Of course, sanctions for stepping out of approved gender boundaries can be severe, up to and including death.

And just as you can find variation in the appropriate gender expression per culture, there are also variations on how much a person can blur the lines between masculinity and femininity within a given culture. Italian culture today features a strong dash of bravado and machismo, but men are also expected to be extremely deferential towards their mothers, in ways that many Italian women find overfeminine. Life is complicated!

The native peoples of North America have a long tradition of the *berdache*, the person who is biologically male but acts and dresses in ways normally reserved for women. Many anthropologists believe that although this practice has never been particularly common worldwide, such behavioral variation was more common before the 19th-century European colonization of much of the rest of the world, when such behavior was so counter to Victorian ideals that it was largely and widely suppressed.

Common gender roles

Although the varying gender roles have changed through time, anthropologists have found several trends in gender roles worldwide. These trends are often related to the gender division of labor, which is more significant in nonindustrial societies than in industrialized societies. *(Non-industrial* refers to traditional societies that aren't deeply involved in the high-technology, mass-productive, high-speed world of Western civilization; it's not the best term, but it's better than the archaic *primitive.*) Non-industrial societies often organize labor according to other factors (including age and social rank), but gender is often important as well. In non-industrial societies, male roles often include fighting/engagement in warfare, hunting and fishing, working with hard substances such as rock, and long-distance trade. Female roles typically include food preparation, domestic activities (maintenance of a home), child-rearing activities, and working with soft substances such as fabric

When social inequalities arise from gender differences, the society is practicing *gender stratification.* This occurs when certain kinds of activities are valued over others, such as hunting over child-rearing. Such evaluations may seem arbitrary from the outside, but each culture has a complex gender ideology serving as a foundation of the practice. Any attempt to change them would require careful work with the society in a way that recognizes the significance of these roles to the culture practicing them.

The gendered division of labor is often more ideological than written in stone. In some societies, women participate in hunting, and in many cases males are engaged in child-rearing. Especially during times of stress, gender roles may be altered, such as they were in the United States during World War II, when women were suddenly welcomed into industrial labor that previously had been largely outside their typical gender expectations. Figure 15-2 shows how women were encouraged to do work that used to be more male-dominated without losing their identity as women; the definition of what it was to be a woman, what was considered appropriate for women to do, changed as a result of cultural change.

Figure 15-2:
Rosie the
Riveter,
a new
women's
gender role
in the
U.S. during
World
War II.

Kinship and Gender Worldwide and through Time

In Chapter 10, I outline the three main subsistence modes humanity has devised: foraging (hunting and gathering), horticulture (low-intensity growing of crops and raising animals), and agriculture (high-intensity crop-growing and animal husbandry). I also describe the distinctive social organization associated with each of these modes, and in each of these kinds of societies you can make some generalizations about how kinship and gender play out. The following sections outline the main trends.

Among foragers

Most foraging societies are small, apolitical bands or tribes that move across landscapes to take advantage of widely dispersed food sources; this mobility de-emphasizes concepts of ownership, material property, and even social ranking and also has affects kinship and gender.

In many cases, foraging society kinship systems are largely based on the nuclear family or small groups of nuclear families called *bands*. Large descent groups, either matrilineal or patrilineal, can't really form because populations are low and the amount of physical property to be handed from one generation to the next (a management task important in descent groups) is limited.

Although men and women do about the same amount of work in foraging societies, the societies often have strict concepts of men's and women's work. Where meat is a large part of the diet (as in the Arctic), men do more hunting; where plant food is a large part of the diet (as in the Congo), women do more foraging. Because foragers aren't prone to warfare, males typically don't serve as soldiers or warriors, though they may take up such roles for short times.

Foraging societies today and historically have some parallels with our prehistoric ancestors because all humans were foragers until the invention of horticulture and agriculture about 10,000 years ago. But there have been many ways to be a forager in the last few million years, and today's foragers have undergone centuries of change since contact with Western civilization, so anthropologists are careful about equating them with some idea of the "original" human society.

Like any anthropological category, the label "forager" masks a lot of variation. Many foragers are (and have been) small in population, and highly mobile, and practicing little in the way of social ranking, but in a few cases (as on the Pacific Northwest Coast of North America) traditional foraging societies were socially ranked, owned property, and were residentially sedentary (rather than highly mobile). Rather than think of these categories as unchanging absolutes, you're better off thinking about them as shades in a spectrum of social and subsistence modes.

Among horticulturalists

Horticulturalists typically appear as chiefdoms that practice low-intensity agriculture, farming small fields (or even garden-sized plots) and raising a small number of animals; these behaviors make them more sedentary than the highly mobile foragers, but they still do move, often cyclically from one farming patch to another on a three-or-four-year rotation. Because of their investment in these patches of land and the tools and facilities used to process grown foods, horticulturalists have more physical material to pass down from one generation to the next than foragers do; social ranking is also present, though not as pronounced as in civilization.

Horticultural society kinship systems are largely based on large, complex descent groups organized into clans or lineages that have elaborate traditions and histories that link them to important ancestral founding figures, such as the revered spirits of ancestors among natives of New Guinea Many are matrilineal (identify themselves with the mother's side of the family), and they're often exogamous (marry outside their bloodlines). Marriage ties are also more important than in foragers, again because of the need to carefully manage the transmission of rights and property from one generation to the next.

Although gender roles vary a great deal, in many cases women in horticultural societies have relatively high status compared to other societies; this tendency is even more prominent in societies where families reside near the wife's family.

Among agriculturalists

Ancient agriculturalists practiced high-intensity agriculture, farming large fields with intensive irrigation and using plows, and raising large numbers of animals. These behaviors made them very sedentary (often living near the bodies of their buried relatives) such that the concept of owning property is strong and deeply ingrained. Agricultural societies were strongly socially ranked, with a small, elite class ruling over many farming peasants.

Agricultural society kinship systems could also be based on large, complex descent groups, but because urbanism (cities) and specialized trades (such as baker or potter) were present, kin connections were sometimes de-emphasized in favor of labor-based social connections. Most of these societies are patrilineal; in fact, males are often dominant in nearly every aspect of life, at least on the surface. However, women in such arrangements can hold considerable power to influence the husband (for example, economically), and this point shouldn't be overlooked. Although gender roles varied enormously, in many cases women focused on domestic work away from the public sphere, which (along with long-distance trade) was the domain of men. In ancient Egypt, for example, males were much more likely to become scribes, where women were more likely to remain child-rearers, or workers in the home. Men also often engaged in warfare, in many cases as full-time soldiers.

Keep in mind that in all these cases, the various gender roles, kinship rules, and subsistence modes were complexly intertwined; try to tweak one factor, and others would be affected. And in most cases, these behaviors were somehow adaptive in that they promoted survival. Now, not all adaptations are good — cultures also have maladaptations that area actually bad for at least some of the members of society — and you can always ask yourself who's benefitting from a particular arrangement Sometimes, the answer is "everyone," but other times things might not be so magnanimous.

Chapter 16

Not at the Dinner Table! Religion and Politics

● ●

● ●

"Men never do evil so completely and cheerfully as when they do it from religious conviction."

—Blaise Pascal

"If you ever injected truth into politics you would have no politics."

—Will Rogers

*W*orldwide, humans have various religious and political views. Strike religion against politics, and the sparks can really fly; few things are as volatile as the friction between religious or political ideas. Why is this? And why does such a diversity of beliefs exist in the first place?

In this chapter I explain just what politics and religions are — as anthropologists understand them — and how anthropologists study them to get at human universals as well as diversity. I also examine, essentially, what anthropologists have discovered about these fields, and what that means for being human.

What Is Religion?

As in many other facets of the human experience, religions are so different worldwide that religion as a whole can be hard to define. At the very least, any given *religion* is a set of beliefs and instructions regarding the *supernatural*, a realm thought to exist beyond the material, concrete realm of daily life. Most anthropologists would agree that all religious systems describe

- **The supernatural world and its inhabitants:** Most cultures have a belief in some kind of supernatural world beyond the material one.

- **How to properly revere and/or interact with the supernatural world and its inhabitants:** The supernatural world is complex and needs to be properly addressed (sometimes to improve life and conditions here in the material world).

- **What's proper behavior for life in the material world and the soul's fate after death:** Most cultures have some concept of a human energy or soul persisting after the death of the physical body.

Religions, then, at the least, are instruction manuals for what the supernatural world is like and what to do about it. This phrasing is very similar to the definition I give for *culture* in Chapter 11; as a subset of cultural information, religion is the system of beliefs and instructions about the supernatural part of the human experience.

Functions of religion

Anthropologists have suggested many reasons for the *functions* of religion in human cultures:

- Religions provide explanations for the unknown; religious myths name and discuss the unknown, which then makes it at least seem knowable.

- Religions reinforce social unity, reminding people of their cultural commonalities rather than their differences.

- Religions provide psychological comfort by offering consolation for injustice, harm, and death.

- Religions provide bedrock principles for life, which give followers security in a world of change.

- Religions provide guidance through the stages of life, reinforcing culturally appropriate changes with baptisms, marriages, and funerals and spirit-assistance sanctified by religious specialists, such as priests.

Religions are significant social institutions that provide guides to a lot of behavior. They often describe the reasons for *taboos*, important social restrictions against things such as incest or blasphemy.

Religious concepts intertwine with other aspects of human life: In the United States, a person may pray to a deity when going to war, or swear an oath on a religious text when in a court of law. This infusion of religious concepts with the rest of society — even in a culture, like that of the United States, which explicitly professes the separation of church and state — shows just how deeply structuring religious ideas really are for most cultures.

One reason the study of religion is so important in anthropology is that religious belief systems have been a central aspect of life for most of the world's people throughout history. The spread of *atheism* (active disbelief in a higher power) and *agnosticism* (belief that a higher power may or may not exist) is a relatively new development; for much of history, religious belief systems are where people past and present have gotten their basic concepts of right and wrong, sin and good deeds, death and life, and so on.

Ideas about right and wrong can come from many sources, such as non-religious philosophy. But for most of history and even today, they don't. Religions have established such a monopoly on defining right and wrong, for example, that my own city's main newspaper *(The Oregonian)* has a section called "Religion and Ethics." But any good philosopher can go on for hours (or days or whole careers) about morality and ethics without ever invoking religious reasons for certain positions. These discussions of *moral philosophy* deal with ethics without bringing religion into it. For example, primatologists have studied social rule systems in nonhuman primates, where systems of moral behavior exist independent of religious beliefs.

Why religion is so powerful

So where do religious systems of belief get their power? Why does every culture have at least one, and why do people believe them so fervently that many are ready and quite willing to kill and die and for them?

The answer of a participant in one of the religions would be that the particular religion is so important, compelling, and powerful because it's right; it derives from the divine and inerrant words of the higher power, so it must be valuable and true.

The scientific perspective suggested by late, great anthropologist Roy Rappaport is that the power of religious systems is found in their self-reinforcement. That is, religions gain their strength and authority through the repetition of religious rituals designed to remind participants of *ultimate sacred postulates*, which are a set of core beliefs about the nature of the universe and human existence. Although the exact contents of each set of ultimate sacred postulates differ in each religion, they're all said to be self-evident, inerrant truths that are so scared they must not be questioned; they're foundations of entire religious belief systems.

Ultimate sacred postulates can be found in the Muslim's statement "There is no god (ilah) but God (Allah), and Muhammad is His prophet" and the Christian prayer, "I believe in God the Father Almighty, Maker of heaven and earth. I believe in Jesus Christ, his only begotten Son, our Lord. I believe in the Holy Catholic Church, the communion of saints, the forgiveness of sins, the resurrection of the body, and the life everlasting. Amen."

In many cultures, religious belief systems are so complex that they require full-time specialists — priests of one kind or another — to handle the various rituals and ceremonies used to reiterate the ultimate sacred postulates. In this way, these religious specialists are the mediators between the material world — in which the human experience is lived — and the supernatural world. I look at these concepts a little more closely in the next section.

The Material and Supernatural Worlds

Every human has a physical body and material needs that they feed through material means like water, food, nutrients, and shelter. I call this world of physical, mundane objects the *material world.* All humans exist in the material world; even the most devout monk or yogi has to drink and eat.

At the same time, though, anthropologists have found that all human cultures have some concept of the *supernatural,* a word referring to a universe of real things beyond the material. In Western civilization, the word *supernatural* indicates beings, processes, and circumstances in the supernatural world that can't be explained by the natural sciences. Because I'm writing this book from the basic perspective of Western science, I'm comfortable saying that a material world exists and that at the same time, many cultures worldwide have strong beliefs about a realm or beings, powers, and circumstances *beyond* this physical realm. It's this beyond that I refer to as the *supernatural* or *ethereal* world.

This topic can get pretty sticky when you consider that some cultures don't subscribe to the notions of Western science; is their supernatural actually their natural? To some extent, any definition of *supernatural* is relative, but for the purposes of this book I'm using the definition laid out in the preceding paragraphs.

The anthropological division of the human experience into what I call material and supernatural realms isn't particularly new. In 1912, Emile Durkheim, a prominent French sociologist of religion, wrote that all religious beliefs exhibited a common distinction between real and ideal things into classes he called the profane (material) and sacred (ethereal). I (and many anthropologists) believe Durkheim was right about some of this stuff, but in this book I'm using my own terms to avoid being lumped in with all of his views.

Now because all cultures and their members live in the material world but also have some concepts of the ethereal world, all humans live in a state of overlap between the two. Figure 16-1 illustrates that access to the ethereal often occurs through mediators, such as shamans or priests, who specialize in religious knowledge.

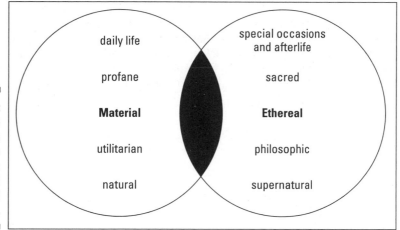

Figure 16-1: Human life is lived in the overlap between the material and ethereal worlds.

daily life

profane

Material

utilitarian

natural

special occasions and afterlife

sacred

Ethereal

philosophic

supernatural

The overlap itself isn't specifically so important — that's just a reality of life. More important is understanding that this position of life between these realms is central to many human lives. More than sheer economics or politics or even biology (though each of these is important), the ultimate sacred postulates encoded in a culture's religion motivate everything from suicide bombings to acts of nonviolence.

Ritual and Religion

A religion's ultimate sacred postulates have to be communicated to the members of a culture — they don't get transmitted through DNA any more than culture does. (See Chapter 11 for more on the transmission of culture.) This communication often occurs in ceremonies or rituals.

I think the most important definition of ritual comes courtesy of anthropologist Roy Rappaport, who wrote that *ritual* is the performance of relatively invariant, traditionally defined acts and utterances; one example is the ceremony of First Holy Communion in the Christian tradition.

This definition may seem pretty vague; like many human behaviors ritual varies enormously worldwide. But the following important commonalities show just how important religious ritual is and reinforce Rappaport's definition:

- ✔ Ritual briefly transports people a little closer to the ethereal or supernatural world, reminding them of their ultimate sacred postulates; it reforges ties they may forget in the rush of daily life here in the material world.

- ✔ Ritual reminds people of their common religious and social values.

- ✔ Ritual normally takes place at special places and times, such that the presentations of the ultimate sacred postulates are remembered as special events (for example, church on Sunday).

- ✔ Ritual doesn't normally present new information but rather reiterates the ultimate sacred postulates (for example, the Lord's Prayer).

Not all ritual is religious, but a lot is, and a lot of nonreligious ritual — such as swearing in an American president — still incorporates religious elements, such as swearing on the Bible.

Ritual can also be used to try to manipulate forces or plead to beings in the supernatural or ethereal realm. For example, Aztec priests ritually sacrificed human beings to satisfy various gods. The priests thought this ritual would bring about better conditions for farming because the gods (in the supernatural realm) supposedly controlled rain and other variables important to agriculture (in the material realm). Many in Western civilization today ask God — through prayer — to assist in everything from daily life to victory in battle . . . just as humans have appealed to the supernatural for thousands of years.

Religious ritual often includes *magic,* an attempt to control some aspect of the supernatural. Magic is normally carried out by religious specialists equipped with special objects, and magic rituals often involve specific sequences of events (such as chants, bodily postures, and so on) called *magical formulae.* Knowledge of magical formulae is normally secretive, and can include things as diverse as appropriate drumming techniques or the use of hallucinogenic substances; long periods of apprenticeship may be necessary to learn them.

Regardless of whether a person believes in what a religion states, the anthropological study of religion has shown that religion is so important because it drives (to a variable degree) a lot of human behavior.

When I say that religious systems are important or significant to human cultures, I'm not saying that they're necessary or that any one of them is correct. I'm simply saying that as things stand today, which is how they have for a long time, religion is a significant factor of human life. Which religion to follow — if any — is (in Western societies, anyway) largely a person's own choice. I'm selling no particular soap here!

The Organization of Supernatural Knowledge

The specific content of a given religion is normally complex and detailed; as human societies become more populous and complex, sometimes religion also becomes more complex. The supernatural beings of religious systems include *gods* (powerful, immortal beings responsible for creation and destruction) and *spirits* (lesser supernatural beings including deceased ancestors, personal guardians, and mischievous — and sometimes friendly — ghosts).

Polytheistic religions have multiple gods and goddesses; people in ancient Egypt worshiped nearly 100 main deities, and Hinduism features thousands of deities. *Monotheistic* religions tend to have one major god (as in the Christian tradition), but also contain other supernatural beings (such as angels and the devil).

Supernatural religious knowledge is often handled by *religious specialists,* people in a given culture who act as repositories of supernatural knowledge and are capable of using it effectively in ritual. Religious specialists include two main types: shamans and priests.

Shamans

A *shaman* is a person who is charged with much special supernatural knowledge and the know-how to use it to create lasting effects in the material world. Shamanism is typically found in cultures with relatively low populations and less-institutionalized religious systems, like small-scale foraging or simple farming societies. Shamans are often outsiders. They're feared as well as respected, and they often live on the margins of society because of their potentially dangerous proximity to the powerful forces of the supernatural realm. Shamans have at least two important roles that recur worldwide. One is that they facilitate physical healing; health problems in the material realm are often thought to originate in the ethereal or supernatural realm, and shamans often are called on to mediate with spirits to solve such problems. They also deal with spiritual healing. What Westerners may call psychological issues are often considered spiritual problems in shamanic societies. Shamans often undertake perilous, ritually marked journeys to the supernatural realm to intervene.

A shaman can be male or female; the word *shaman* derives from a Tungus (native Russian) word used to designate Tungus ritual-religious specialists, but the word is now used for any such specialist. People with shamanic roles are found worldwide.

Shamanic rituals often involve the shaman entering a state of altered consciousness, or a *trance* state. This state can be accomplished in many ways, such as with repetitive chanting, drumming, self-deprivation of food or water, or the use of hallucinogenic substances such as the fly agaric mushroom in Siberia and North America, *peyote* (a cactus found mainly in Mexico), and *ayahuasca* (a visionary tea brewed by shamans in South America). In the trance state, the shaman is transported to the spiritual realm; on coming out of the trance, the shaman is returned to the material realm.

Shamanism isn't a religion itself; it's more of a technique for influencing the supernatural world to have effects in the material world.

Figure 16-2 shows a traditional Tungus shaman. He wears special clothing and holds a drum used in his healing ceremonies.

Figure 16-2:
A traditional Tungus shaman photographed in Siberia around 1890.

© Bettmann/CORBIS

Priests

A *priest* also possesses special supernatural knowledge, but a priest normally has less direct access to the supernatural world than a shaman does.

Additionally, they serve more as conduits or guides to the supernatural instead of directly contacting or influencing it. Priests are more common in cultures with relatively large populations and institutionalized religious systems, such as large-scale agricultural societies (but more on that a bit later). Priests come in different forms (such as Christian ministers, Jewish rabbis, or Muslim imams), but their functions as part of the religious system are normally roughly the same. Two common services priests provide are giving official blessings to social events such as marriage (and one Russian Orthodox priest blessed a new missile system) and offering guidance to the supernatural ramifications or origins of problems.

Priests often carry out complex religious rituals involving special material objects and substances, like the wine and wafer in Christian communion or the obsidian blades in Aztec sacrifice. What's important to remember here is that these religious specialists are necessary for the maintenance and proper carrying out of the religious system; if the priestly classes aren't supported, the religion may crumble.

Priests are typical of large *institutionalized religions* — official religions of certain political units, such as states or civilizations — that they sustain through delivering the ultimate sacred postulates to the lay public. Although not all civilizations or states today have official religions, the ancient civilizations normally had very strict rules as to what religions citizens could practice. In Aztec civilization, for example, police would patrol the suburbs on important ritual days to ensure that everyone was attending the state-sponsored religious activities.

Institutionalized religions are normally complex and arranged hierarchically. For example, consider the modern Roman Catholic Church, which employs thousands of people worldwide. Its religious specialists are hierarchically arranged to most effectively communicate the religion's ultimate sacred postulates. The ranks include

- **The pope,** an official who orchestrates structural changes in the church and has the most direct access to the supernatural (God)
- **Archbishops,** 45 of whom oversee and govern the activities of the church in the United States
- **Priests,** who most directly communicate the ultimate sacred postulates to the lay public by performing rituals

The Origins of Religion

Where did these ideas of the supernatural world come from in the first place? Again, these questions can have emic or etic answers.

Lucretius on the invention of religion

One of the first recorded statements that the gods were invented by humans (rather than the other way around) appears in the writings of Lucretius, a first-century BC Roman philosopher. In his fascinating treatise *De Rerum Natura* (sometimes translated as *On the Nature of the Universe*), Lucretius suggested that humanity had invented gods and religion first to account for their dreams and then to account for some of the (then) mysteries of the natural world. The following excerpt was translated by R.E. Latham and published in 1951, but the ideas are more than 2,000 years old:

"Let us now consider why reverence for the gods is widespread. . . . The explanation is not far to seek. Already in those early days men had visions when their minds were awake, and more clearly in sleep, of divine figures. . . . To

these figures they attributed feeling . . . . credited them with eternal life . . . . pictured their lot as far superior to that of mortals . . . because in dreams they saw them perform all sorts of miracles without the slightest effort."

"[M]en noticed the orderly succession of celestial phenomena and the round of the seasons and were at a loss to account for them. So they took refuge in handing over everything to the gods and making everything dependent on their whim. They chose the sky to be the home and headquarters of the gods . . . . What griefs they hatched then for themselves . . . . This is not piety, this oft-repeated show of bowing a veiled head before a stone . . . this deluging of altars with the blood of beasts; this heaping of vow upon vow. True piety lies rather in the power to contemplate the universe with a quiet mind."

purpose B a contemplating this peace which passeth . . . .

The *emic* perspective (which considers the supernatural to be a real realm) is that the ideas about the supernatural world came from the gods and goddesses themselves, either directly or sometimes through mediums such as prophets. For these billions of folks, the supernatural world that Western science would call unprovable or not demonstrable is as real as the book in your hands.

The *etic,* anthropological perspective (though some anthropologists have religious convictions of their own) is that the supernatural was essentially invented by humanity. Why would humanity create these religious, some of which are unfathomably complex to all but the most learned, and some of which have guided humanity through one war after another?

In the past century, anthropologists have proposed many reasons for the invention of religion. The possible origins of religion have been arranged into several main types:

✓ **Explanatory/rationalizing origins:** Religion was invented to account for the unknown, to explain the inexplicable, to account for the unaccountable, to give order to a world that can be disorderly, and/or to account for order that seemed to have been created by something far more powerful than humanity.

 ✔ **Self-actualizing origins:** Religion was invented as a system of beliefs that gave shape to human culture and could maintain that shape through time. This idea is exemplified by Emile Durkheim's statement that "religion is society worshipping itself;" and although prereligious cultures certainly had shape and could survive, religion was a further adaptation, a new way of making human cultures function more efficiently.

 ✔ **Social control origins:** Religion was invented as a way to better control human behavior. A fascinating twist on this old idea is Rappaport's concept that the rituals and restrictions of religion were invented to dampen out the potential for social chaos presented by the rise of human language, which can be used to create new thoughts and interpretations that challenge social harmony.

So far, none of these models has completely swept the anthropological community. Some of the factors in each model may have contributed to the evolution of the first religion; other religions were affected by all three factors in varying degrees. Right now, anthropologists just don't know how the first religion originated.

Just because anthropologists *don't* know something at the moment doesn't necessarily mean they *can't* know it. Many things take a lot of time to understand.

What does archaeology say about the origins of religion? More these days than in the past century, but still not much. More than likely, early peoples exercised religious thoughts without using a lot of artifacts; without artifacts, archaeologists will be hard-pressed to find traces of early religions.

Still, some new approaches to cave art have been interesting. Many archaeologists are now convinced that *cave art* (images in European caves, dating to over 40,000 years ago) are depictions of shamanic rituals — specifically, shamanic voyages to the supernatural world, where they encounter animals and beings not found in the material world. Though this argument hasn't been completely developed, some of the evidence for this interpretation is pretty compelling.

Archaeologically, the first unambiguous evidence of religious systems is the temples of the ancient civilization of Sumer, dated to just over 6,000 years ago; and since then (as you can read in Chapter 10) large, organized state religions have flourished more or less worldwide. Some kinds of religion must have served as foundations for these institutionalized state religions, but right now archaeological evidence for them is pretty thin on the ground.

Types of Religions

As with many aspects of human life, religions vary a lot worldwide, but they can be classified into various types. One influential classification of world religions (published by Anthony F.C. Wallace) recognizes four main types, based on their relative complexity:

✔ **Shamanic** religions allow people to have direct, unscheduled contact with their supernatural world; sometimes they're assisted by a shaman who may work magic for various purposes, and sometimes they're assisted by a lifelong guardian spirit. Shamanic religion is most commonly practiced by the most mobile of human societies.

Examples of shamanic religions include those of the native peoples of the Arctic, including the Canadian Inuit and the peoples of Arctic Siberia. These folk have a strong tradition of powerful shamans, and their world is *animistic,* populated by supernatural beings that inhabit both animate (living) and inanimate (nonliving) objects. They have no real supreme god, although some deities are more powerful than others; among the Canadian Inuit, for example, Sedna, the keeper of the sea animals (seals, whales, and others that are very important to Inuit subsistence) is particularly important.

✔ **Communal** religions feature regular rituals carried out in special places and at special times to give members access to a supernatural world populated by many gods and goddesses. Followers continually use magic to assist in any activity that involves risk, and although magic may be performed by religious specialists such as shamans, community members themselves carry out many religious tasks. This religion is associated with slightly less-mobile societies, including horticultural societies that practice low-intensity farming. Communal religion is or was practiced by many groups including most Native Americans, many Africans, and the peoples of Australia and Oceania (the Pacific islands).

✔ **Olympian** religions have a very complex supernatural world accessed largely by religious specialists such as *diviners* (people who attempt to predict the future). Numerous subdivisions of the religious system can include *ancestor cults* (focusing on the worship of ancestor spirits) and *great god cults* (focusing on the worship of specific principal deities).

An Olympian religion was practiced by the traditional agricultural chiefdoms of Dahomey, West Africa, a society with higher population and less mobility than the polar Inuit or the native Australians. In Dahomey, elaborate ceremonies carried out by nearly full-time religious specialists venerated the ancestor spirits of the living and made sacrifices to the great gods. As in the religions of ancient Greece, Egypt, and Babylon, Dahomey had a complex pantheon of many gods.

✔ **Monotheistic or ecclesiastic** religions are those in which a single supreme god is venerated above all else (though other supernatural beings, such as angels, may exist). These religions support a hierarchy of full-time religious specialists who have the most continual and richest communication with the supernatural world.

Monotheistic or ecclesiastic religions include the Judeo-Christian and Islamic traditions, each of which venerates a single, ultimate God and are organized as complex churches staffed by career religious-knowledge specialists who have high social status. The lay public, though they take regular part in religious ritual, have less direct access to the supernatural realm than in other types of religion and look to the clergy to interpret that realm.

Figure 16-3 shows the varieties and locations of many of the world's religions.

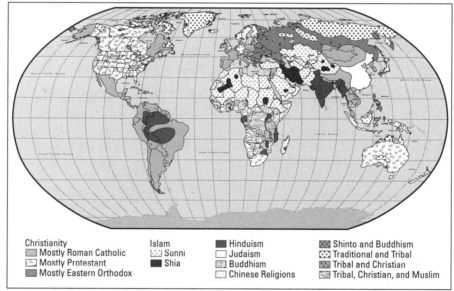

Figure 16-3:
Modern distribution of world religions.

Christianity	Islam	Hinduism	Shinto and Buddhism
Mostly Roman Catholic	Sunni	Judaism	Traditional and Tribal
Mostly Protestant	Shia	Buddhism	Tribal and Christian
Mostly Eastern Orthodox		Chinese Religions	Tribal, Christian, and Muslim

The Relations of Power: Politics

Although many believe that in some distant past, humans lived in social harmony, archaeology and anthropology indicate that this is a myth. Even the chimpanzees, our closest relatives in the animal kingdom, maintain strict social hierarchies in which social power isn't equally distributed but rather held by individuals until . . . well, until they lose that power and status, often by losing a physical challenge issued by another chimpanzee.

In the human world, *power* is the ability to constrain the options of or impose will on others. The constraints and impositions can be material, as when food is withheld from a population, or social, as when a powerful group refuses to recognize the legitimacy of a less-powerful group. The following section delves into the acquisition and exertion of power.

I've got the power (and I know how to use it)

Anthropologists studying power relations have identified two main ways that power is *acquired* by individuals and organizations. One is by *force,* or the use or threat of violence to achieve power (such as invasion of one group's territory by another). The other is by *authority*, or the use of socially recognized status to achieve power (such as movement of a governmental official up through the ranks of the political system).

When most Americans hear the word *politics*, they think of the Republican or Democratic parties— but I'm not touching these with a ten-foot boathook! Anthropologically, *politics* simply refers to the relations of power in a culture and how these relations affect decision-making.

An important aspect of power in human culture is *social status*, a person's rank as measured by prestige in the culture. In some cases social status is *achieved* by an individual's deeds in the course of life. In other cases, it's *ascribed* at birth, such as when one is born into a royal family, for example, or a lower *caste* (a term some cultures give social statuses).

Anthropologists have also identified some main ways that the powerful wield their power:

- ✔ **Leadership selection:** How power is transferred among individuals — for example, via elections placing leaders into positions versus leaders being born into positions of power

- ✔ **Regulation of social behavior:** The use of communal power to maintain social cohesion through social customs, prohibitions, and norms versus the use of institutionalized power through laws

- ✔ **Conflict resolution:** The use of power to resolve differences

- ✔ **Relations with neighbors:** The use and negotiation of power in dealing with neighbors, be they ally, enemy, or neutral

Power plays: How various societies apply power

Anthropologists have also spent a lot of effort identifying the main kinds of political systems worldwide and through time. Although anthropologists always debate about exactly how to define the main kinds of political organization, most would agree on the four main kinds I summarize in the following sections. For more on the basic characteristics of these societies, head to Chapter 10. To read more about small- and large-scale societies' approaches to conflict, check out Chapter 17.

Bands

The key political characteristic of bands is their *egalitarian* character, in which power is distributed rather than concentrated. But remember, bands members have to work at this arrangement because individuals sometimes try to build social power by bragging about their hunting prowess or some other attribute; in fact, bands typically handle justice through social channels rather than formal codes of law. Therefore, they often squash such attempts at self-aggrandizement with ridicule. One native hunter of southern Greenland who attempted to lord over his fellows on the strength of his great hunting abilities was given the derogatory name "Dog Diarrhea" to cool his heels.

Tribes

Politically speaking, tribes (often consisting of loosely allied bands) are also typically egalitarian, although they allow a bit more leeway for the accumulation of power by individuals. They follow a somewhat more formal law system than bands do, but this system is still pretty simple. The main political characteristic of tribes is that their slightly larger and more sedentary populations have more complex political interactions — internally and with their neighbors — than those of bands. Whereas bands may have headmen who wield a limited amount of power, tribes can have more powerful chiefs. But tribal chiefs can only exert their will so far, and they aren't as powerful as they are in chiefdoms.

Chiefdoms

Politically, chiefdoms are normally *ranked* societies; although all members normally have equal access to material resources (such as food), access to social resources such as high social rank is limited. These societies have clear *social ranks*, different levels of prestige in the society. Because of these ranks, the key political characteristic of chiefdoms is that power is concentrated in the hands of certain members, often *elites*, who are born into positions of power, simply by being members of a ruling family. Chiefs, who could be male or female — female chiefs were common in Southeastern Alaska in the 19th century — had considerable power to coerce or influence their constituent populations. However, they had direct, violent power of life or death over slaves only. They didn't have such power over commoners; in fact, they couldn't even prevent commoners from moving away, an important distinction from states. Finally, note that a chiefdom's concentrated power structure supports a much more complex, formal legal system than bands or tribes operate.

States

The most important political characteristic of a *state* (also called a *civilization*) is that it's typically a *class* society, meaning it doesn't guarantee all members equal access to social and material resources. In other words, states concentrate power in certain hands and not others. Individuals are often born into classes that may be difficult to migrate out of. States have far-ranging political dealings, and they often express their power through a military composed of full-time military specialists including soldiers and officers. States are large and tend to dominate and assimilate surrounding political units of lesser power. Whereas the most important personal and economic bonds in bands, tribes and chiefdoms center on *kinship* (family connections), states emphasize professional and trade connections.

Although in some parts of the world bands have taken up farming and become chiefdoms (and then states), that's not an inevitable course for all human societies. States depend on agriculture to support a high population density, which just isn't possible in places like the Arctic or much of Australia. For more on the evolution of human political systems through time, have a look at Chapter 10.

Part IV
So What? Anthropology, the Modern World, and You

The 5th Wave   By Rich Tennant

"So, how long have you two been in Ghana studying the apes?"

In this part . . .

The study of humanity is fascinating, but it isn't confined to the ivory towers of academia. The lessons of anthropology are useful in your daily life; in this part, I show you how you can apply anthropological concepts to modern problems like climate change and cultural conflict.

Chapter 17

Kiss or Kill? Diversity, Conflict, and Culture

*L*ike any social animal, humans have conflict. But alone in the animal kingdom, humans have very distinctive cultural identities, each with its own set of ideas of what's appropriate in the world. When these different ideas come into contact (or even have interior disputes), humans are capable of dragging conflicts out into feuds, military strikes, and wars that kill millions.

In this chapter I discuss the long history of human conflict and how anthropology addresses the questions of diversity and conflict. You also see how anthropology can help solve problems of cultural conflict worldwide, an important point considering that globalization and mass, rapid communications make the world smaller every day by bringing all humans into closer and more frequent contact.

The Anthropology of Conflict and Conflict Resolution

By definition, social animals — including humans — live in communities. This arrangement brings individuals into close contact, and that can cause friction — for example, when two individuals want the same thing. For anthropologists, *conflict* occurs when negotiation fails to resolve differences between people or groups of people. Although most animals limit conflict to short episodes related to competition for mates or basic resources such as food and water, humans seem to have more (and more extensive) conflicts over a wide variety of cultural issues.

One of the goals of anthropology — and therefore a central message of this whole book — has been to combat, at least in modern civilization, the universal habit of *ethnocentrism*, judging other cultures by one's own standards. Most often, anthropologists combat ethnocentrism by promoting relativism in everything they write, including communications with the nonacademic world.

Cultural relativism is the anthropological perspective that sees each culture as being morally independent, not subject to moral judgment by others. Though this practice is useful in many ways, it can cause moral difficulties because, as anthropologist Conrad Kottak has pointed out, it would place Nazi Germany on the same moral level as Athenian Greece.

Considering how hard getting along with others can be, in some ways it's amazing the world isn't completely consumed in war. Of course, war is expensive in terms of lives and money, so for most cultures it's a later rather than earlier response to cultural friction. Table 17-1 shows American war deaths in many major conflicts over the years. The United States has been engaged in some kind of conflict quite a bit since 1775.

Table 17-1	American War Deaths	
War	**Years**	**Deaths**
Revolutionary War	1775–1783	4,435
War of 1812	1812–1815	2,260
Mexican War	1846–1848	13,283
Civil War	1861–1865	623,026
Spanish-American War	1898	2,446
World War I	1917–1918	116,708
World War II	1941–1945	407,316
Korean War	1950–1953	36,914
Vietnam War	1964–1973	58,169
Invasion of Grenada	1983	19
Persian Gulf War	1991	269
Afghanistan	2002–ongoing	350+
Operation Iraqi Freedom	2003–ongoing	4,000+
Totals	52 years+	1,269,195+

Source: U.S. Army Military History Institute, Carlisle, PA.

So, how does peaceful conflict resolution work? Anthropologists have identified that worldwide, one of the first resorts is normally some kind of *negotiation*, which is nonviolent resolution of differences, otherwise known as a *settlement*. Negotiation actually attempts to avoid conflict in the first place, so technically speaking it comes before conflict. To achieve settlements, humans must practice some degree of relativism even if the other side's point of view isn't precisely aligned with their own interests.

Negotiations aren't the only way to resolve conflict, however. Carol and Melvin Ember, two prominent conflict anthropologists, have identified the following peaceful means of conflict resolution (see the list that follows). Understanding these methods helps anthropologists advise governmental agencies on how to deal with conflict in many situations:

- ✓ **Avoidance:** Parties experiencing conflict move apart; the move may be literal, and in small-scale societies — such as the Inuit foragers of the Arctic — families may simply pack up and leave a village to avoid conflict for a time.

- ✓ **Social sanction:** A society uses any of a wide variety of social means to prevent conflict; these methods include ridicule of individuals who attempt to impose their will on others in the group.

- ✓ **Mediation:** A neutral *mediator* may come in to assist in negotiations.

- ✓ **Ritual:** Rituals may invoke the culture's spiritual resources and/or guides (gods) to sanctify any resolutions to conflict; because the sanctification is by definition very important, the parties are less likely to violate it.

- ✓ **Law and courts:** These formal systems of conflict resolution have the authority to enforce their rulings.

- ✓ **Post-conflict reconciliation:** Though it doesn't strictly prevent conflict, post-conflict reconciliation — in which the conflicting parties interact peacefully — decreases the likelihood of further conflict in some cases.

Post-conflict reconciliation is common in nonhuman primates; for example, a baboon that has attacked another often signals peaceful intentions after the conflict by gentle grunting and sitting quietly with the victim.

Unfortunately, when negotiation fails, conflict begins; the following section presents some principles of the anthropology of conflict.

Scales and consequences of conflict

Although human conflict comes in many forms, important basic scales and consequences exist in most human conflicts. In any given conflict, you need to understand how each of these factors is playing out to better devise a solution, and this is precisely what people trained in cultural anthropology do when helping governmental agencies avoid or deal with conflict.

Many anthropologists recognize the following common scales of conflict:

- **Intrafamily conflict:** Personal conflict in a family unit, including parent-offspring and spousal conflicts; in the U.S., these range from strife over what music teens are allowed to listen to (are the lyrics appropriate or offensive?) to friction between in-laws at Thanksgiving dinner.

- **Intracommunity conflict:** Conflict between descent groups or families within a community; one example would be when some families support a local economic change (such as a building a new mega-supermarket), and others (who may in this case own small mom and pop stores) oppose such a change.

- **Intercommunity conflict:** Large-scale conflict between communities within a culture; think about the conflicts between different racial communities in the U.S. today or between Catholic and Protestant communities of Northern Ireland in the not-so-distant past.

- **Intercultural conflict:** Conflict between different cultures; consider major wars fought over religion, such as the 14th-century Crusades in which Christians battled adherents of Islam.

Anthropologists have also noted that conflict beyond the intrafamily level involves *groups of people* rather than just individuals. At first these groups may share many values, but as conflict increases, groups differ more with time, showing

- **An increase in group solidarity:** Social bonds within each competing group become tighter, and pre-existing tensions within each competing group may be put aside, at least temporarily.

- **An increase in stereotyping:** Group members increasingly objectify opposition groups, often with dehumanizing language that clearly marks the opposition as "Other."

- **An increase in groupthink:** *Groupthink* is an interesting phenomenon that suppresses individuality (implicitly and/or explicitly) and promotes using a rigid and uncompromising way of thinking (defined by the conflict group) for all decision-making. Some characteristics of groupthink include increased use of bumper-sticker-type slogans and unrealistic optimism that things will work out preferably, as well as a decrease in rational thinking, demand for evidence, and personal moral accountability.

Knowing that human conflict normally involves these elements, anthropologists have better equipped themselves to understand conflict. The following section details what they've discovered.

Cultural conflict among small-scale societies

Many have suggested that if humans had remained mobile foragers, they never would've experienced the horrors of war. Although warfare waged by civilizations normally lasts longer and takes place on a larger scale than warfare among people living in smaller societies, small-scale societies aren't always peaceful. In fact, archaeologists have evidence for interpersonal violence going well back into the Stone Age:

- ✔ A 7,700-year-old site in Germany once occupied by hunter–gatherers has yielded 38 skulls bearing distinctive execution-style crushing to the back of the head.

- ✔ Throughout the Neolithic period in Mediterranean Europe, an increasing number of males show evidence of interpersonal violence. One archaeologist interpreted this pattern not as an increase in violence but as an increase in the cultural assignment of males to violent roles.

- ✔ The 9,400-year-old Kennewick man skeleton found in Washington State has a stone point imbedded in his hip, as though he'd been shot from behind (a good indicator of interpersonal violence). See Chapter 8 for more on the Kennewick man.

Although many *Homo erectus* bodies show evidence of butchery (such as at Bodo, Ethiopia, where 600,000-year-old skeletal material bears distinctive cut-marks from butchery with stone tools), this doesn't necessarily indicate violence. The hominid may have died naturally.

There are plenty of other indications of interpersonal violence in ancient and small-scale societies. What makes this conflict different from conflict as you know it today? The answer is largely a matter of scale, both in time and space. If not solved by the nonviolent means noted earlier in this chapter, cultural conflict among small-scale societies is shorter in duration and takes place over smaller distances. This is largely because the foragers, herders, and small-scale farming people of these societies simply *can't* carry out long-term warfare; they have to keep their food-production systems working. Without massive granaries to feed standing armies (each a characteristic of every ancient civilization), small-scale societies have to solve their violent conflicts quickly and over a short distance so they can get back to the food quest.

Figure 17-1 shows Native American Indian warriors from the 16th century. Although becoming a warrior was an important part of the life of many Native North Americans, their violent conflicts were normally short and occurred over relatively small distances compared to modern, state-supported warfare.

Figure 17-1:
Native North American warriors in a 1590 engraving by Theodore de Bry.

© Bridgeman

Melvin and Carol Ember point out some common violent means of conflict resolution in such small-scale societies. *Feuding* is a protracted conflict between kin groups that may go on for generations because people born into one kin group are bound by that blood tie to carry on the conflict with some other kin group. Although feuding can be protracted, it's *low-intensity* and not what one would call open war. *Raiding* is making short, target-specific, highly concentrated attacks on an enemy group, often to steal material goods or kill a certain individual or individuals.

So although nonindustrial, smaller-scale societies don't wage war for as long as or across such large distances as bigger civilizations do, you should be careful with the idea that only large, industrial societies wage war.

Although violent conflict sometimes seems inevitable because humans live in groups and interactions lead to friction, some anthropologists believe that violent conflict is largely absent from some small-scale societies such as the Semai of Southeast Asia, who essentially forbid violence as a means of solving conflict. Although anthropologists have identified more than 20 human societies as having little to no significant violent conflict, they are in the minority, and conflict remains common in human culture.

Cultural conflict in larger-scale societies

Conflict between (or within) *states* — large political units equipped with military forces — is normally called *war*. Compared to the violent conflict in small-scale societies, the main characteristic of war in large-scale societies is that it normally takes place over longer distances and longer time periods than in smaller-scale societies. Larger-scale societies are simply equipped with more material and social resources, including *standing military forces* whose members are engaged in military affairs full-time.

Just because warfare is more protracted in larger societies, however, doesn't mean that it's more frequent than in smaller societies; in fact, nonindustrialized societies wage war about as often as larger societies. In general, humans have fought wars for many reasons, and anthropologists have attempted to identify patterns in these reasons for warfare by looking at cultures worldwide and throughout history and determining whether they exhibit recurring reasons for war. They came up with several main kinds of war, but note that the following aren't the only kinds of war:

- ✔ **State-building:** One state attempts to conquer another to expand its own territory.

- ✔ **Civil:** Groups within a state war among themselves; these wars are usually more for political than material gain.

- ✔ **Imperial:** States explicitly seek material wealth.

- ✔ **Religious:** States make war over points of religion.

- ✔ **Ethnic:** States (or units within states) make war over ethnic identity.

Natural-born warriors?

In August 2006, genetic epidemiologist Rod Lea of New Zealand's Lea Institute of Environmental Science and Research announced that Maoris — the native people of New Zealand — had higher incidences of "a gene associated with risk-taking and aggressive behaviors," according to Boonsri Dickinson of *Cosmos Online.*

Does a gene predispose certain people to violence? Many 19th-century anthropologists believed that they could identify so-called criminal types by physical characteristics such as the shape of the skull. Others believed that upbringing was far more important than any genetic factor. The battle between those who disagree whether nature (genes) or nurture (socialization and upbringing) is most responsible for unusual aggression hasn't been resolved. Many say that both are involved and that the search for nature or nurture as the sole influence in behavior is a red herring. Still, in 2003, researchers identified the gene Pet-I, which seemed to strongly correlate with anxiety and aggression in mice; in humans, however, the genetics of human aggression are still poorly known, and Lea's statements have been criticized as oversimplifying a complex issue.

For his part, Lea also commented that "This gene has been linked to different anti-social behaviours and risk taking behaviour, but the link that is usually quite weak, and only present in association with non-genetic factors, like sociological upbringing lifestyle factors. . . . There are lots of lifestyle, upbringing-related exposures that could be relevant here so, obviously, the gene won't automatically make you a criminal." In other words, the link is far less substantial than it may sound, and socialization in a culture that reveres its warrior past, for example (like that of the Maoris) is probably the more important factor influencing aggression.

Whereas small societies tend to fight wars for purposes of revenge or other similarly specific reasons, larger societies have political structures that people attempt to increase in size by means of conquest warfare, where neighboring territories are swallowed up by the conqueror. In a study of all ancient civilizations, the late archaeologist Bruce Trigger found that most ancient civilizations expanded outward and annexed any neighboring society that couldn't resist military attack. Check out Chapter 10 for more on warfare in ancient civilizations.

Modern warfare extends over thousands of miles and kills not only intended targets but also civilians. It employs highly technical weapons and many labor specialists who work to design, build, maintain, and deliver the weapons. Figure 17-2 shows a modern bomber airplane, which is only one of these weapon-delivery advances.

Figure 17-2: Modern military aircraft dropping bombs.

© Werner Forman/CORBIS

Some anthropologists have suggested that all wars are, ultimately, about access to resources; this *materialist/ecological* explanation for war has its merits, but other anthropologists say a specific *historical* explanation is necessary for every war. So far, no general theory for the cause of war has convinced all anthropologists. I'm betting that many *justifications* exist for war but that in the end, material gain is often (though not always) an important factor.

Humanity and justice

Every human culture has rules for regulating social behavior, and these guidelines include rules and behavioral formulas for administering justice and righting wrongs. The late anthropologist Roy Rappaport called the deepest foundational norms of a culture its *ultimate sacred postulates*, a set of ideas — often linked to religious or supernatural concepts about the order of the universe — on which all else rests. (See Chapter 16 for more on these postulates.) A given culture's concepts of justice are built on the framework of these ideas.

As early as 3,700 years ago some human cultures were writing down their legal rules; at that date, in central Iraq, the Babylonian God-King Hammurabi had the rules of his kingdom encoded in a stone monument. Legal solutions to all kinds of problems were prescribed. For example, one dealt with what I suppose today you would call medical malpractice: "If the doctor has treated a gentleman for a severe wound with a lancet of bronze and has caused the gentleman to die, or has opened an abscess of the eye for a gentleman with the bronze lancet and has caused the loss of the gentleman's eye, one shall cut off his hands."

As cultures become more complex, their justice systems become more complex. This simplicity doesn't necessarily mean that smaller-scale cultures' systems of justice aren't effective, however; they have to be to keep peace. But because fewer people interact in these societies, justice is often meted out by elders or councils rather than the legal specialists — such as lawyers — of larger-scale societies.

Globalization and Human Culture

As communications and transportation become faster and more extensive, connecting (at least potentially) more and more people around the globe, the world seems to shrink. Anthropologists, naturally, are interested in this phenomenon of globalization.

Globalization can be defined many ways, but most anthropologists would agree that it's a worldwide process of increasing cultural interaction and integration, made possible in part by increasing economic ties. For example, Americans calling computer companies for technical support may end up speaking with people in India. Or cotton grown in the U.S. is often shipped to other countries (such as Honduras), assembled into garments there, and then shipped *back* to the U.S. and sold in American stores; this situation has economic effects (and therefore cultural effects) on each society here, and what one culture does has effects on the other. British sociologist Anthony Giddens explains globalization as ". . . the intensification of worldwide social relations which link distant localities in such a way that local happenings are shaped by events occurring many miles away, and vice versa."

Anthropologists recognize at least three main dimensions of change in the process of globalization:

- **Social/cultural** changes include the rapid spread of ideas among all the connecting societies, such that culture change may be very rapid.

- **Economic** changes include the rapid change of economic conditions in one region because of previously unfelt activities in another area. For example, the rapid growth of the technology-support jobs in India resulted from the rapid abundance of consumer electronics in the United States.

- **Demographic** changes include migrations into and out of political boundaries (often driven by economic concerns) leading to the complexities of cultural contact between migrants and the populations they move into. For example, Mexican migrants may move rapidly over long distances to take advantage of job opportunities in places that may or may not welcome them with open arms.

Although cultures have always been changing and in contact with other cultures, the changes brought about by globalization are particularly rapid, which may not give cultures time to adjust to the new conditions. Some *applied anthropologists* — anthropologists who apply their knowledge to real-world problems — focus on assisting local populations with the rapid changes imposed by globalization.

Globalization and ecological justice

Much globalization is driven by consumer demand in the industrialized First World and fulfilled by manufacturing centers in the developing Third World.

To keep consumer product prices as low as possible, companies pay developing-world workers less than they would pay workers in the developed world. Also — and importantly — many developing-world countries, desperate for cash, trade their ecological wealth for monetary wealth in very unsustainable ways; for example, in Borneo ancient forests that could be used for many years to draw ecotourists are cut down for one-time payments for logs. *Ecological justice* is the concept that a country's ecological resources are as precious as its monetary wealth and that citizens have the right to healthy ecological conditions. People trained in anthropology — and some applied anthropologists — are increasingly working to ensure that cultures of the Third World, including many indigenous cultures, are ensured ecological justice.

Globalization and cultural assimilation

Cultural assimilation — the absorption of one culture into another so that the characteristics of the first culture are diluted beyond recognition over time — is an alarming aspect of globalization. As cultural diversity decreases, everyone loses because each culture has unique perspectives, histories, languages, cuisines, costumes, and habits — all the spices of life. Although many indigenous and small-scale cultures actively resist assimilation into Western civilization, it's usually a losing battle, and many cultures have already disappeared forever. Today, for example, the cultural identity of Portugal is threatened by the global demand for plastic wine-bottle corks. Portugal has been the world's leader in making wine-bottle corks from real trees for centuries, and making these items by hand is part of their traditional culture; although obviously not every Portuguese is a cork-maker, cork-making, naturally, is important to the Portuguese. The increasing worldwide demand for cheaper, plastic corks has brought globalization to Portugal's doorstep. This loss of culture is one of the hidden costs of globalization. Cultures traded in for low prices . . . in my estimation, that's no bargain.

Globalization and nativistic movements

Over the past five decades, *nativistic movements* — the organization of indigenous peoples into political groups capable of lobbying for their own interests — have been very common. Many native groups, from the Inuit of the Canadian Arctic to the Philippines' National Council of Tribal Elders, have organized into political entities and pooled funds to send their own children to college and then law school, allowing them to fight for their rights in the legal arena. As the processes of globalization increasingly require new natural resources, many native groups who live on such land and are now recognized in international courts of law find themselves — to a degree — in a powerful position. The United Nations even has a Permanent Forum on Indigenous Issues, which deals specifically with "indigenous issues related to economic and social development, culture, the environment, education, health and human rights," according to its Web site (www.un.org/esa/socdev/unpfii/). Their work, and that of many other such organizations, is assisted by many people trained in anthropology, and it's certainly informed by decades of anthropological research, worldwide, into the lives of indigenous peoples.

Globalization and forced migration

As resources like forests are depleted and new ones are sought on an international, globalized raw-material market, many native people find themselves in the position of being forced (by military or political manipulation) off their traditional territories. Such displacement is called *forced migration*, and it's such a problem worldwide that Oxford University's Department of International Development has started an online organization — Forced Migration Online (www.forcedmigration.org/) — to help coordinate efforts both to reduce such migrations and to make the *back migration* — return to traditional lands when circumstances permit — an easier transition. Again, this undertaking involves many anthropologists, from cultural anthropologists familiar with how cultures react to migration to linguists knowledgeable about the misunderstandings that can arise as refugees speaking one language move into areas occupied by people speaking another language, and so on.

Chapter 18

Looming Disasters? From Overpopulation to Space Debris

Anthropology has done a good job — if I may say so myself — of sketching out where humanity came from and when, and basically how our species has turned out up to the present. Of course, how things are today wasn't an evolutionary goal and isn't necessarily how they'll be tomorrow. Looking into the future can be a tricky business, but you don't have to look too far to see some major challenges. In this chapter, you find out a few of these major challenges, and what anthropology can do to help overcome them.

The Only Constant Is Change

Many have believed that the purpose evolution was essentially to create the modern world and, with that task completed, that evolution is somehow over or finished. But this just isn't true. Humanity continues to evolve, both bodily and (even more so) culturally.

Many previously thought that as humanity increasingly relied on technology to adapt to its world, its genetic evolution would slow because humanity wouldn't need biological adaptations any more. But recently a number of studies have shown that human biological evolution is continuing, and has even accelerated over the past 50,000 years or so as the human population has exploded — more people means more mating and offspring, and every offspring presents the chance for a new variation on the parental form. So, the human species continues to evolve.

Evolution is simply a process of change through time, and it doesn't mean that that change is going to be good, bad, or anything else. It just means change.

Human environments change, too. Only 15,000 years ago, all of Canada was essentially under a sheet of ice; when these glaciers (and other ice caps worldwide) melted away by 10,000 years ago, global sea levels rose by about 300 feet, radically changing the many habitats occupied by people around the world. For example, Britain was cut off from mainland Europe as the water rose, forming today's English Channel.

And our environments change today as well; the Arctic, for example, is warming. Of the 10,000 known bird species worldwide, one becomes extinct every year, and by the end of the century — according to Peter Raven at the Missouri Botanical Garden — ten are likely to become extinct every year. Many of the plants and animals you see on a hike today are different from what your grandparents would have seen; there are fewer plants and animals and fewer *kinds* of plants and animals.

A problem of our own making: The Sixth Extinction

Although some threats to humanity come from out of the blue — like potentially civilization-destroying comets that may be headed for Earth — many problems are of our own making. Many scientists believe that due to massive overuse of resources (such as overfishing), clearing land for agriculture and other purposes (destroying natural environments), and polluting the natural environments that are left, the human species is causing the extinction of about 30,000 species per year. That's about three per hour, the fastest extinction rate in tens of millions of years. Although the last five mass extinction events on Earth have been due to natural causes — such as the planet being struck by comets or asteroids — this sixth extinction is caused by humanity.

Palaeoanthropologist Niles Eldredge has written an essay called "The Sixth Extinction" (available at www.actionbioscience. org/newfrontiers/eldredge2.html. In it he makes the bleak facts perfectly clear:

"The world's ecosystems have been plunged into chaos, with some conservation biologists thinking that no system, not even the vast oceans, remains untouched by human presence. Conservation measures, sustainable development, and, ultimately, stabilization of human population numbers and consumption patterns seem to offer some hope that the Sixth Extinction will not develop to the extent of the third global extinction, some 245 million years ago, when 90% of the world's species were lost."

"Though it is true that life, so incredibly resilient, has always recovered (though after long lags) after major extinction spasms, it is only after whatever has caused the extinction event has dissipated. That cause, in the case of the Sixth Extinction, is ourselves — *Homo sapiens*. This means we can continue on the path to our own extinction, or, preferably, we modify our behavior toward the global ecosystem of which we are still very much a part. The latter must happen before the Sixth Extinction can be declared over, and life can once again rebound."

This situation matters to humanity because no species is an island; the science of ecology has shown that all species are connected in a massive web of complex interactions. Why does it matter that some obscure bug is becoming extinct? Because some kind of bird feeds on that bug, and that bird in turn helps to distribute the seeds of plants it consumes. It's not just a bug going extinct — pretty soon, a whole ecosystem is affected.

Clearly, both humanity and the environments we call home are always changing.

Some of these changes threaten the way humanity lives today. Millions of people, for example, live in low-lying areas that will flood if sea levels continue to rise. Those people will have to move somewhere. Other threats to humanity include the human immunodeficiency virus (HIV) that causes AIDS and has already killed close to 30 million people. And some cultural trends don't bode well either, such as the alarming loss of traditional languages worldwide. A traditional saying in Madagascar is that "An old person dying is a library on fire," and every language lost is another perspective on humanity gone up, so to speak, in smoke.

Because anthropology has studied humanity so closely for so long, I think you can reasonably ask how it can help with these challenges. The American Anthropological Association thinks so, too; a recent issue of its *Anthropology News* newsletter was devoted to climate change and what anthropologists have to say about it.

The rest of this chapter looks at six major problems facing humanity today. Some are connected with others in complex ways, but anthropology has something useful to say about all of them:

- Overpopulation
- Climate change
- Language loss
- Food and water availability/famine
- Disease
- Space debris (yes, space debris)

Overpopulation

Just over 10,000 years ago, the human population was probably around 5 million — 5 million hunter–gatherers spread across a vast globe. Today,

7 billion is a more accurate count. Figure 18-1 shows the growth of the human population over the past 10,000 years. Remember, it's around 10,000 years ago that farming was first invented, and the first civilizations occur around 5,000 years ago. The rapid growth in human population after about the year 1900 has a lot do with the invention of modern medicines and agricultural techniques. Plant and animal species can show this kind of rapid population growth, but they're normally checked by natural limitations of the environment.

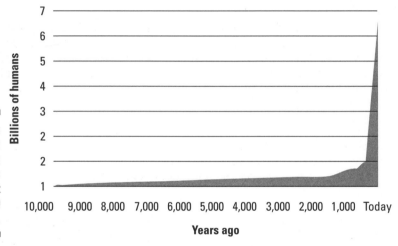

Figure 18-1:
Human population growth in the last 10,000 years.

The road to overpopulation

In the late 1700s and early 1800s, an Englishman named Thomas Malthus published a number of papers on the relationship between a species' population and its food supply. Essentially, Malthus said that populations will tend to expand at a geometric rate (such as doubling every so many years) and food supplies will tend to expand only at an arithmetic rate (increasing by a fixed amount in a fixed amount of time). Populations, Malthus said, are limited by a lack of food. More individuals are born than can be supported by the environment, and those that can't find food perish.

In practice, though, humanity works a little differently. Humans store up food after they harvest it and can feed many more mouths than a given plot of land could naturally support. This ability to store food has helped offset the normal *Malthusian limit* (named after Malthus's argument) to population growth, and the human population has gone through the roof. Between 1900 and 2000, the human population has increased fourfold, from 1.6 billion to more than 6 billion, an astonishing increase in the animal kingdom.

Over 200 years after Malthus, anthropologist J.K. Smail argued that even if zero-population-growth measures were enacted immediately, stabilizing the human population would take more than 50 years. He agreed with other estimates that by 2050 the population would be close to 10 billion, an increase of 50 percent in just two generations.

One *generation* is the period of time between a person's birth and when he or she has children; though it varies a lot worldwide, a 20 to 30-year range is about right.

Smail also noted that the era of cheap energy (fossil fuels), adequate food supplies (from wood to fresh water), and plentiful fresh water was coming to an end, and rapidly. Combining these facts with the staggering increase in the human population would spell disaster. The human species won't become extinct, but billions — not just hundreds of millions — will suffer and die horribly.

The world's leaders know all of this: Today 70 percent of leaders in the developing word — where population growth is highest — report their concern with overpopulation (compared to 25 percent just 30 years ago) and many have implemented measures to limit population growth.

The Third World, a term dating to 1952, refers to countries that don't have the infrastructure (roads, water systems, and so on), technology, and high standard of living found in the more highly developed First World, which consists of countries such as the United States, Canada, Australia, and most of the countries of Europe. Some consider the term derogatory, and *developing world* is increasingly used.

Hope on the horizon

That's all the bad news; is there any good news? Smail was actually cautiously optimistic about limiting human population growth, but made it clear that efforts had to be real and immediate, and had to supersede any other issues — medicine, famine, health care — because "fixing" these in overpopulated countries wouldn't do any good if the population continued to increase.

The most important part of Smail's argument was pointing out that humans, too, are subject to Malthusian limits; sooner or later, humans will have to face the terrible consequences of having too many mouths to feed. Keeping human population in line with what the Earth can support (about 2 billion people, according to Smail) — basically, living sustainably as a species — is a reasonable priority. Reducing human population growth would

✔ Decrease stress on nonrenewable resources

✔ Prevent famine

✔ Provide reasonable employment

✔ Provide basic social services (health and education)

So what can anthropology do to help keep the human population living sustainably?

First, anthropologists can monitor and document population change as demographic anthropologists. (*Demography* is the study of populations.) Demographic anthropologists, accustomed to the ins and outs of understanding human migration and other population-related phenomena, could be very helpful.

More importantly, anthropologists can help population-growth-limiting efforts on the local and community levels because cultural anthropologists are most familiar with this level of the human experience. Instead of simply having impersonal decrees coming down to the community level from national governments, anthropologists can help those at government levels better understand the needs, culture, and values of people living at the community level.

Climate Change

Unless you've been living under a rock for the past few years, you've heard that the Earth's climate is changing. Most scientists agree that the changes are related to the *greenhouse effect*, a warming of the Earth due to the introduction of carbon dioxide into the atmosphere from burning fossil fuels. The United Nation's Intergovernmental Panel on Climate Change lists many lines of evidence for climate change:

✔ **Increasingly volatile weather:** Droughts, tropical cyclones, heat waves, and storms in general have increased in intensity; the Mediterranean, parts of Southern Asia, and part of Africa have become increasingly dry, and increased incidences of flooding (such as floods in central Europe in 1996 and 1997 and floods in Bangladesh in 2004 that left half the country flooded) are evidence of more powerful storms.

✔ **A warming Arctic:** The average Arctic temperature has increased nearly twice as fast as in the rest of the world over the past century, and many believe that sea ice on the ocean will melt completely during summers by 2050, and the Northwest Passage will remain ice-free throughout the year.

> ✔ **Glacier melting:** Globally, glaciers are in retreat — for example, in the past century, two-thirds of Switzerland's glaciers have essentially melted away.

> ✔ **Plant and animal changes:** More than 400 plant and animal species are known to have been affected by modern climate change; for example, butterflies, dragonflies, moths, beetles and other insects are found farther north than ever as the climate warms. (Now *that* could be a soap opera.)

In November, 2007, the UN called these changes "unequivocal," so well-documented that debating them would be like debating about gravity. The world's climate is changing. Whatever humanity decides to do about it — switching to clean, non-greenhouse-gas-emitting energy sources, for example — is a question I don't want to tackle; it's too big for this book. But what I do want to mention is how anthropology will be able to help implement the changes that are sure to happen.

The American Association for the Advancement of Science on Climate Change

In December 2006 the American Association for the Advancement of Science released a statement on the reality of climate change, excerpts of which are reprinted here; head to www.aaas.org/news/releases/2007/0218am_statement.shtml for the whole thing.

"The scientific evidence is clear: global climate change caused by human activities is occurring now, and it is a growing threat to society. Accumulating data from across the globe reveal a wide array of effects: rapidly melting glaciers, destabilization of major ice sheets, increases in extreme weather, rising sea level, shifts in species ranges, and more. The pace of change and the evidence of harm have increased markedly over the last five years. The time to control greenhouse gas emissions is now."

"The atmospheric concentration of carbon dioxide, a critical greenhouse gas, is higher than it has been for at least 650,000 years. The average temperature of the Earth is heading for levels not experienced for millions of years. Scientific predictions of the impacts of increasing atmospheric concentrations of greenhouse gases from fossil fuels and deforestation match observed changes. As expected, intensification of droughts, heat waves, floods, wildfires, and severe storms is occurring, with a mounting toll on vulnerable ecosystems and societies. These events are early warning signs of even more devastating damage to come, some of which will be irreversible."

"The growing torrent of information presents a clear message: we are already experiencing global climate change. It is time to muster the political will for concerted action. Stronger leadership at all levels is needed. The time is now. We must rise to the challenge. We owe this to future generations."

The December 2007 issue of the American Anthropological Association's *Anthropology News* was devoted to climate change research and how anthropology could be involved in finding ways to cope with climate change.

One article by anthropologist T.J. Finan made the important point that although anthropologists have had a long history of researching human interaction with the environment, a somewhat antiscientific atmosphere in anthropology over the last 20 years or so has left a whole generation of anthropology graduates with a sense that hard science, typified by climate change science, was outside the view of anthropology. That, Finan says has to change. I agree. Anthropology can help with understanding, reacting to, and perhaps planning to reduce climate change in several ways:

✔ As in population-growth-limiting work, anthropologists could help by easing the transition on the community level from old ways of doing things to new ways of doing them. Governmental attempts to implement change often fail because they come from the top down and are alien to the needs and concerns of communities. Anthropologists can facilitate better communication between communities and higher levels of organization.

✔ *Ecological anthropologists* — those focusing on human interactions with their environments and resources — have a deep knowledge of the principles of evolution and adaptation and can help to make climate-change-related adjustments more sensitive to the local conditions and ecologies of human communities.

✔ Anthropologists would be well suited to understanding how humans change and adapt over time. Therefore, they may be best suited and equipped to evaluate plans of action that will take time and affect human communities.

✔ Ecological anthropologists can document environmental change over time, as well as track how humans have dealt with it in the past and in the present.

Whatever changes are implemented or considered globally to deal with climate change, I think calling on anthropologists to help facilitate those changes on the human level is a no-brainer.

Say What? The Loss of Linguistic Diversity

Can the loss of languages be as disastrous to humanity as climate change or overpopulation? Although language loss may not cause as much suffering or death, losing languages is like losing entire archives of human experience.

And it's happening at an alarming rate; of about 6,000 languages spoken today, half are spoken by so few people that they'll be forgotten by the end of this century. One anthropologist has estimated that about two languages vanish every month. One example of a terrible loss is in Australia, where some estimate that 90 percent of the native languages will be extinct in the next 20 years. It's staggering to think that after 40,000 years, these languages — each one a set of ways of looking at survival, philosophy, love, art, music, humor, drama, and everything else humans love so much — will just suddenly be gone. That's a tragedy.

How do languages go extinct? Normally it happens in the process of *cultural assimilation*, in which one culture adopts the customs, habits, values, traditions — and language — of another. To conform to new surroundings, immigrants often assimilate into a larger culture, losing their traditional language in the process.

Why does this matter? Wouldn't it be good for all people to share a common language? Wouldn't that facilitate better communications and maybe even peace? Probably, but that doesn't mean that rarer languages should die out. Because any human infant can acquire several languages with ease, humans have no reason not to preserve the world's heritage of unique experiences, recorded in each distinctive language. Because the words a language uses to describe the world make for a unique perspective, each language represents an alternative way of understanding humanity. Losing languages is a human problem, not just a problem of a single culture. Losing a language is like losing a culture.

What can anthropologists do to help to preserve languages? They can spread the word that language diversity is important and threatened. And, knowing the goals, values, and lives of native and traditional peoples worldwide better than any government bureaucrat, anthropologists are best equipped to advocate for those native and traditional peoples so that assimilation and language loss aren't the only options in a rapidly globalizing world. Linguistic anthropologists have already done this in many cases, recording endangered languages and developing programs for preserving and teaching those languages.

Food and Water Availability/Famine

Famine — a general food shortage that reduces individual human caloric intake below about 1,000 calories per person per day — and *drought* (water shortage) have accounted for millions of deaths in the last century and a half as the human population in developing countries has exploded. The deaths of millions of human beings make these issues concerns of anthropology. Famines occurred in the ancient civilizations as well, but they're pretty much restricted to agricultural societies that depend on stored foods; mobile hunter–gatherers facing a food shortage simply move on to other hunting and foraging grounds, One of the significant consequences, then, of humanity's general shift to agriculture has been a susceptibility to famine (and drought, which affects agricultural crops, of course).

Sometimes, famine is a genuine result of the population exceeding the food supply, but in many cases, anthropological studies have found that famines have been politically sponsored. For example, the famines in the former Soviet Union in the early 1900s killed between 5 and 8 million, and many believe Soviet officials allowed this to happen regardless of whether they politically engineered it. More recently, food shortages in certain areas are the result of the processes of globalization, in which states sponsor farming for export rather than to feed the population.

Anthropologists are involved in many attempts to better understand and cope with famine. One frightening finding of anthropology is that famines tend to divide populations internally, which could sponsor civil war; famine can lead to a domino effect of one miserable consequence after another. Another finding, made in a cross-cultural study by anthropologist Robert Dirks, is that states that tend not to have famine (such as the U.S.) aren't necessarily spared famine because their farming systems are better than anywhere else; they avoid famine because they have systems in place to offset food and water shortages, such as unemployment assistance, market-price guarantees, and many other aid programs supported by taxes. Knowing this, anthropologists can help implement such programs in countries where famine is more common; once again, the anthropological approach is important to implement programs with a greater understanding of local conditions and cultures than is normally had by government administrators.

Disease

Humanity is susceptible to many diseases. Some are *endemic* (always present in a population), and some sweep rapidly through widespread populations as *epidemics*. Only in the last century or so — when diseases were well-enough understood by science — have large-scale disease-eradication programs been implemented. In some cases, this has radically changed disease situations that had been present for centuries, if not thousands of years. Technological eradication of certain diseases has in effect removed one limit to human population growth that was in effect for a very long time, contributing (along with modern medicine and agriculture) to the recent world population boom.

Some diseases already eradicated (or nearly so) in the United States remain a problem in other countries; the Centers for Disease Control estimates that 1 million people per year die of malaria. That's nearly 3,000 per day, or several every minute. That's a serious problem. So is AIDS (acquired immune deficiency syndrome), the result of the sexually transmitted HIV virus. The UN has estimated that more than 40 million humans worldwide (most of them in Africa) carried the HIV virus at the end of 2001. However, the disease is also common in Asia; at the end of 2006, the UN estimated a population of nearly 1 million HIV carriers in China and another 1.5 million in India. Such numbers indicate a global epidemic.

Anthropological approaches to helping prevent disease include studies of the cultural dimension of disease. In some African countries, for example, males feel the use of a condom isn't masculine, so sexually transmitted diseases continue to spread. In this case, although a technological solution — the use of condoms — is present, a cultural condition (male views of what's masculine) is the most important factor in controlling disease. In such cases, cultural change has to occur if disease is to be controlled, and it's anthropologists who are best equipped to understand and even help guide that cultural change. Once again, this is important to do from the ground up — from understanding cultural conditions in local communities — rather than from the top down by mandates from government agencies that may not be in touch with cultural realities.

Space Debris

Several telescopes today monitor space for potentially harmful space debris, such as comets and asteroids. These pass by the Earth all the time, and NASA currently considers about a thousand asteroids ranging in size from basketballs to mountains to be *potentially hazardous.* This means they will probably pass very close to the Earth in the foreseeable future and have a chance of impacting the Earth. If an item about 2 kilometers (1.2 miles) across impacted the Earth at the proper velocity, the explosion would raise so much dust that it would block out the sun, an event that would cripple agriculture to the point that humanity may starve before the dust settled. Figure 18-2 illustrates what could happen if one of these objects impacted the Earth.

To protect humanity against such disasters, many have advocated colonizing space. In a 1982 book titled *Interstellar Migration and the Human Experience,* several anthropologists and other scientists speculated on why and how humanity may choose to move off Earth to other planets and, eventually, other solar systems. In the long run, this plan seems like the only option for humanity. It's not science fiction, nor is it necessarily running away from our problems here on Earth (although some may try to do just that); new colonies would have to be self-sufficient, harmonious, and extremely efficient. They would be the epitome of environmentally conscious culture.

Figure 18-2:
Artist's
conception
of a massive
space-
debris
object's
impact with
the Earth.

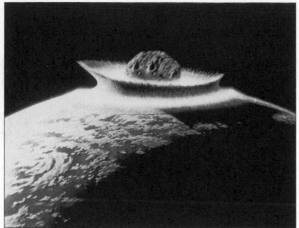

© Goodshoot/Jupiterimages

In 2006 astrophysicist Stephen Hawking advocated that humanity seek a second home, echoing the late astronomer Carl Sagan's comment that humanity should become at least a "two-planet species" — not to plant a flag on Mars, or just look for fossils of exotic life forms there, but to move to at least one other planet to prevent humanity from having all its eggs in one basket.

After all, nothing lasts forever, and that includes our solar system. The Earth isn't as safe as it's seemed for the last 5,000 years of recorded history. Truly catastrophic space debris could pop up unexpectedly at any time; it happened to the dinosaurs around 65 million years ago as the Fifth Mass Extinction. In several billion years, the sun will become a red giant and incinerate the Earth. That's worth thinking about.

Anthropology can help with nearly every aspect of planning the human colonization of space, from societal concerns to those of human nutrition, evolution, conflict resolution, and so on. I cover the anthropological implications of many of these topics throughout this book.

Chapter 19

Eve and the Iceman: The Cutting Edge of Physical Anthropology

*F*or much of its history, physical anthropology was mainly concerned with studying the fossils of humanity's early ancestors. Physical anthropologists trained in biology — particularly skeletal biology — anatomy, and evolution, focusing on how evolutionary forces shaped the bodies of ancient humans, as reflected in the fossil record.

For the last two decades, however, there's been a new game in town: *molecular anthropology*, focusing on how DNA (*deoxyribonucleic acid,* the molecule of life) can help anthropologists understand human evolution. This new field has reinforced some old theories, toppled others, and continues to hold great promise for the understanding of the human species.

Because molecular anthropology is so prominent today and shows more signs of growing than fading away, in this chapter I introduce you to the principles of this exciting new field as well as some of its results.

Molecular Anthropology

Molecular anthropology is a relatively new branch of physical anthropology that focuses on human genetics to investigate — in the words of one evolutionary anthropology bigwig — "... the origin, relationships, history, structure, and migration patterns of human populations." Other prominent research institutes have very similar goals.

How it works

The basis of most molecular anthropology is the fact that DNA, the molecule that directs the building of a living thing's physical body (whether that body is an acorn, fish, or gibbon) changes over time; when the parent generation have offspring, the DNA of those offspring aren't — in the great bulk of all cases — identical to the DNA of the parents. I get into why the DNA is different in a moment, but let me mention the next significant point first.

Although parent and offspring DNA will have some differences, they're still very similar because the offspring are just one generation removed from the parents: The apple hasn't fallen far from the tree, genetically speaking. Examining the DNA "fingerprint" for parents and their offspring has shown this time and again. And that fingerprint will be more similar between the parents and their offspring than the parents, say, and the offspring of some other parents. This key is one of the keys to molecular anthropology.

Knowing that the DNA fingerprint for an individual is more like his parents than any other individual, you can trace the movements of and relationships among various peoples based on the similarities of their genetic fingerprints. For example, the genetic fingerprint for native people of the Pacific Islands and those of Southeast Asia should be quite similar because archaeological evidence shows that Southeast Asians first colonized the Pacific Islands more than 3,000 years ago, and the Pacific Islanders are their descendants. At the very least, Southeast Asian and Pacific Islander DNA should be more similar to each other (because Pacific Islanders are descended from Southeast Asians) than either is to, say, European DNA, because these populations just haven't been interbreeding with Europeans until comparatively recently (and certainly not 3,000 years ago).

So why does the DNA differ between the parent and offspring generations, and how does that help anthropologists? This question has several answers.

First, the *nuclear* DNA (the DNA that you inherit from both parents) differs between parent and offspring because the male and female parents' DNA are shuffled in the egg and sperm cells before they unite. That is, before the male's and female's DNA come into contact (at the moment of conception), they reorder themselves to a degree, introducing new combinations. This process is called *recombination*, and the new variations on the basic parental DNA fingerprint are called *mutations*.

Although in popular use the word *mutation* has negative connotations, in biology mutation simply means a novelty, a change in the DNA. Genetically speaking, mutations can be *negative* (not beneficial to the bearer), *positive* (beneficial to the bearer), or *neutral* (have no significant negative or positive consequence for the bearer).

Second — and of great interest to the molecular anthropologist — is the fact that *mitochondrial DNA,* the DNA that humans inherit from their mothers only, differs between parent and offspring because it slowly accumulates changes — mutations — simply as a function of time, as DNA replication errors accumulate. I come back to this topic later.

Third — and also of great interest to the molecular anthropologist — is the fact that *Y-chromosome* DNA, the DNA that only males inherit from their fathers, differs between parent and offspring much like mitochondrial DNA, slowly accumulating changes as DNA replication errors accumulate. I come back to this subject later, too.

How anthropologists use it

How can this information help anthropologists? For one thing, they use it to identify the genetic distance between individuals, or the genetic population to which some human remains belong, as in the case of the Pacific Islanders and the Europeans I mentioned earlier. If anthropologists can extract good (undamaged and uncontaminated) DNA from a skeleton (or, more commonly, from a tooth root) they have a good chance of telling what human population it came from. This process can help in tracking ancient migrations.

Second, anthropologists can use what's called a *molecular clock* to identify how long ago two populations diverged. That's because in some types of DNA — such as the mitochondrial DNA I discuss later in this chapter — genetic differences accumulate over time at a known and stable rate. Knowing the rate at which changes accumulate (and that the rate doesn't change significantly over time) allows the molecular anthropologist to count up the genetic differences between two individuals by comparing their DNA "bar codes" or fingerprints. This counting can determine when, in terms of years ago, the two individuals were in the same genetic population.

In short, then, molecular approaches allow anthropologists to analyze DNA to identify the degree of genetic similarity between individuals and the time since two individuals were of the same genetic population (which in turn helps them figure out when and at what rate ancient populations migrated).

The studies of human genetics used by molecular anthropologists generally include the following:

 ✔ **Mitochondrial DNA (mtDNA) studies** focus on the DNA passed from mother to offspring and are widely used to estimate the degree of similarity or difference between two samples of human DNA. Anthropologists can then convert this difference into an estimate of how long ago the two populations diverged genetically.

✔ **Y-chromosome DNA studies** focus on the DNA passed from father to son only, and are used in much the same way as mtDNA studies.

✔ **DNA sequencing studies** identify the sex and global population of origin of a given DNA sample.

✔ **Human leukocyte antigen (HLA) studies** focus on a group of genes related to the production of *antigens* (molecules used by the immune system) and can aid in tracking migration and the geographical origin of populations.

The appearance and flourishing of a genetic component to anthropology is in keeping with a larger trend. In biology in general, recent advances in understanding DNA and the ability to study it have led to a tremendous shift in the life sciences, generally speaking, toward molecular approaches. In 1992, after more than 120 years as a general-science research publication, the journal *Nature* launched *Nature Genetics* to keep up with advances in this field.

Molecular anthropology is widely popular today and has provided great information on human migration and evolution worldwide; some examples include the following:

✔ A study by Italian scientists has shown that the population of Sicily is genetically so similar that they seem to all have come from a single founding population.

✔ A synthesis of many studies of Native North and South American DNA has shown that the first colonists of the Americas came from East Asia and probably arrived around between 20,000 years ago and 14,000 years ago, a finding that coincides well with the archaeological and geographical evidence (see Chapter 8 for more on the first colonization of the Americas).

✔ A study by American and Russian scientists has found that Alaska's Aleutian Islands were colonized by people genetically most related to Russia's Kamchatka peninsula, just a few hundred miles to the west of the Aleutians. What's surprising is that the migration didn't come from the west, but from the east, suggesting that ancient Kamchatkan pioneers entered the Alaskan mainland long before back-migrating west to discover the Aleutians.

An excellent online resource for tracking human migration as revealed by DNA can be found at *National Geographic*'s Genographic Project Web site, at www3.nationalgeographic.com/genographic/index.html. And Figure 14-2 in Chapter 14 shows you a genetic map of the world's populations according to recent findings in molecular anthropology.

DNA detectives

The last two decades have seen a veritable explosion of anthropological interest in genetic studies. Due largely to advances in the ability to read DNA fingerprints of both modern and ancient DNA, the once low-tech field of physical anthropology (characterized by studying fossils excavated from the ground) has been transformed into an expensive, high-tech endeavor. Although fossil studies haven't been abandoned (because the fossils can reveal things the DNA can't), they have been joined by molecular anthropology.

Because every person's DNA is unique, molecular anthropologists can identify anyone's recent genetic history. For less than $300, commercial laboratories can test your DNA to identify where your ancestors came from thousands of years ago. DNA is also useful in forensics to identify criminals or absolve people accused of crimes, as well as to identify human remains from crash sites and other disasters where normal identifying characteristics — such as dental records — aren't available. The Innocence Project, based at The Benjamin N. Cardozo School of Law at Yeshiva University, uses DNA evidence to exonerate falsely accused (and often imprisoned) people. As of this writing, the project has cleared 215 wrongly convicted individuals.

Why some say it doesn't work

Molecular anthropology has its problems, and you have to keep them in mind until they're worked out.

First, some say the rate at which genetic differences accumulate isn't so stable. Instead of DNA having a known, stable rate of mutation in humans, some argue, the rate can be highly variable. Therefore, critics argue, molecular anthropologists need to go back to the drawing board and fully investigate the idea that the mutation rate among humans is both known and stable.

Some scientists have done exactly that, but their findings haven't supported the idea that mutation rates are as variable as critics say. At the least, proponents of the molecular clock say, highly variable mutation rates are a very recent phenomenon (for all kinds of reasons), and beyond a few hundred years ago mutation rates *were* stable and *are* well known. This issue hasn't been entirely sorted out, yet, but I'm willing to bet it will be in the next few years. Also keep in mind that most of the findings of the molecular-clock studies support the information in the fossil and archaeological records. That fact helps support the idea that anthropologists understand the molecular clock pretty well understood — it's not just a crude "sundial," as one critic put it.

Another potential problem is contamination. When first excavating human remains in field settings, workers' DNA can contaminate the ancient bones because they rarely wear protective garments. I can't blame them; the outfits are hard to work in — imagine excavating a site in sweltering central Panama wearing a hazardous-material suit! Unfortunately, this contamination leaves many human remains studies in jeopardy. Even in the lab, contamination can be a problem, and studies that show very little difference between modern and ancient DNA are immediately suspect. For this reason, many labs take DNA samples from their own workers to be sure they aren't contaminating the archaeological material.

Yet another issue is the fact that DNA, an organic molecule, decays over time. In the film *Jurassic Park*, characters extract 100-million-year-old dinosaur DNA from an ancient mosquito preserved in amber. This practice is possible in principle, but only in very rare cases. The oldest DNA yet recovered is about 500,000 years old, and even this age is rare: Most DNA studies occur on specimens less than 10,000 years old. Still, DNA recovery from several Neanderthal remains, each over 30,000 years old, has been successful. DNA decay (which really means degradation into pieces so small that not much can be learned from them) is a limiting factor to molecular anthropology, not something that stops it entirely.

DNA and the Mitochondrial Eve

In 1987, the venerable scientific journal *Nature* published a paper by biochemists Rebecca Cann, Mark Stoneking, and Allan C. Wilson titled "Mitochondrial DNA and Human Evolution." This exciting paper signaled the coming of age of molecular anthropology, even though it immediately divided the anthropological community into those who believed in its methods and implications and those who rejected them.

What the paper proposed was this: Mitochondrial DNA, which is inherited only from the mother, had been shown to accumulate mutations over time at a known and stable rate — about 2 to 4 percent per million years, or about one significant mutation every 6,000 to 12,000 years. The authors proposed that this knowledge, combined with the degree of genetic diversity worldwide today, could help track ancient migration. Populations with similar DNA would be more recently related (because they had been accumulating genetic differences for relatively little time), even if they were genetically distinctive (say, Scandinavians and Britons). Populations with very different DNA would be more distantly related (say, Africans and East Asians) because they had been accumulating genetic differences for a longer period. With such data, a human genetic family tree could be diagrammed. Furthermore, because the rate of mutation was known and stable, the number of mutations differentiating two groups could be read like a molecular clock to identify how long the two groups had been apart.

To demonstrate these points, the authors had collected mitochondrial DNA samples from human populations worldwide and compared them, with startling and exciting results.

Out of Africa: African diversity and extra-African similarity

The paper reported several main discoveries:

- ✔ Genetic diversity was greatest within Africa, indicating that African populations had been accumulating mitochondrial DNA mutations for a relatively long time.

- ✔ Genetic diversity was relatively low outside Africa, indicating that all populations outside Africa had been accumulating mitochondrial DNA mutations for a relatively short time.

- ✔ Modern human populations had been accumulating mutations for about 200,000 years, and around 200,000 years ago a maternal ancestral group — the "mitochondrial Eve," located somewhere in Africa — donated the mitochondrial DNA that all humans carry today

Basically, the authors of the paper had made the remarkable claim to have identified the last common ancestor of all living people, somewhere in Africa around 200,000 years ago. The study also strongly supported the "out of Africa" theory of human origins, which said that modern humans emerged from Africa about 100,000 years ago, replacing all prior extra-African migrants — such as, for example, the Neanderthals, who already existed in Europe.

The inevitable debates

As Carl Sagan used to say, extraordinary claims should be backed up by extraordinary evidence, and so in the best tradition of science, researchers worldwide began to take Cann and her colleagues' paper apart piece by piece. How carefully had the DNA been collected? Did the statistics check out? Why didn't they consider this factor or that one? The main contention has been that that the overall rate of mutation in mitochondrial DNA isn't constant, and therefore the paper's molecular clock was suspect. The clock was suspect (no anthropologist believes the rate of mutation was entirely stable or completely constant over hundreds of thousands of years), but research has shown that the clock is reasonably accurate.

Genetic trails

By genetically "fingerprinting" thousands of people around the world who represent different ethnic populations and using the molecular clock to identify when they originated, anthropologists have identified more than 20 main mitochondrial DNA groups, called *mtDNA haplogroups*. Groups L1, L2, and L3, for example, are African in origin (with an origin date of around 150,000 to 170,000 years) and are at the root of all other groups including group U5, which appears in Europe around 50,000 years ago, likely originated in the Near East, and probably represented the individuals that replaced the Neanderthals. As researchers refine their methods and studies, anthropologists are increasingly able to track the migrations of ancient peoples in detail never before thought possible.

And although much of molecular anthropology has focused on mitochondrial DNA inherited only from the mother, recent advances have allowed anthropologists to also track the evolution of the Y-chromosome inherited only by sons from their fathers. *Y-chromosome haplogroups* have also been identified and are currently being compared with mtDNA haplogroup data, with promising results.

Debate went on for some years, and today some questions remain, but later research largely backed up the out of Africa/mitochondrial Eve models. In fact, they were backed up not only by further genetic studies but also by independent lines of archaeological and fossil data that also suggest an African origin for all modern humans around 150,000 to 200,000 years ago. Now, I have to admit that I'm more convinced by the "Out of Africa" model for modern human origins than any other, but remember, the debate rages on; for more on that the debate, check out Chapter 7.

Neanderthals and You: The Neanderthal Genome

In recent years, molecular anthropology has also set its sights on one of archaeology's greatest enigmas, the question of the fate of the Neanderthals.

Neanderthals first appear in Europe and the Near East around 200,000 years ago, as one of the many regional variants of proto-human that had emerged from Africa for around 2 million years. For the next 170,000 years, Neanderthals were great survivors, adapting to the ice-age conditions of Europe by living in protective caves, using fire, wearing a basic kind of animal-hide clothing, and hunting as effectively as cave lions and other top predators. But suddenly, around 30,000 years ago, the Neanderthals vanished, their tool types disappeared, and their fossils stopped. In their place are the moderns, *Homo sapiens sapiens* — you and me. For a long time, anthropologists have wondered whether the Neanderthals evolved into *Homo sapiens sapiens*, were replaced by *Homo sapiens sapiens*, or were done in by something in between.

But by the late 1990s it was technically possible to extract DNA from the unfossilized remnants of some Neanderthal bones and compare them with modern human DNA. Since the first paper on Neanderthal DNA was published in 1997, several other studies have followed, examining DNA from relatively recent Neanderthals (within the period 50,000 years ago to their extinction around 30,000 years ago). What molecular anthropologists have found has helped solve the mystery of the Neanderthal's demise. The main findings to date include the following:

- ✓ **Neanderthal DNA is substantially different from modern human DNA.** This fact strongly suggests that Neanderthals didn't interbreed substantially with the modern humans, which supports the out of Africa model mentioned earlier.

- ✓ **However, studies show Neanderthal DNA is over 99 percent identical that of modern humans.** Although this similarity shows how genetically "human" Neanderthals were, remember that a 1 percent difference can be significant: Chimpanzee genes are also about 99 percent identical to those of humans.

- ✓ **The divergence between Neanderthals and modern humans occurred somewhere around 300,000 years ago.** That is, Neanderthals appear to have been an offshoot or branch of the lineage *Homo erectus*, which many believe also gave rise to modern humans around 100,000 years ago.

Of course, not everyone buys the Neanderthal DNA data. Some say the samples have been contaminated, some say that the DNA analysis methods are faulty, and some say that DNA over about 10,000 years old is so degraded that anything that may be read from it would be highly suspect.

Despite these criticisms, though, Neanderthal genetics is a flourishing field. By the time this book goes to press, the full Neanderthal genome is expected to be completed by researchers at Germany's Max Planck Institute for Evolutionary Biology and 454 Life Sciences, a biotech company in Branford, Connecticut. I'm sure the next decade will be as exciting as the last.

The Iceman

In 1991, two hikers discovered a body eroding from the ice of a glacier in northern Italy. Initially thought to be the corpse of an unlucky and forgotten mountaineer, the strange artifacts near the body — including a fur hat, a copper axe, and a stone knife — indicated that the find was much more interesting. When radiocarbon dating set the age of the Iceman at 5,300 years ago, archaeologists went wild: Here was a well-preserved human who was 700 years dead when the first stones of the great pyramids of Egypt were just being laid. What could the Iceman tell humanity about the past?

At first, not much. Nobody could tell, just from looking at the relatively well-preserved, naturally mummified body where he came from, where he was going, how he died, or whom he may be related to. Although speculation flew wildly (and still does today), DNA analysis answered some important questions and revealed a few facts that nobody expected:

- ✔ **The Iceman's arrows and clothing had the blood of several humans on them,** strongly suggesting that the Iceman was in a fight just before death and didn't simply freeze to death, as first believed. This evidence was backed up by the discovery of a stone arrowhead in the Iceman's back and other wounds on his body.

- ✔ **The Iceman may have been infertile,** with a low sperm mobility; some have suggested that this characteristic may have had something to do with the circumstances of his death, though no case has been assembled yet.

- ✔ **Mitochondrial DNA showed that the Iceman's mother had come from the K Haplogroup,** a European group originating around 16,000 years ago and spreading widely throughout the continent after a dramatic recession of the great ice sheets.

As DNA extraction and analysis methods improve, I'm sure anthropologists are in for more exciting discoveries. Personally, I'm waiting for a frozen Neanderthal to be found thawing from the Siberian permafrost.

Chapter 20

Stonehenge and You: Why Archaeology Matters

● ●

In This Chapter

▶ Understanding why historical records can't always be trusted, and how archaeology can help

▶ Discovering how archaeology has revealed the lives of common people through the ages

▶ Looking at the strides archaeology has made toward answering some age-old questions

● ●

*A*rchaeologists are often depicted as crusty old professors obsessed with artifacts and working away, buried deep in some university basement. Although that's sometimes the case — I've spent entire winters basically confined to my basement lab, analyzing artifacts — it's not always. Many applications of archaeology are relevant to modern daily life. Take tourism, for example. Go to the British Tourist Authority Web site and you immediately see ancient castles; nearly any Web site dealing with travel in England mentions Stonehenge. Tourism is a major industry contributing well more than 119 billion dollars per year to England's economy, and much of it's geared to visiting sites like Stonehenge. The same goes for a lot of other countries: Think of the pyramids of Egypt, Mexico, or Central America. Finding such archaeological sites and investigating them in detail is important to maintaining a healthy tourist industry, and doing so demands a steady flow of archaeologists.

Archaeology is also useful for learning about your ancestors. Unless you're royalty, you're probably related by blood to the essentially voiceless multitudes of citizens from the ancient civilizations, people living in a world where only the elites were literate. Without books or the ability to write, the peasants and common citizens of the ancient world — your ancestors — have for a long time gone without representation. But archaeology can tell you about their lives.

And what about the historical record? Many are wary of official accounts of contemporary events because, frankly, they've been lied to so many times. So, big surprise, ancient state records also highlight the best times, glorify their leaders, and so on. For these reasons, archaeology can help you understand your history better than official records alone. Archaeology can test the historical record by comparing what was written down with actual physical evidence of what happened in the past.

In 1934, the Society for American Archaeology formed as a professional organization "dedicated to the research, interpretation, and protection of the archaeological heritage of the Americas." Among its Principles of Archaeological Ethics is a statement written to ensure that archaeology reaches out from the so-called ivory tower to the general public; Principle Number 4, public education and outreach, states that "Archaeologists should reach out to, and participate in, cooperative efforts with others interested in the archaeological record with the aim of improving the preservation, protection, and interpretation of the record. . . . explain and promote the use of archaeological methods and techniques in understanding human behavior and culture, and communicate archaeological interpretations of the past."

For all these reasons and more, archaeology is an important part of any civilization that values and wants to learn from its past. To understand how, in this chapter I share some examples of how archaeology can impact people in daily life.

History Is Written by the Winners: The Importance of Archaeology

You often hear that history is written by the winners, and indeed, a lot of history is recorded from a biased point of view; but archaeology seeks the truth. One benefit of archaeology, then, is that it can help correct the official record or even flesh out incomplete records. Archaeology can also speak for those who had no voice in the ancient world, and this goal is important for many archaeologists. Because official histories are features of civilizations and therefore only come after the millions of years of prehistoric archaeology, the kind of archaeology that investigates the accuracy of historical records is called *historical archaeology*.

For example, an official battle account describes the 8th-century BC God-King Sargon of Assyria laying waste to his opponents with a handful of men at his side: "[L]ike a mighty javelin I fell upon Rusash, his destruction I accomplished, I routed him. The bodies of his warriors like malt I brewed. . . . Two hundred and fifty of the royal seed, his governors, his officials and his cavalry in my hands I took and I broke his battle line." A pretty remarkable account, and it's backed up by official Assyrian sculptures that always show glorious Assyrian victories (but never defeats). Figure 20-1 shows an official state depiction of a 7th-century BC battle.

Historical archaeology and written history

What actually happens in the world and what gets written down as history sometimes conflict, whether it's because of deliberate mischaracterization, selective memory, or just generally incomplete record-keeping. Luckily, historical archaeology can help resolve these conflicting stories and lead to a better understanding of history.

Historical archaeology combines the field and laboratory methods of prehistoric archaeology with the research methods of history to paint a more complete picture of the past. This examination particularly involves the analysis of both *primary documents* (original accounts of an event by an eyewitness) and the context in which those documents were written. Is this document a personal journal or government record? Did a peasant write it, or was it a state scribe? These kinds of questions give historical anthropologists a better idea of a document's historical significance.

Note also that historical archaeologists also often analyze quite a bit of *oral tradition* in their investigations; this tradition is the history of people who don't read or write but pass their histories from one generation to the next through stories, myths, and so on. See Chapter 11 for more on oral tradition.

The following sections give you some examples of how archaeology can help people understand the past better than simply relying on official records can.

New York's forgotten African burial ground

For more than 100 years beginning in the late 17th century, a 5-acre plot of what is today Lower Manhattan was used as a cemetery for more than 20,000 African Americans. By the late 19th century, the site was paved over and forgotten as New York City grew. Only in 1991 was it rediscovered and investigated as an archaeological site.

The scientific excavation of the site, where over 400 skeletons were discovered and carefully excavated, was one aspect of the project. Analysis focused on the human remains, revealing relatively short lifespans for the adults (who rarely lived past their mid-thirties and often died between the ages of 15 and 25) and a high death rate for children; in fact, nearly half of all the bodies were prepubescent children. Those who lived to adulthood were worked hard; adult bones often bore signs of torn muscles. Despite these terrible realities, these early African Americans retained elements of their original cultures, such as decorating their teeth with distinctive filing patterns, and using West African motifs in decorating at least one coffin.

After analysis, in October 2003, the human remains were reburied. Excavating the site to learn about the lives of these largely forgotten slaves showed how archaeology can be relevant in the real world, where slave descendants powerfully felt the reconstruction of their ancestors' stories. The African burial ground is now a national monument in downtown Manhattan. You can find out more at www.nps.gov/afbg.

Commoners of ancient Egypt

Until the last few decades, archaeologists have focused on large, spectacular finds like the tombs and palaces of Egypt's kings and queens. But, of course other stories exist, stories that haven't been told for thousands of years. Only archaeology can tell these tales, the stories of the common folk who built the great monuments, farmed the fertile soils, and supported the priestly classes who venerated Egypt's hundreds of gods and goddesses.

For example, excavations at the ancient Southern Egyptian village Dier el Medina have revealed that workers lived in two-story apartments, each with several rooms, that were normally furnished with beds, a hearth and kitchen for grinding grain to flour, a storage cellar, and often a small shrine to the goddess Bes. Entire families may have lived in some of the buildings, called up to perform work for the state. For this work, citizens were paid in food, including wheat grain, fish, vegetables, salt, oil, and — occasionally, as a bonus — poultry or other special foods.

Although most Egyptians didn't read or write — that was a special skill of elites such as priests and scribes — villagers of Dier el Medina occasionally did mark business transactions and legal decisions on small *ostraca,* or pieces of clay marked with hieroglyphs found scattered throughout the site. Still, these records are few and far between, and they don't flesh out the lives of commoners nearly as well as careful archaeological excavation.

Studies of Dier el Medina's graffiti, the quality of its pottery and the types of food people ate, and the afflictions and diseases revealed by their skeletons shows that Dier el Medina's population included all kinds of tradespeople, such as masons to work the stone for the tombs, draftsmen to design them, artists to decorate them, and carpenters to work with wood. Work was generally plentiful because a new pharaoh's first task was usually to command the design and building of elaborate tombs and temples.

Although pharaohs were buried in the tombs built by the citizens, citizens were buried in a graveyard just outside the town wall. Work group leaders and other people of relatively high status were sometimes buried beneath miniature pyramids, but most workers were buried in simple graves. Analysis of some bones has shown that workers received good medical care for the inevitable injuries received when working with heavy stone blocks. This consideration alone shows that the people of Dier el Medina weren't slaves, because Egyptian slaves didn't receive good medical treatment.

Skeletal analysis revealed that Dier el Medina was often mainly populated by women because males were off working on construction projects. And architectural analysis has shown that the town appears to have had its own judiciary system for solving disputes, and archaeologists have found ostraca bearing records of typical concerns: a minor theft, someone not paying for something, and so on.

When work was nearby, workers walked to the construction site in the morning and back home in the evenings. Each work group had a scribe who made sure that everyone showed up — these Egyptians were punching the clock just like many people do today. Thousands of clay jug pieces show that they also shared a love of a minor luxury: beer, one of Egypt's greatest products. Once again, this is a detail often overlooked in official state records, but a facet of life that was important to the common person.

The archaeology of American slaves

As slave archaeology in the Americas continues to find and document sites, the details of lives long-forgotten will continue to emerge. Between the 1520s (when Africans were first brought to North America as slaves) and Abraham Lincoln's 1863 proclamation freeing slaves held in territories still fighting the Union, at least half a million slaves were forcibly invited into North America. These ancestors of many African Americans today lived lives of terrible hardship. Most never learned to read or write (at one point, teaching them was illegal), and what was written about them and their lives was rarely impartial. Some slave journals do exist in American history, but they're pretty rare and tell only a little of the story. Archaeology helps to tell the rest.

Reconstructing the lives of American slaves has been an important goal of many historical archaeologists over the last few decades. Many excavations have focused on slave quarters, often located on the edge of old plantations, far from the luxurious homes of their masters. Others, including excavations in Mississippi and Jamaica, have focused on the settlements established by *maroons*, which were escaped slaves. In fact, some archaeologists have shifted their focus away from enslavement and toward Africans' freedom and resistance.

Excavations at George Washington's estate at Mount Vernon, Virginia, have focused on a large house, near Washington's own, that housed some of the 60 to 80 slaves he owned at any given time. Artifacts found include buttons, probably indicating that some of these slaves wore somewhat finer European clothing than most, as well as a set of pottery of a style that had gone out of fashion; Washington probably gave the slaves this castoff set when he ordered newly fashionable Wedgewood ceramics from England. Further analysis at Mt. Vernon showed that slaves often ate from bowls rather than plates, suggesting stew-like foods; the small, highly-processed bones of animals, such as fish, beef, and pork, show that they often ate substandard foods. They apparently hunted to supplement their diet.

But these were the high-status slaves who lived near their master; life wasn't the same for those who lived further away in small structures described by Polish visitor Julian Niemcewicz in 1798: "We entered one of the cabins of the Blacks, for one can not call them by the name of houses. They are more miserable than the cottages of our peasants. The husband and wife sleep on a mean pallet, the children on the ground; a very bad fireplace, some utensils for cooking, but in the middle of this poverty some cups and a teapot."

Other important historical archaeology sites

In Peru, archaeologists have recently found evidence that conquistador Francisco Pizarro enlisted some native Peruvians to help in his conquest of the Incan empire. In a burial ground where more than 70 Incan skeletons were discovered, nearly half showed evidence of injury or death having come from native weapons rather than conquistador weapons. These new discoveries confirm a previously held theory that Pizarro had some help from native Peruvians in conquering the Inca.

In December 2007, archaeologists using ground-penetrating radar discovered the remains of two Great Halls in southern Norway. Dating to around 700 to 900 AD, the massive buildings would have been palaces where Viking kings lived, held court, entertained guests, and administered their kingdoms. This discovery requires historians to reevaluate the common concept that southern Norway wasn't a seat of power during the Viking age.

In the 13th century, several hundred Vikings settled in south Greenland, barely eking out a living as they farmed on the northernmost margin of the farmable world. They survived until around 1410, when suddenly mention of these settlements stops in all historical sources. Archaeologists have tried for decades to explain the disappearance of these settlements with theories as diverse as death by the Black Plague and murder by pirates or the native Inuit. Cemetery excavations have revealed a little evidence of interpersonal violence, with one man buried with a knife still imbedded in his body; however, this find isn't evidence for widespread chaos.

Excavations of the farms have revealed that life slowly became worse for the Vikings as their livestock overgrazed the land. Excavations of houses showed that as the climate worsened, the Vikings put up walls inside their houses to make rooms smaller and easier to heat. One excavation showed that some Vikings ate their livestock one winter, which was unusual. But archaeologists haven't found any mass graves, discounting the Black Plague as the killer of the Vikings. Similarly, no evidence of attack by either native Inuit or pirates has surfaced; rubble and unburied bodies are typical of such circumstances but were all absent. In the end, the Viking mystery appears to be solved: as the climate worsened (as evidenced by precise environmental records collected from ice cores nearby), their farms simply failed. According to archaeologist Thomas McGovern, they failed to adapt to changing conditions, which they could have done by hunting seals like the Inuit.

Historical archaeology isn't just limited to filling in gaps in the histories of specific groups of people. It can also clear up misconceptions about ancient humanity as a whole. For example, a lot of archaeological evidence contradicts the idea that people in the ancient world lived in a state of noble harmony with nature and one another. In fact, warfare appears to have been a human occupation for a depressingly long time.

In Sudan, 14,000-year-old skeletons excavated in the 1960s have recently been reexamined and discovered to bear fractures and other evidence of interpersonal violence. At the site of Qermez Dere in Northern Iraq, discoveries of skeletons with violence-related injuries, defensive architecture, and war weapons all date to about 10,000 years ago. Australian rock art dated to 10,000 years ago depicts conflict between individuals, and by 6,000 years ago the depictions show large groups of individuals combating one another. And in China, 4,600-year-old farming villages have defensive architecture and scalped skeletons.

Widespread excavations in the Near and Middle East have shown that writing didn't appear suddenly around 6,000 years ago, as many histories suggest, but as the result of a long evolution of longer-lasting communication systems that have roots going back to 9,000 years ago. The earliest writings appear to have been encoded on small clay tablets or tokens that early archaeologists dismissed as toys or gaming pieces. But new analysis — not believed by all archaeologists — suggests these objects were the precursors to *Sumerian cuneiform* (the world's earliest known writing system), which is found on thousands of clay tablets after 6,000 years ago.

Conversation Stoppers? Archaeology and the Unknown

People often theorize what's best for mankind and base these theories on what they know of humanity's past. "Well, if we ate the Palaeolithic (Stone Age) diet, we'd be just fine!" some may contend, as others lament that "We should never have come down from the trees in the first place." Yet others may base their ideas of what men and women should do in the workplace on deeply held ideas about what people "have always done."

In a lot of friendly discussions (which can become pretty heated because basic ideas of the past are at stake), people begin to look at the origins of things. Presumably, archaeology can serve as a guide. I often think these discussions could be smoothed out with a handy encyclopedia of archaeology, even if that encyclopedia had to often say, "We just don't know yet."

Just because archaeology hasn't yet answered a question doesn't mean the question is unanswerable. It will probably take time and energy; whole careers may be used just to answer simple questions about the past.

Archaeology can still be useful, even when it doesn't provide concrete answers. For example, archaeology tells us that the idea of some ancient, pure Palaeolithic diet just isn't possible. The *Palaeolithic* period (the "old stone age") lasted for millions of years and was lived in by millions of hominids across vast and diverse landscapes, and peoples' diets would have reflected this diversity. Some Palaeolithic folks would have focused on hunting reindeer, or horses (like some European Neanderthals), and others may have had a broader diet; most foragers eat plenty of things other than mammal meat, including shellfish, nuts, fish, roots and tubers, and lots of other plant foods.

So what has archaeology done to (start to) answer some of the basic questions about the human past? In the following sections I want to show you the progress archaeologists have made toward answering two pretty big questions about fundamental aspects of humanity, even though they haven't fully answered them yet. People have floated some good ideas, but none have convinced all anthropologists that the essential questions have been answered.

Why did humanity take up farming?

Farming (which you can read much, much more about in Chapter 9) is a way of making a living based on raising plants and animals for food. It's only about 10,000 years old and was invented after humans had spent millions of years as foragers. The obvious question is what compelled people to give up foraging and take up living in one place? Naturally, the world has turned to archaeologists to answer this question; because farming was invented long before writing, only archaeologists are equipped to investigate it.

But not even archaeologists are sure — or, more specifically, they think they may know, but they aren't sure yet. None of their models seems to explain the advent of farming worldwide. Although archaeologists still don't know why farming originated, they've at least proven the following theories, once accepted, as false:

- **Farming is the easiest way to live:** Foragers have a good living; in fact, they have less work than most farmers and also have better health than the first farmers.

- **Farming is the most efficient way to use the land:** This statement assumes that foraging isn't efficient, which just isn't true. If foragers keep their populations low and remain mobile, they very efficiently utilize their landscapes.

- **Farming is part of civilization, and all societies are on a single track evolving towards civilization:** Each human society has its own adaptive solutions to its environments, and no internal engine drives all humans towards being farmers or anything else.

How did humans go from having leaders to having rulers?

Another big question: How is it that human societies went from being led (by someone who has the group's best interest at heart) to being ruled (by a tyrant who's mainly looking out for number one)? Why put up with tyrants in the first place? Archaeologists have tackled this topic as well, striking down other theories:

- **Social hierarchies are part of civilization, and all societies in the past were on the single track towards civilization:** Stop me if you've heard this one, but all societies aren't on the same track toward any ideal state. Archaeology has shown that each society worldwide has found its own ways to survive, and the idea that the same engine drives them all just doesn't fly.

✔ **Humans are inherently hierarchical:** This statement may actually be true — all primates have pretty rigidly structured societies that include some degree of status recognition. However, many human societies have managed to remain *egalitarian*, meaning that all members of the culture have basically the same rights and the same access to resources; although egalitarian societies do have to work to prevent individuals from gaining power, they manage to do it. Unfortunately, this presents an entirely new question: In societies that are now ruled, how did this egalitarian mindset get overturned in the first place?

As you can see, archaeology can answer a lot of questions, but it hasn't answered them all. It also introduces more questions that need answering as well. And this is good news for archaeologists because it keeps them employed.

Does history repeat itself?

History, people often say, repeats itself. And looking at the historical records of the ancient civilizations, some things do seem to happen again and again: Civilizations expand, get overextended, and then collapse (as in the cases of Rome, which went under in 476 AD, and the British Empire, which fell apart more than a thousand years later in the post-WWII era.

But is this always the case? If so, archaeology would be pretty boring; one thing would happen again and again. But that's not what archaeologists see. Some civilizations end abruptly, like the Aztec and Inca, conquered by invaders in the 1520s AD; those empires never had the chance to collapse as a result of overexpansion. So in the case of civilizations, "history repeats itself" seems to be an oversimplification.

The statement has another problem: What about prehistory? What does it say about the millions of years of human or at least proto-human life that preceded historical records? As an archaeologist, I can tell you that prehistory says very little about those millions of years. Archaeology, then, has shown that this short and somewhat satisfying statement may be true about some things, but it's just too short, too "bumper-sticker" to account for the whole human story.

Part V
The Part of Tens

The 5th Wave   By Rich Tennant

DOREEN AND JANICE WERE EXCITED TO SEE A TOOL-USING HOMINID AT THE END OF THE BAR THAT NIGHT.

In this part . . .

This is the fun part. Head swimming from all that anthropological goodness? Check out Chapter 21 for a concise list of the ten most important (in my opinion) anthropology topics. Ready to take the next step? Head to Chapter 22 for ten great anthropology-related careers. Just need a break? Chapter 23 gives you ten enjoyable, nontechnical books and movies starring anthropology.

Chapter 21

Ten Things to Remember about Anthropology, Whatever Else You Forget

Can a person boil the results of a four-field academic discipline over 100 years old down to ten statements? Well, I'm going to try. For me, these are the most important lessons of anthropology to date.

We're Not Just Like Apes, We ARE Apes

Humans aren't mineral or vegetable, so we must be animal; of the animals, we're clearly members of the primate order. Forget monkeys and small, cat-like prosimians — genetically and anatomically, we humans are clearly most like the living apes, the chimpanzee, gorilla, orangutan, and gibbon. And although we diverged from them millions of years ago, we don't just *look* like them — we share much of their DNA. For all practical purposes, we are apes. (For more on our simian brethren, check out Chapter 4.)

Nobody Knows Why Hominids First Walked Upright (Yet)

Although someday anthropologists may find good evidence for exactly why hominids first walked upright, at the moment they just don't know. (You can read about some theories in Chapter 6.) What they do know is that bipedalism would have presented early hominids with both pros and cons including (but not limited to) the following:

- ✔ Pro: Ability to stand and look over tall grasses
- ✔ Pro: Ability to carry items such as tools
- ✔ Con: Less able to climb (to escape predation) than before
- ✔ Con: Slower and less maneuverable than main predators (like big cats)

Remember, just because anthropologists *don't* know why hominids started walking on two legs doesn't mean they *can't* know, and it also doesn't mean that all theories are equally valid.

Everyone Is in the Human Race

Biologically speaking, race is a slippery concept. Individuals capable of mating and having offspring that are themselves healthy enough to have offspring are considered members of the same *species*. Races or subsets exist within species — like different breeds of dogs, or people of slightly different skin colors or hair types — but, biologically speaking, these differences are quite insignificant. That hasn't stopped humanity from making a big deal out of the differences between, say, native Africans and native Europeans and using those differences for all manner of mischief. But it's all smoke and mirrors, from racial stereotyping to misguided attempts to engineer so-called super races. Everyone is in the human species, *Homo sapiens sapiens*. I discuss the intricacies of race in more detail in Chapter 14.

Tool Use Separated Behavior from Anatomy

For every living species aside from humanity, evolution is a matter of how well the body fits the environment. Complex behaviors can help nonhumans survive, of course, but for most animals anatomy pretty well constrains behavior. In stark contrast, humans make and use tools (and have done so for at least 2.5 million years) to allow survival in situations where the body couldn't normally survive; that is, humans have severed the anatomical bonds of their behavior by relying on tools rather than their bodies. Now that's what I call food for thought! Head to Chapter 6 for more on tools and behavior.

Civilization Is Brand-New

From about 2 million years ago to about 10,000 years ago, humans didn't plant crops and raise animals; as a species we *foraged,* or hunted and gathered, for our calories, water, and nutrients on a daily basis. Lacking substantial storage technologies, our ancestors had to keep moving around their resource landscapes, which prevented the rise of cities or even villages. For most of our ancestors, life was a trek across vast landscapes in a continual food quest.

But the way people live today — moving thousands of miles per year in cars, freely choosing from various religions, even voting to choose their leaders (more or less) — is an extremely new way for humanity to live; for millennia, humans were hunter-gatherers (which I discuss in the next section), and even in the ancient civilizations things were very different. The ancient civilizations were dynasties, ruled for centuries and longer by royal families controlling the fates of millions, enslaving further millions, and dictating everything from taxes to worship schedules to the kinds of clothing people of different social ranks could wear. Today's new civilization has many problems, but it has largely solved some as well. Check out Chapter 10 for the lowdown on civilization.

There Are Many Ways to Be Human

At its most basic level, being human is having modern anatomy and using symbolism, and these have been with us for at least the last 50,000 years. And every human today, from China to Nigeria to Finland, is equally human. Although humans everywhere have adapted their cultures to new circumstances by devising, inventing, and evolving different ways to survive, ultimately each of these cultures is just another variation on the human theme, another way of being human.

Culture Doesn't Ride on Genes

Culture — the whole set of ideas about what the universe is like and what you're supposed to do about it — isn't encoded in your genes. It's not passed on biologically but rather socially through language. Culture is transferred from one generation to the next largely through written and spoken words. And because studies have shown that language isn't hard-wired — any healthy human infant can learn any human language by about three years of age — culture clearly isn't hard-wired either. An infant born in Japan but quickly moved to Denmark will grow up Danish, not Japanese. Chapter 11 deals with culture in more detail.

Language and Metaphor Are the Keys to Human Success

Although lots of animals communicate in all kinds of ways — using scent, bodily postures, and even sounds — human communication by spoken language is particularly fast and conveys more information (and more subtle information) than any other system of communication. Importantly, human language also uses metaphor, in which one word can have several meanings. This flexibility in communication has many effects, one of the most important of which is the fact that no two humans are identical in their thoughts. Because each mind interprets the language in slightly different ways, humans are distinctive and individualistic and not interchangeable automatons, a fact that has its own effects on the shape of human culture. Clearly, language is central to what it means to be human. See Chapter 13 for a more complete discussion of language.

Absolutely, There Are No Absolutes

Being human is a messy business; try as they might, anthropologists have had a hard time making any but the most basic universal statements about the biology or behavior of members of the human species. Yes, every society has rules for marriage, but they vary from *polyandry* (multiple husbands to one wife) to *polygyny* (multiple wives for one husband). Yes, every society traces biological descent — but the processes vary from *matrilineal* (tracing descent through the female line) to *patrilineal* (tracing through the male line). And so on. Humanity is characterized by diversity; themes and patterns do emerge, but not much is written in stone.

There Is No Ladder of Progress

For a long time, people thought that all human societies were evolving in the same direction, climbing a ladder of progress that passed through the stages of Savagery and Barbarism to finally arrive at the pinnacle of Civilization. But as it turns out, each society is really on its own path and has its own solutions to survival, and you just can't compare one culture to another anthropologically. Now, this doesn't mean that all cultures are perfectly adapted to their environments; some cultures clearly have self-destructive habits, and I personally think having a Universal Declaration of Human Rights is a good thing (see the sidebar "The Universal Declaration of Human Rights" in this chapter). Still, anthropology has found that cross-cultural comparisons have more to do with justifying colonialism or imperialism than honest recognition of the fact that over many millennia, humanity has found many ways be human. Check out Chapter 17 for more on cultural diversity and human rights.

The Universal Declaration of Human Rights

In 1948, the United Nations — an organization founded to foster international cooperation during World War II — presented the world with its Universal Declaration of Human Rights, calling on all member countries "to cause it to be disseminated, displayed, read and expounded principally in schools and other educational institutions, without distinction based on the political status of countries or territories." Among the 30 articles of the Declaration are the following:

✔ Article 1: All human beings are born free and equal in dignity and rights. They are endowed with reason and conscience and should act toward one another in a spirit of brotherhood.

✔ Article 4. No one shall be held in slavery or servitude; slavery and the slave trade shall be prohibited in all their forms.

✔ Article 16.1. Men and women of full age, without any limitation due to race, nationality or religion, have the right to marry and to found a family. They are entitled to equal rights as to marriage, during marriage and at its dissolution.

You can imagine that even as well-meaning as they truly are, some of these articles can be subject to some debate regarding definitions. This discrepancy emphasizes the importance of intercultural understanding generated by understanding the lessons of anthropology themselves.

Chapter 22

Ten Great Careers for Anthropology Majors

· ·

In This Chapter

▶ Identifying some good careers for people interested in any of the four fields of anthropology

▶ Looking at the educational requirements of anthropological careers

· ·

*W*hat can anyone do with a degree in anthropology? Can you actually have a career in studying humanity? Sure you can. Here are ten suggestions. Personally, I think that if you're fascinated by the human species and your passion is studying humanity, you should find a way to make a living at it.

Academic Anthropology

If you're really hooked on the study of humanity, you need to know two things: You'll need a PhD, and you'll need to specialize in one of the four main fields of anthropology. Remember, the field has four main divisions:

> ✓ **Physical (or biological) anthropology:** The study of human biology and biological evolution through fossils and (increasingly) DNA
>
> ✓ **Linguistic anthropology:** The study of human communication
>
> ✓ **Cultural (or social) anthropology:** The study of living human societies through participant observation
>
> ✓ **Archaeology:** The study of the human past through the remains of ancient people and their civilizations

Academic anthropologists in any of these fields normally work in a Department of Anthropology at a college or university. Being a professor requires a PhD and is normally a career-long decision because the PhD can take so much time and effort to earn. The jobs are scarce and include a lot more than just teaching and research, but if you're hooked, this is one way to go. Be prepared to work long and hard for the coveted title of professor.

Cultural/Human Resources

Increasingly, corporate America is recognizing the value of improving intercultural communication in its growing multicultural workforce. Students interested in cultural anthropology and working with people may be interested in careers in cultural or human resources, facilitating and improving workplace communication and understanding. For this career, a bachelor's degree in anthropology may be sufficient, but increasingly a master's degree is necessary.

Medical Examination

The popularity of crime novels and TV shows in America reveals a deep interest in human fallibility and the solving of mysteries. Many of my students tell me they're interested in becoming a medical examiner, a profession that investigates the cause of a human's death in detail. The road to becoming an ME is long and difficult, but I imagine it could be a very rewarding career for the right person. Although requirements vary, most MEs need a bachelor's degree (a BS in anthropology with a focus on physical anthropology would be perfect), then a medical degree, and then several years of post-MD training focusing on pathology. So, this career track isn't for everyone, but it's a possibility for those dedicated to understanding this facet of humanity. Try checking out www.thename.org/, the Web site for the National Association of Medical Examiners.

Crime Scene Investigation

Anthropology students who focus on physical anthropology, particularly human skeletal anatomy, are well-prepared for further training as a crime scene investigator (CSI) who specializes in documenting and investigating crime scenes involving human remains. A bachelor's degree is normally sufficient to begin the CSI certification process. Still, most CSIs are actually police officers who apply for the CSI position after a few years on the force (according to the International Crime Scene Investigators Association — check out www.icsia.org/, the association's Web site). Still, I feel a good background in human culture and anatomy must be a good background for anyone interested in law enforcement careers, particularly when that law enforcement has to do with human beings.

Primate Biology

Zoos, research facilities, and other places that maintain populations of nonhuman primates all employ biologists to maintain the primates' health and well-being. Although you must consider serious ethical concerns — conditions for the primates are better today than they have been in the past, but many abuses continue — you could argue that primate biologists are in the best position to better conditions from the inside. Primate biologists require a graduate degree in biology, but a good start would be a bachelor's degree in anthropology with a focus on physical anthropology, particularly the physical anthropology of the nonhuman primates.

Primate Ethology

Zoos, research facilities, and other places that maintain populations of non-human primates also employ ethologists to study nonhuman primate behavior. (*Ethology* is the study of nonhuman animal behavior.) The same ethical considerations apply here as to primate biologist. Primate ethologists will need a graduate degree in biology (focusing on nonhuman primate ethology) or anthropology (focusing on the same field).

Diplomacy

Anthropology students focusing on cultural anthropology are good candidates for careers in international relations and conflict resolution, and it seems clear enough that humanity could use a lot of that. The lessons of anthropology include statements about our unity as a species, the importance of genuine mutual respect between cultures, and recognition of some absurdities and aberrations like racism and slavery. (See Chapter 21 for a discussion of anthropology's most important lessons.) These ideas shouldn't be based on political grounds but on what we know of *what it is to be human*. The field of conflict resolution is new and thriving and may be particularly good for anthropology majors wanting to pursue graduate degrees that take advantage of the anthropological perspective.

Museum Work

Lots of anthropology graduates find positions in museums and historical societies managing collections of old documents and artifacts. For these positions, a general interest in the past, facilitated by an anthropological appreciation for the ancient past of our species, could be a good foundation.

Get started as early as possible by taking internship positions in museums and libraries while you're an undergraduate to get a feel for what the work is really like.

Library Science

Because anthropology is such a massive field, with interests in so many facets of human existence, anthropology students tend to be Jacks- (or Jills-) of-all-trades. They tend to have a good knowledge of where to go for information, and this quality can be a big advantage in working in libraries. A bachelor's degree in anthropology can be a good background for getting a master's in Library Science (MLS), which is commonly necessary for higher positions in library work in the United States.

Contract Archaeology

Contract archaeologists work for private firms hired to evaluate whether construction projects will harm archaeological sites. They form a large portion of the professional archaeologists in the U.S., and, as opposed to academic archaeologists, they don't necessarily need a PhD. You'll need a master's degree in the field of archaeology, focusing on Cultural Resource Management (CRM). A bachelor's degree will be sufficient if you want to excavate for only a few years, but moving up into administrative positions will most likely require the MA. A PhD can be useful but isn't necessarily required.

The American Anthropological Association on careers in anthropology

The American Anthropological Association is a professional society founded to promote the results and study of anthropology. About careers in anthropology, the AAA says, "More than 350 U.S. colleges and universities offer an undergraduate major in anthropology, and many more offer coursework. Because the subject matter of anthropology is so broad, an undergraduate major or concentration can be part of a broad liberal arts background for men and women interested in medicine, government, business, and law. More information on college and university anthropology can be found in the American Anthropological Association's *AAA Guide,* published yearly."

The AAA Careers Web site is at www.aaanet. org/careers.htm. This site lists many jobs and job databases.

Chapter 23

Ten Great Anthropologically Themed Movies and Books

*W*e humans are fascinated by ourselves, and the themes and findings of anthropology have permeated our popular culture. In this chapter I recommend ten of my favorite anthropologically themed books and movies. I give each of them two thumbs up.

Once We Were Warriors (1995)

This film, produced and set in modern New Zealand, follows the story of an urban Maori (native New Zealander) family struggling to overcome addictions and poverty, problems common to native people worldwide who have been moved from their ancestral lands to city environments. In the film, as in real life, one solution to these problems is a reconnection with traditional values and culture. The film's scenes of grinding poverty and violence can be hard to watch, but they're a reality. Directed by Lee Tamahori.

Gorillas in the Mist: The Story of Dian Fossey (1988)

This Hollywood film depicts part of the career of Dian Fossey, one of the three main women in living-ape studies. Fossey, played by Sigourney Weaver, diligently (or obsessively, depending on your perspective) studies gorillas in central Africa, eventually spending as much time trying to protect them from poachers as study them. Fossey was murdered in 1985, and the scene depicting this event in the film leaves the mystery open; to date, nobody has been charged with her death. Directed by Michael Apted.

Neanderthal (2005)

This BBC production for the television series *Horizon* presents some of the most interesting recent work on just what the Neanderthals were and how they may have become extinct. Of course, the documentary contains lots of theories, and each one will have some palaeoanthropologist or another shaking her head; however, this movie demonstrates how ingenious anthropologists are with the bits of archaeology used to reconstruct the past and both how much and how little they really know. Some of the most prominent Neanderthal researchers appear in the video, which includes many realistic reconstructions of Neanderthal life. Directed by Cameron Balbirnie.

Quest for Fire (1982)

This French-produced film follows the lives of a band of hunter–gatherers attempting to find a new source of fire after their own is catastrophically snuffed out. The film is pretty dramatic, and many archaeologists would cringe at some of the technical details. Nevertheless, the film is thought-provoking and I think in many ways a good depiction of what foraging life was like for our ancestors many thousands of years ago. Directed by Jean-Jacques Annaud.

Koyaanisqatsi (1982)

This film, with no narration or script, is an audio-visual meditation on humanity and its relationship to the natural world. By simply showing scenes of that natural world, with and without humanity, and then scenes of humanity alone without apparent connections to the natural world, the film forces you to think deeply about what our species is, for better and worse. *Powaqqatsi,* a later film in the same trilogy, focuses more on humanity than *Koyaanisqatsi.* Both films directed by Godfrey Reggio.

The Places in Between (2006)

This book traces Scotsman Rory Stewart's adventurous walk across Afghanistan in 2002. Yes, that Afghanistan, in 2002, with the Taliban holding sway in many regions. But most of the people Stewart meets aren't Taliban members; they're Afghan peasants who want to live the way they have lived for centuries, and he finds their attitudes of hospitality and generosity nearly everywhere he goes. He also comes across the remains of an ancient city being looted by pot hunters, the description of which is tremendous. *The Places in Between* won several awards and was on the *New York Times* Top Book Review list for 2006. Stewart has also published *The Prince of the Marshes* about his time in Iraq.

Shadows of Forgotten Ancestors (1993)

In this grand tour of the human species, the late, great astronomer Carl Sagan and his still-living wife, Ann Druyan, bring the reader from the origins of life up to the present day, beautifully and accurately describing the fascinating details of every aspect of being human, from DNA to cell division to primate behavior and human evolution. Although some elements of the book are out of date today, none of these are critical errors that lead the reader astray; most of what the authors present here is profound and timeless.

Anyone enjoying this book will probably also like *Cosmos,* Sagan's 1980 TV series (cowritten with Stephen Soter and Ann Druyan). It's the most humanistic perspective on the cosmos, and humanity's place in it, that I've ever seen. It's recently been digitally remastered from the original, 25-part TV series. Directed by Adrian Malone.

Maps and Dreams (1981; 2nd edition 2002)

Writer-anthropologist Hugh Brody recounts his travels and investigations of the vast sub-Arctic regions of Canada in this beautifully-written book that puts the reader right on the tundra. This book made me realize just how important it is as an archaeologist to be careful about how much I believed in models (mine or anyone else's) about human behavior in the ancient world. The decisions that Brody's native hunting informants make — about hunting or anything else — are affected by subtle but powerful cultural factors that can be difficult to imagine.

We, the Navigators: The Ancient Art of Landfinding in the Pacific (1972; 2nd edition 1998)

David Lewis-Williams was a sailor and amateur anthropologist fascinated by traditional Polynesian navigation methods, including steering craft by the stars and detecting far-off islands by cloud formations and swells in the ocean. He spent years learning these methods among the traditional navigators of the Pacific. His book details these astounding methods and is sure to thrill and educate anyone interested in Polynesia, ancient sailing, or details of how human cultures have adapted to life on the Pacific. Some of the methods Lewis-Williams describes are probably more than 3,000 years old, originating when the first Lapita people began to colonize the Western Pacific from Southeast Asia.

Lord of the Flies (1954)

In this novel by William Golding, a group of young boys stranded on an island try to build a society without any parental guidance. Golding uses this scenario to speculate on how human society would naturally shape up if boys old enough to have ideas about how culture "should" be arranged were isolated in a cultureless area. Whether or not Golding accurately depicts human nature, this book is thought-provoking and forces readers to ask themselves what human nature really is. Is it a product of our surroundings, or is it more deeply rooted in the fact that we're basically large social primates? The book was adapted into films in 1963 (directed by Peter Brook) and 1990 (directed by Harry Hook.)

Index

BUSINESS, CAREERS & PERSONAL FINANCE

0-7645-9847-3

0-7645-2431-3

Also available:
- Business Plans Kit For Dummies
  0-7645-9794-9
- Economics For Dummies
  0-7645-5726-2
- Grant Writing For Dummies
  0-7645-8416-2
- Home Buying For Dummies
  0-7645-5331-3
- Managing For Dummies
  0-7645-1771-6
- Marketing For Dummies
  0-7645-5600-2

- Personal Finance For Dummies
  0-7645-2590-5*
- Resumes For Dummies
  0-7645-5471-9
- Selling For Dummies
  0-7645-5363-1
- Six Sigma For Dummies
  0-7645-6798-5
- Small Business Kit For Dummies
  0-7645-5984-2
- Starting an eBay Business For Dummies
  0-7645-6924-4
- Your Dream Career For Dummies
  0-7645-9795-7

HOME & BUSINESS COMPUTER BASICS

0-470-05432-8

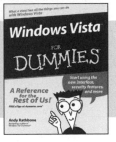

0-471-75421-8

Also available:
- Cleaning Windows Vista For Dummies
  0-471-78293-9
- Excel 2007 For Dummies
  0-470-03737-7
- Mac OS X Tiger For Dummies
  0-7645-7675-5
- MacBook For Dummies
  0-470-04859-X
- Macs For Dummies
  0-470-04849-2
- Office 2007 For Dummies
  0-470-00923-3

- Outlook 2007 For Dummies
  0-470-03830-6
- PCs For Dummies
  0-7645-8958-X
- Salesforce.com For Dummies
  0-470-04893-X
- Upgrading & Fixing Laptops For Dummies
  0-7645-8959-8
- Word 2007 For Dummies
  0-470-03658-3
- Quicken 2007 For Dummies
  0-470-04600-7

FOOD, HOME, GARDEN, HOBBIES, MUSIC & PETS

0-7645-8404-9

0-7645-9904-6

Also available:
- Candy Making For Dummies
  0-7645-9734-5
- Card Games For Dummies
  0-7645-9910-0
- Crocheting For Dummies
  0-7645-4151-X
- Dog Training For Dummies
  0-7645-8418-9
- Healthy Carb Cookbook For Dummies
  0-7645-8476-6
- Home Maintenance For Dummies
  0-7645-5215-5

- Horses For Dummies
  0-7645-9797-3
- Jewelry Making & Beading For Dummies
  0-7645-2571-9
- Orchids For Dummies
  0-7645-6759-4
- Puppies For Dummies
  0-7645-5255-4
- Rock Guitar For Dummies
  0-7645-5356-9
- Sewing For Dummies
  0-7645-6847-7
- Singing For Dummies
  0-7645-2475-5

INTERNET & DIGITAL MEDIA

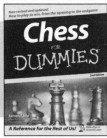

0-470-04529-9

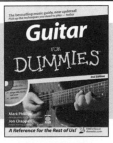

0-470-04894-8

Also available:
- Blogging For Dummies
  0-471-77084-1
- Digital Photography For Dummies
  0-7645-9802-3
- Digital Photography All-in-One Desk Reference For Dummies
  0-470-03743-1
- Digital SLR Cameras and Photography For Dummies
  0-7645-9803-1
- eBay Business All-in-One Desk Reference For Dummies
  0-7645-8438-3
- HDTV For Dummies
  0-470-09673-X

- Home Entertainment PCs For Dummies
  0-470-05523-5
- MySpace For Dummies
  0-470-09529-6
- Search Engine Optimization For Dummies
  0-471-97998-8
- Skype For Dummies
  0-470-04891-3
- The Internet For Dummies
  0-7645-8996-2
- Wiring Your Digital Home For Dummies
  0-471-91830-X

* Separate Canadian edition also available
† Separate U.K. edition also available

Available wherever books are sold. For more information or to order direct: U.S. customers visit www.dummies.com or call 1-877-762-2974.
U.K. customers visit www.wileyeurope.com or call 0800 243407. Canadian customers visit www.wiley.ca or call 1-800-567-4797.

SPORTS, FITNESS, PARENTING, RELIGION & SPIRITUALITY

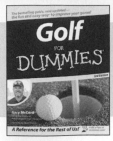

0-471-76871-5

0-7645-7841-3

Also available:
- Catholicism For Dummies
  0-7645-5391-7
- Exercise Balls For Dummies
  0-7645-5623-1
- Fitness For Dummies
  0-7645-7851-0
- Football For Dummies
  0-7645-3936-1
- Judaism For Dummies
  0-7645-5299-6
- Potty Training For Dummies
  0-7645-5417-4
- Buddhism For Dummies
  0-7645-5359-3

- Pregnancy For Dummies
  0-7645-4483-7 †
- Ten Minute Tone-Ups For Dummies
  0-7645-7207-5
- NASCAR For Dummies
  0-7645-7681-X
- Religion For Dummies
  0-7645-5264-3
- Soccer For Dummies
  0-7645-5229-5
- Women in the Bible For Dummies
  0-7645-8475-8

TRAVEL

0-7645-7749-2

0-7645-6945-7

Also available:
- Alaska For Dummies
  0-7645-7746-8
- Cruise Vacations For Dummies
  0-7645-6941-4
- England For Dummies
  0-7645-4276-1
- Europe For Dummies
  0-7645-7529-5
- Germany For Dummies
  0-7645-7823-5
- Hawaii For Dummies
  0-7645-7402-7

- Italy For Dummies
  0-7645-7386-1
- Las Vegas For Dummies
  0-7645-7382-9
- London For Dummies
  0-7645-4277-X
- Paris For Dummies
  0-7645-7630-5
- RV Vacations For Dummies
  0-7645-4442-X
- Walt Disney World & Orlando
  For Dummies
  0-7645-9660-8

GRAPHICS, DESIGN & WEB DEVELOPMENT

0-7645-8815-X

0-7645-9571-7

Also available:
- 3D Game Animation For Dummies
  0-7645-8789-7
- AutoCAD 2006 For Dummies
  0-7645-8925-3
- Building a Web Site For Dummies
  0-7645-7144-3
- Creating Web Pages For Dummies
  0-470-08030-2
- Creating Web Pages All-in-One Desk
  Reference For Dummies
  0-7645-4345-8
- Dreamweaver 8 For Dummies
  0-7645-9649-7

- InDesign CS2 For Dummies
  0-7645-9572-5
- Macromedia Flash 8 For Dummies
  0-7645-9691-8
- Photoshop CS2 and Digital
  Photography For Dummies
  0-7645-9580-6
- Photoshop Elements 4 For Dummies
  0-471-77483-9
- Syndicating Web Sites with RSS Feeds
  For Dummies
  0-7645-8848-6
- Yahoo! SiteBuilder For Dummies
  0-7645-9800-7

NETWORKING, SECURITY, PROGRAMMING & DATABASES

0-7645-7728-X

0-471-74940-0

Also available:
- Access 2007 For Dummies
  0-470-04612-0
- ASP.NET 2 For Dummies
  0-7645-7907-X
- C# 2005 For Dummies
  0-7645-9704-3
- Hacking For Dummies
  0-470-05235-X
- Hacking Wireless Networks
  For Dummies
  0-7645-9730-2
- Java For Dummies
  0-470-08716-1

- Microsoft SQL Server 2005 For Dummies
  0-7645-7755-7
- Networking All-in-One Desk Reference
  For Dummies
  0-7645-9939-9
- Preventing Identity Theft For Dummies
  0-7645-7336-5
- Telecom For Dummies
  0-471-77085-X
- Visual Studio 2005 All-in-One Desk
  Reference For Dummies
  0-7645-9775-2
- XML For Dummies
  0-7645-8845-1

EALTH & SELF-HELP

0-7645-8450-2

0-7645-4149-8

Also available:

- Bipolar Disorder For Dummies
  0-7645-8451-0
- Chemotherapy and Radiation
  For Dummies
  0-7645-7832-4
- Controlling Cholesterol For Dummies
  0-7645-5440-9
- Diabetes For Dummies
  0-7645-6820-5* †
- Divorce For Dummies
  0-7645-8417-0 †

- Fibromyalgia For Dummies
  0-7645-5441-7
- Low-Calorie Dieting For Dummies
  0-7645-9905-4
- Meditation For Dummies
  0-471-77774-9
- Osteoporosis For Dummies
  0-7645-7621-6
- Overcoming Anxiety For Dummies
  0-7645-5447-6
- Reiki For Dummies
  0-7645-9907-0
- Stress Management For Dummies
  0-7645-5144-2

DUCATION, HISTORY, REFERENCE & TEST PREPARATION

0-7645-8381-6

0-7645-9554-7

Also available:

- The ACT For Dummies
  0-7645-9652-7
- Algebra For Dummies
  0-7645-5325-9
- Algebra Workbook For Dummies
  0-7645-8467-7
- Astronomy For Dummies
  0-7645-8465-0
- Calculus For Dummies
  0-7645-2498-4
- Chemistry For Dummies
  0-7645-5430-1
- Forensics For Dummies
  0-7645-5580-4

- Freemasons For Dummies
  0-7645-9796-5
- French For Dummies
  0-7645-5193-0
- Geometry For Dummies
  0-7645-5324-0
- Organic Chemistry I For Dummies
  0-7645-6902-3
- The SAT I For Dummies
  0-7645-7193-1
- Spanish For Dummies
  0-7645-5194-9
- Statistics For Dummies
  0-7645-5423-9

Get smart @ dummies.com®

- **Find a full list of Dummies titles**
- **Look into loads of FREE on-site articles**
- **Sign up for FREE eTips e-mailed to you weekly**
- **See what other products carry the Dummies name**
- **Shop directly from the Dummies bookstore**
- **Enter to win new prizes every month!**

* Separate Canadian edition also available
† Separate U.K. edition also available

Available wherever books are sold. For more information or to order direct: U.S. customers visit www.dummies.com or call 1-877-762-2974.
U.K. customers visit www.wileyeurope.com or call 0800 243407. Canadian customers visit www.wiley.ca or call 1-800-567-4797.